Hardship
to
Homeland

Hardship
to
Homeland

Pacific Northwest Volga Germans

**RICHARD D. SCHEUERMAN
& CLIFFORD E. TRAFZER**

**PHOTOGRAPHS BY JOHN CLEMENT
ILLUSTRATIONS BY JIM GERLITZ**

WSU
PRESS

Washington State University Press
Pullman, Washington

WSU PRESS
WASHINGTON STATE UNIVERSITY

Washington State University Press
PO Box 645910
Pullman, Washington 99164-5910
Phone: 800-354-7360
Fax: 509-335-8568
Email: wsupress@wsu.edu
Website: wsupress.wsu.edu

First printing 2018

Library of Congress Cataloging-in-Publication Data

Names: Scheuerman, Richard D., author. | Trafzer, Clifford E., author.
Title: Hardship to homeland : Pacific Northwest Volga Germans / Richard D.
    Scheuerman and Clifford E. Trafzer.
Other titles: Volga Germans.
Description: Pullman, Washington : Washington State University Press, [2018]
    | Includes bibliographical references and index.
Identifiers: LCCN 2018015313 | ISBN 9780874223620 (alk. paper)
Subjects: LCSH: Russian Germans--Northwest, Pacific--History. | Russian
    Germans--Northwest, Pacific--Folklore. | Northwest, Pacific--History. |
    Northwest, Pacific--Folklore
Classification: LCC F855.2.R85 S33 2018 | DDC 305.83/10795--dc23
LC record available at https://lccn.loc.gov/2018015313

Originally published as *The Volga Germans: Pioneers of the Northwest* by the University
Press of Idaho, Moscow, Idaho, 1980, *Hardship to Homeland* is revised and expanded to
include drawings by Jim Gerlitz, photographs by John Clement, and stories retold by
Richard D. Scheuerman.

Publication of this book was made possible with generous support from the
Washington State Libraries Schneidmiller Endowment for Palouse Regional Studies

On the cover: German Immigrants in St. Petersburg, c. 1770. Engels Museum, Saratov,
Russia. *Photo by John Clement*

For Don and Rod

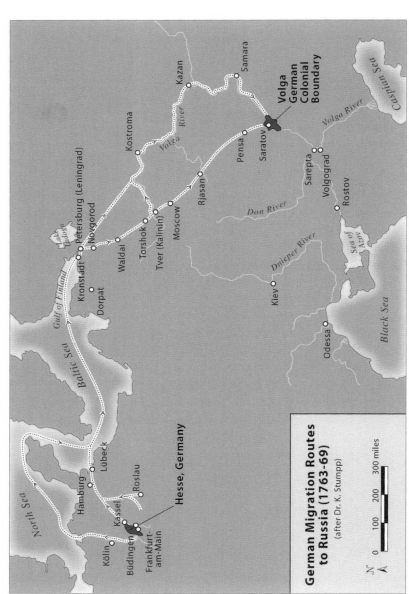

German Migration Routes to Russia (1763-69)

(after Dr. K. Stumpp)

0 100 200 300 miles

Map by Chelsea Feeney, cmcfeeney.com

Contents

Illustrations and Maps

Preface to the 2018 Edition

Andrew gently grasped the half-dozen brittle heads of the Saxonka grain and marveled as if viewing a talisman. "So this is what they brought with them back in Catherine the Great's time?" he asked. That fall day of 2013 my nephew Andrew Wolfe and I were inspecting an array of samples of heirloom grains we had raised at Palouse Colony Farm near Endicott, Washington, with the help of Washington State University agronomists Stephen Jones and Steve Lyon. Through them we learned that a USDA globe-trotting botanist had obtained the sample responsible for our test plot in 1936 from Saratov, Russia. At that perilous time of the Soviet purges, Saratov was the capital of the Volga German Republic—a jurisdiction eradicated by Stalin in the wake of World War II five years later.

This single accession ensured the germplasm of the grain Andrew held would be kept vital for generations of researchers throughout the world. Saxonka had not been commercially raised anywhere in the world for over a century, and we had planted at the very place where the Northwest's first Volga Germans settled in the 1880s. The variety is highly significant to the heritage of *usu Leut* (pronounced *ooza loit*— "our people"), the Germans from Russia, and to world agricultural history. Also known in Russia as "Colonist wheat," cultural lore holds that Saxonka kernels were brought to Russia in the 1760s by German colonists invited by Tsarina Catherine the Great to secure Russia's southwestern frontier borderlands.

In the decade following Catherine's 1763 Manifesto of the Empress, offering generous conditions of settlement to Europeans seeking land and stability in the aftermath of the Seven Years War, some 27,000 Germans left to establish 104 agricultural colonies on the Volga. The Russian government's colonist campaign on the faraway Volga suffered from a host of administrative and logistical failures, and many settlers felt abandoned upon reaching their destinations on the largely uninhabited and undeveloped steppes as winter approached. Many survived only by fashioning crude *zemlyanki*, or dugout earth homes, nearly impossible to keep warm and dry in the harsh Russian elements. The

xii   *Hardship to Homeland*

foresight of those who brought the golden treasure for seed stock may well have spared their lives long before spring planting.

The year 2018 marks a pivotal year in the decade commemorating the 250th anniversary of this epic immigration. Andrew and others have worked in recent years with a dedicated team of WSU agronomists like Jones and Lyon, and others from The McGregor Company of Colfax, Washington, to revive some of the heirloom grains associated with our people's Russian experience. Legendary USDA "plant explorer" Mark Carleton published a series of scholarly articles between the 1890s and 1920 describing how Eastern European grains had revolutionized North American agriculture. Volga Germans had perpetuated Saxonka and other high quality bread wheats in Russia. A succeeding wave of German farmers to Russia's Black Sea region under Tsar Alexander I in the early nineteenth century contributed to widespread production of famed Turkey Red, the wheat that Russian-German Mennonites brought to Kansas in the 1870s.

As a young man raised on a Palouse Country farm between the communities of Endicott and St. John, I had heard many times from first-generation immigrant elders about Old World farming methods and our ancestors' historic trek from Germany to Russia during the reign of Catherine the Great. Her name was mentioned with pride by our elders as "*die Kaisarina Katarina*," and sometimes with a sense of familiarity that enhanced tales of how she had taken time to personally greet them upon arriving in St. Petersburg. Stories retold many times with details of trial and triumph on the epic journeys to Russia, and then to the United States and Canada, have woven this enduring legacy now evident in the lives of my children and grandchildren, nephews and nieces, and other members of their generation. They want to walk inside the cellar-like *zemlyanki* that their ancestors built into hillsides, to hear about the struggles our people endured as civilians during wartime, and about those who perished in service to their country. They want to go to Germany and Russia, and to know where our people fit in American history. They want to eat Saxonka bread, and to know the stories.

Beginning in the 1970s, my wife, Lois, and I began interviewing Russian-German immigrant elders who had settled in Washington, Idaho, and Oregon. Over delicious fare of freshly baked rye bread and homemade berry jams with tea, we asked about their Old World traditions and American settlement experience. We found the fellowship of these elders who had been raised in our grandparents' Volga German colonies of Yagodnaya Polyana (Berry Meadow) and Norka to be of special value because many stories handed down among our families were associated with these places and the rural communities they established in the Pacific Northwest. Along with their tales, they often brought forth bulbous amber necklaces, hand-carved wooden spoons, multicolored embroidered headscarves, and other family heirlooms safeguarded since leaving the colonies.

Northwest places like Moscow, Idaho, and Odessa, Washington, suggest Russian origins, as do smaller rural hamlets like Tiflis and Batum. The story of how our people relocated to the United States and Canada is fascinating not only because of the complex backdrop of East-West tensions since the late nineteenth century, but also because Russian-German immigration to North America began at a time when the Far West was just emerging from the frontier era. The curry comb of Eastern culture had not stroked the open ranges our people first encountered in the 1880s when they began arriving in the Pacific Northwest. In 1881, a vanguard of families from the lower Volga's east bank *Wiesenseite* (Plains Side) traveled from Kansas to San Francisco by rail, and continued on to Portland by steamship. The following year, some of the newcomers traveled by wagon across the Cascades to establish homes in eastern Washington Territory's fertile Palouse Country.

Other Russian-Germans from the western Volga *Bergseite* (Hilly Side) crossed trails with them in 1882 in the boomtown of Walla Walla after they had traveled from Nebraska to Utah by rail and then over the Oregon Trail by wagon train to Washington. The epic journeys undertaken by these and subsequent German colonies from Russia are replete with tense encounters with Native Americans, hazardous trail drives, near fatal mountain crossings, and fraudulent land speculators. While some who "wested" also "busted," the majority endured hardships and prospered to the extent that over 21,000 Russian-Germans were living in the three Northwest states by 1920. (Almost half were first-generation.) Thousands more lived in British Columbia and Alberta. The number of their descendants in the greater Pacific Northwest reached approximately 100,000 by the mid-twentieth century.

Many German names are synonymous with Northwest history: artist Gustavus Sohon who illustrated Isaac Stevens' epic Pacific Coast Railway surveys; timber baron Fredrick Weyerhaeuser; and Henry

Villard, the Bavarian financier who made and lost a fortune establishing the Northern Pacific Railroad. Less known are men and women like Phillip and Anna Green, Frederick and Maria Rosenoff, J. R. Schrag, and Cornelius Jantz. Stories of their exploits are not well known beyond their rural communities, though they led substantial immigrant groups to the varied landscapes of the Northwest from their homelands in Russia—the Volga, Black Sea, and Volhynia regions.

After the initial publication of this book as *The Volga Germans: Pioneers of the Pacific Northwest* in 1980, tumultuous change took place in Eastern Europe with the collapse of the Soviet Union a decade later. These events led to unprecedented access to archival collections in Russia and Ukraine. This has shed considerable light on Volga German history from the time of settlement since the 1760s, to circumstances of daily life and policies influencing emigration that took place between the 1870s and First World War. In the 1990s I retrieved microfilmed copies of some 10,000 pages of administrative and census documents from Russian archives on these topics on behalf of the American Historical Society of Germans from Russia.

The most significant collection of primary source material about Pacific Northwest Germans from Russia since publication of *The Volga Germans* was the discovery in 1986 of a cache of sixteen letters from the 1870s and 1880s. This long lost correspondence, found in an old wooden file cabinet of a farm home near Endicott, provides rare insight into the lives of the Northwest's original vanguard of Volga Germans. Family members referenced in the letters include the Brachs/Bracks, Rothes, and Ochses from Schönfeld; the Greens from Rosenfeld; Klavenos/Klewenos and Schiermans/Scheuermans from New Yagodnaya; Aschenbrenners from Brunnental, and others. Although reflecting a range of village origins, these families shared a spiritual identity through involvement with the *Brüderschaft* (Brotherhood) Movement, a pietistic lay renewal that engulfed the Volga in the 1870s. Its origins were in the missionary activities of two Moravian missionaries who traveled throughout the region in 1868.

Another motivating force behind the movement was a Reformed pastor, Wilhelm Stärkel of Norka, whose family later settled in Portland, Oregon. In many Volga villages, the evangelical minded "Brethren" were derided by local clergy. Most *Brüder*, however, sought to remain within the established Lutheran or Reformed churches; they merely wanted to hold weekly prayer meetings and Bible studies. But such pietistic lay gatherings drew the wrath of many villagers, and the homes of eventual Northwest pioneers Henry Green and Henry Rothe were attacked for harboring Brethren missionaries.

The association of the earliest Russian-German families in the American West with the Brotherhood Movement in Russia suggests that a principal motivation for their emigration was not primarily economic or to avoid service in the Russian army. Indeed, many of the newcomers were military veterans. Rather, they came seeking religious freedom. The collection of letters also aids in tracing the peregrinations of these early Volga German families from 1875 to 1882 when they experienced the hazards of Atlantic sailings, life on Midwestern prairies, and the epic trek to the Pacific Northwest.

A letter fragment penned on January 24, 1882, appears to have been written in Kansas by Henry Rothe to his daughter and son-in-law, Henry and Anna Green, who had recently arrived in Portland. The date provides firm documentation that Volga Germans were in Oregon at that time. Rothe's query about Hussenbach, Russia, native Conrad Dewald, who had recently arrived in Walla Walla via Nebraska, also confirms that the Kansas and Nebraska Volga German "colonies" were acquainted with each other. The letters also reveal that the Northwest did not initially represent the immigrants' long sought land of milk and honey. On December 18, 1883, Rothe's son, Johannes, wrote to relatives who had relocated from Portland to Washington's Palouse Country and mentioned intentions they had recently expressed about returning to the Midwest. But "life yielded little" in Kansas, and Rothe suggested instead that his family might soon follow the pathfinders to the Northwest.

The folk stories featured in this book are based on oral histories related to me by Volga German elders and published here for the first time. Accounts I heard from my youth of peculiar happenings like our ancestors' encounter with Catherine the Great or rescue from a Northwest blizzard came to sound far-fetched in the light of scholarly skepticism. Yet time after time I would encounter documentation and physical evidence in many forms to confirm what were often the strangest parts of these tellings. Following each tale is a brief postscript on informants and related information. I am deeply grateful to Seattle artist Jim Gerlitz, himself a descendant of Volga Germans from Yagodnaya Polyana, for wonderfully illustrating these stories.

This book is based on oral histories and primary sources provided by individuals and institutions in the United States, Canada, Russia, and Germany. I am especially grateful to historian Clifford Trafzer of the University of California, Riverside for informing my understandings of Euro-American settlement in the American West. I also thank Brent Mai, founder of the Concordia University Volga German Studies Center, for his efforts to preserve and perpetuate Northwest Volga German culture. Significant contributions to this work were also made by Igor Plehve, Rector of Saratov State Technical University, and Elizabeth Yerina, Director of the Engels Volga German Archives in Russia; Henny Hysky of the Vogelsberg Heimat Museum in Schotten, Germany; Rev. Horst Gutsche, Calgary, Alberta; and Richard Rye and JoAnn Kuhr of the American Historical Society of Germans from Russia Center in Lincoln, Nebraska.

I also acknowledge the important contributions of Jean Roth, Harland Eastwood, Jim and Sandra Stelter, Jim Repp, Art Kelly, and the late Evelyn Reich, Don Schmick, and Elaine Davison. Oral historians whose experiences, insights, and encouragement contributed most to this work have all now passed on. They included my grandfather, Karl Scheuerman, Alexander Reich, Eva Litzenberger Baldaree, Katherine Morasch, Leta Ochs, Mollie Bafus, Roy Oestereich, Conrad Blumenschein, David Schierman, Daniel and Grace Ochs, Donald Schmick, Alvin Kissler, and Jacob Weber. I owe special thanks to folklorists Timothy and Rosalinda Kloberdanz, authors of *Thunder on the Steppes: Volga German Folklife in a Changing Russia*, for their research on the customs, language, and folk music of *usu Leut*. I am also grateful for encouragement given to me in this work over the years by longtime colleagues and friends Arthur and Maria Ellis, R. D. Ochs, Dan and Kathey (Lust) Birdsell, Gary Schneidmiller, Marlene Michel, Edwin Reich, Connie (Lust) Taylor, Larry Morasch, Jerry Bernhardt, and Marvin Schnaible. Finally, no work of this nature would have been possible without the abiding support of my wife, Lois Jean, and our three children and their families.

Richard D. Scheuerman
Palouse Colony Farm
Endicott, Washington
March 2018

Preface to the 1980 Edition

One of the largest migrations to the Pacific Northwest by a single ethnic group took place in the late nineteenth and early twentieth centuries. That saga, told here, follows the Volga Germans from Germany to Russia and across the Atlantic. Their European origins in the eighteenth century and remarkable program of colonization inaugurated in the 1760s under the Russian empress, Catherine II, comprise a tale of resilience and initiative. When the Russian Senate in 1871 revoked the original terms of settlement, more than 100,000 Volga Germans immigrated to North America. They joined other immigrant waves to the New World, transforming the United States and Canada into centers of Western productivity while influencing North American religion, politics, and social development.

The Volga Germans first settled in the Midwest but many were drawn to the Pacific Northwest in the early 1880s, when railroads arrived in the region. Their involvement in the westward movement provides a valuable case study of the settlement campaigns undertaken by the northwest railroads, principally Henry Villard's Northern Pacific. It also illustrates the interaction between ethnicity and geography in determining regional settlement patterns.

Without the assistance of many helpful people, this narrative could not have been completed. We are deeply indebted to Dr. Philip Nordquist of Pacific Lutheran University in Tacoma, Washington, for his advice concerning the organization and writing of this work. His many helpful suggestions involving aspects of European history and his encouragement have been greatly appreciated. We are equally grateful to Dr. Emmett Eklund for his most enlightening remarks on religious history and his abiding interest in this project. The guidance of Dr. Arthur Martinson and the late Dr. Herman Deutsch in matters relating to Northwest history is gratefully acknowledged. We would also like to thank Donald Messerschmidt, David Stratton, William Willard, and Thomas Kennedy of Washington State University, who have supported our research endeavors.

Several noted authors on the subject of Volga German history have rendered great service by providing relevant materials, notably Mrs.

Emma S. Haynes, Arlington, Virginia, and Mr. Fred Koch, Olympia, Washington. Mrs. Haynes' untiring devotion to this project resulted in the documentation through passenger ship manifests of virtually every family in the original Kansas and Nebraska colonies that immigrated to the Pacific Northwest between 1881 and 1882. Our sincere gratitude is expressed to Dr. Karl Stumpp, Tübingen, West Germany, the eminent authority on the Germans from Russia, for his encouragement and permission to use his excellent series of maps. Ye Galleon Press proprietor Glen Adams, whose name is synonymous with Northwest Americana publishing, and Professor Earl Larrison at the University Press of Idaho (Moscow) deserve thanks for supporting Russian German studies and bringing them into public view. We also thank the many western chapters of the American Historical Society of Germans from Russia (AHSGR) for providing both photographs to illustrate this work and a forum in which to conduct many hours of oral interviews.

No work of this nature could ever have been possible without the cooperation of capable local historians who led us to valuable contacts, new information, and warm friendships. We thank Mr. and Mrs. Roy Oestreich of Ritzville; Mr. and Mrs. Alvin Kissler (Seattle), formerly from Odessa; Miss Jean Roth (Seattle) and Mrs. Elaine Davison for their help on the Walla Walla settlement; Mrs. Anna Weitz, Endicott; Mr. and Mrs. Ray Reich, Colfax; and Alec Horst, Tacoma. Mr. Fred Kromm of Spokane, Mr. William Scheirman of Overland Park, Kansas, and Mrs. Leon Scheuerman of Deerfield, Kansas, also provided valuable source materials. Information gleaned through interviewing first generation immigrants formed a vast reserve of detail essential to this study; participants are listed in the Bibliography. Informants of special note include Mrs. Catherine Luft, Sheboygan, Wisconsin; Mr. Martin Lust, Walla Walla; Mr. Conrad Blumenschein, St. John; Mr. Dave Schierman, College Place; Mr. C. G. Schmick, Colfax; and the late Mr. Alec Reich and Mr. Karl Scheuerman, both of Endicott. In addition, a number of pastors and their families have willingly cooperated and permitted access to most useful sources of information. Appreciation is extended to the Rev. H. Reike family, Rev. K. A. Horn family, Rev. Albert Hausauer, and other pastors and laymen involved in this study.

Staff at several institutions were greatly appreciated, particularly at Pacific Lutheran University Mortvedt Library, Mr. Richard Grefrath and Mrs. Helen Leraas, librarians; Esther Fromm at the Archives of the American Historical Society of Germans from Russia in Greeley, Colorado; John Guido and Terry Abraham, archivists, Holland Library, Washington State University; Rev. Robert C. Wiederaenders, Church Archivist, the American Lutheran Church Archives, Dubuque, Iowa, and its North Pacific District Archive in Seattle. Thankfulness is also extended to Mrs. Henny Hysky, curator, the Vogelsberg Museum in Schotten, West Germany, for her cooperation and assistance and to Mrs. Bob Griffith of Cashmere, and Wayne Rosenoff of Monterey for their encouragement.

Several individuals generously shared their expertise in translating letters and other rare materials; we thank Mrs. Selma Muller, Tacoma; Mrs. Hilda Weirich, Dryden; and Miss Marite Sapiets of the Institute for the Study of Religion and Communism in London. Unless otherwise indicated, the chapter epigraphs were translated by Mrs. Muller from Volga German folk songs included in Erbes' and Sinner's *Volkslieder und Kinderreime aus den Volgakolonien* (1914). Invaluable assistance in the preparation of this manuscript was given by Lois Scheuerman and Cindy DeGrosse and the encouragement extended by our parents is also gratefully acknowledged.

• • •

A variety of names for the Germans from Russia are commonly used in historical sources. In the course of this study, the term "Russian German" is used in a collective sense as a German from any part of Russia. The term "Volga Germans" indicates only those Germans who lived along the lower Volga River, and similarly qualified terms (e.g., Black Sea Germans) refer to Germans of specific geographical origin in Russia.

Until 1918 the Julian calendar was still used in Russia. By the twentieth century it had fallen thirteen days behind the Gregorian calendar of the Western World, losing one day per century between 1700 and 1900. Dates registered in Russian sources during that time reflect the Old Style system (OS) and will be used in reference to that period throughout this study unless indicated otherwise by the initials NS (New Style). When both German and Russian terms appear following their translation in the text, they will be indicated in sequence as follows: (Russian/German).

When both German and Russian terms appear following their translation in the text, they will be indicated in sequence as follows: (Russian/German).

Abbreviations used in footnoting books and serial publications include the following (complete documentation for each is provided in the Bibliography):

DWD—Krause and others, *Denkschrift zum SilberJubilaum des Washington Distrikts der Ev. Luth. Ohio Synode, 1891–1916.*

VRS—Schwabenland, *A History of the Volga Relief Society.*

LS—*Lutheran Standard.*

AHSGR—American Historical Society of Germans from Russia.

Richard D. Scheuerman
Clifford E. Trafzer
Pullman, Washington
April 22, 1980

PART I

Pacific Northwest Volga Germans

Isenburg Castle, Büdingen, the 1766 *Sammelplatz* (gathering place) for emigrants.
John Clement

Volga River near Saratov. *John Clement*

Introduction

In the German village of Nidda in the state of Hesse stands a small stone structure with a single entrance, its massive wooden door crowned by a plaque on which is inscribed: *Der Johanniterturm: Ältestes und ehrwürdigstes Baudenkmal der Stadt...Im 30 jährigen Krieg zerstört.* Built during medieval times, St. John's Tower was once part of the palatial residence of a prominent family but since its destruction in the Thirty Years War (1618–48), it stands alone in the town as a silent reminder of a period in German history when wars ravaged the region. It was from such villages in Hesse and Rhine Palatinate that thousands of people set out in the 1760s to seek new lives elsewhere. While many migrated to the American colonies, others looked eastward to Russia.

Several factors led to this movement, many of which were a culmination of events that began with the Reformation. Martin Luther's remarks in 1521 at the Diet of Worms essentially questioned the authority of the Roman Catholic Church, but thousands of peasants perceived the spirit of reform and Luther's concern for Christian liberty as challenging the very foundations of the oppressive feudal system. German princes and nobles realized the political implications of Luther's theology and sought to assert their political ambitions by breaking away from the control of the Holy Roman Empire. In short, the Reformation advanced a three-fold revolution involving religious, social, and political upheaval.

Early Lutheran converts in the German nobility included Phillip of Hesse, Ulrich of Württemburg, John of Saxony, and others.[1] The German Diet soon became hopelessly divided over religious issues, which continued to be debated while popular discontent seethed in the countryside. Sporadic peasant revolts against ecclesiastical and secular authorities from 1522 to 1524 finally erupted in the ruinous Peasants' War (1524–26).

In 1526 the landgrave of Hesse, Phillip the Magnanimous, formed the League of Gothe and Torgau with John the Steadfast of Saxony in order to solidify and extend Lutheranism. Within two years the Lutheran Church had been established in half of Germany. This did not prevent internal struggles, however, as later in the sixteenth century

1

Lutherans and Calvinists often alternated roles in princely capacities, expelling one another from positions of authority while expecting a corresponding change in the theology of the citizenry. Protestants did unite in the last great religious war in Europe, arising out of a dispute with the Hapsburgs in 1618 over a successor to the Bohemian throne. Over the decades of fighting in the Thirty Years War, no region suffered as much as Hesse and the Rhine Palatinate.[2] Their strategic location between the opposing forces of the southern Catholic states and the Protestants in the north with their ally France, exposed them to ravaging by invading armies. Though the German princes eventually asserted themselves over the Catholic Hapsburgs, the cost in human suffering was horrendous.[3]

Recovery after the Treaty of Westphalia (1648) was further compounded in Hesse-Cassel and Hesse-Darmstadt as the two states became embroiled in a fratricidal war, the *Hessenkrieg*.[4] Foreign expansion into the area was renewed by the French under Louis XIV in 1688 when he dispatched troops to the Rhine after the League of Augsburg refused to accept his claim to a portion of the Elector Palantine's estate. The aggressive policies of the French king led to a full scale invasion of the Rhineland resulting in disastrous conflagrations in the major cities along the Rhine from Phillipsburg to Bingen.

In the ensuing struggles, the French laid waste to large areas of southeast Germany, and although hostilities in the War of the Palatinate (1689–97) were suspended through the Peace of Ryswick, French designs on the area contributed to renewed outbreaks of fighting in the Wars of Spanish Succession (1701–13) and Austrian Succession (1740–48). Each successive campaign exposed a new generation to the ravages of warfare, and while the peasantry bore the cruel consequences, their rulers soon made arrangements to profit from the situation.

Hesse-Cassel in particular provided thousands of mercenaries at foreign expense to fight in Europe during the Seven Years War (1756–63). Although the two Hessian states were again divided by political alliances, the leadership of both houses was characterized by corruption and extravagance, notably Hesse-Darmstadt under Ludwig VII and Ludwig VIII. Whenever burdensome taxes could not support the opulent life of the baroque court, the selling of mercenaries to foreign powers became a convenient method of raising the needed revenue.[5]

The Seven Years War had a major impact on emigration from Germany to Russia for two principal reasons. First, Hesse again became the scene of great decimation throughout the conflict, and second, this period witnessed the ascension of Catherine II, a former German princess, to the Romanov throne in Russia. Prussian advances against the French had been challenged in Hesse by the Duc de Broglie in the spring of 1759 when French forces repulsed the Prussians under Ferdinand of Brunswick northwest of Frankfurt am Main at Bergen. These gains were reversed however when on August 1, 1759, Ferdinand routed the French in a decisive victory at Minden. The retreating French soldiers wreaked havoc on the German countryside, destroying crops and ransacking villages.

Russia entered the conflict under Tsarina Elisabeth, allied with France and Austria against the Prussians and English. Despite heavy losses on all sides, the war continued for years until the balance of power unexpectedly shifted with the Tsarina's death in January 1762 (NS). At her request a nephew, the feeble-minded Peter III, then assumed power and immediately reversed the Russian position into an alliance with Frederick II of Prussia whom he admired as the ideal monarch.[6]

The struggles continued into the next decade, exacting a catastrophic loss of human life. Assistance rendered Frederick by Russia in 1762 was short-lived as a coup d'etat on June 28 in St. Petersburg established Catherine II as "Empress and Autocrat of all the Russians." Her husband, Peter III, was killed days later under circumstances never officially explained. Catherine ordered her generals out of the war. Battle-scarred Europe was exhausted and ready for peace but the settlements reached in 1763 did little to ease the plight of the peasants. Prussian hegemony would become increasingly evident in northern Europe although near the end of the eighteenth century Germany seemed hopelessly divided into over 1,700 states, principalities, and free cities.

The Hessian states were bankrupt and resorted to a program of heavy taxation while returning soldiers formed marauding bands that terrorized the populace.[7] A report from Hesse-Darmstadt dated April 4, 1767, reported:

> The excessive burden of debt and the poverty prevailing at present among the prince's subjects originating partly in the last destructive war, partly in the cattle epidemic existing in many places, partly in the disastrous fluctuating of money values, the creditless and impoverished conditions of the royal subjects; and in addition to this, the present low price of grain, all taken together make the poor subjects unable to pay their present debts or to save themselves from those previously made.[8]

Local magistrates suggested various schemes through which taxes could be reduced, problems between creditors and debtors ameliorated, public granaries established, and various other programs that could alleviate the tragic situation of the peasantry. Unfortunately the princes only listened, taking little action as the masses wasted away in misery or wandered off in attempts to create new lives.[9] Fully a half-dozen generations in such areas of Germany had experienced the deprivation and atrocities of European wars and while many remained, others prepared to emigrate.[10]

In *Briefe über die Auswanderung der Unterhanen besonders nach Russland* [*Letters about the Emigration of Subjects, especially to Russia*] (Gotha 1770), twenty letters appear dealing with the emigration and one by a Herr von Loen reveals the pitiful conditions of the German peasants while blaming the princes themselves for causing their subjects to flee.

> In our time the farmer is the unhappiest of beings; the peasants are slaves; and their labor we can scarcely distinguish from that of the animals which they herd. If you visit a village, you will see children running about half-naked, loudly begging you for alms; their parents have only a few rags to cover their nakedness; two or three scrawny cows must plow the fields and furnish them milk; their granaries are empty; their huts are on the verge of collapsing, and they themselves present a most pitiful appearance. Woe to those princes who by their lusts, tyranny, and mismanagement bring misfortune on so many people! The peasant is always threatened with feudal serfdom, pressed service as messengers, hunting service and digging fortifications. From morning to night he must work the fields over and over, whether the sun remains in the fields, almost becoming a wild beast himself in order to frighten off wild beasts so they do not destroy the crops. That which he saves from the wild beasts is taken by the cruel officers for arrears of taxes.
>
> What is he to do? The most justifiable course consistent with his duty is to leave the land which is unworthy of good citizens and seek another where such citizens are valued and sought after. So he leaves, though willingly, his homeland, his acquaintances and friends, the social life he enjoys, and so on. With a sorrowful heart, he chooses, as a wise man, the lesser of two evils; he prefers to risk his fortunes rather than remain in a country where his ruin is inevitable.[11]

1

The Program of Colonization under Catherine II

Das Manifest der Kaiserin,
Es dachte nach den Deutschen hin,
Sie sollten pflanzen Brot und Wein,
Und sollten auch Kolonisten sein.

The Empress Catherine's Manifest
It thought the Germans would be best.
They were to raise both wine and bread,
And also be colonists, it said.

—*"Das Manifest,"* verse 1

Shortly after the close of the Seven Years War, Catherine II of Russia (1762–96) issued on July 22, 1763, the Manifesto of the Empress, which succeeded in luring thousands of Germans to the vast southwest frontier of her empire. As early as 1752, Tsarina Elisabeth Petrovna (1741–62) had considered peopling the Turkish border region with French Protestants at the suggestion of a French immigration official, de la Fonte.[1] A committee was appointed to consider the project and an active program was formulated, only to be tabled when the Seven Years War broke out in Europe, without any French being settled in the area.

The idea was perpetuated and given new vigor after Catherine II, who had long held grandiose plans for modernizing Russia, was crowned tsarina. Even as a grand duchess married to the heir to the throne, she wrote, "We need people. We must make our wide spaces teem with swarms of people if this be possible."[2] Peter the Great (1689–1725), a century earlier, had launched an ambitious campaign to modernize his backward nation. After centuries of cultural isolation

5

from Europe, Russia in the eighteenth century was just emerging from a quasi-medieval existence. The Petrine reforms succeeded in instituting limited technological and social change by opening the door to Western thought and culture. Under his reign, the capital was moved from Moscow to St. Petersburg, Russia's new port on the Baltic and Peter's "Window to the West." In addition Peter induced over 1,000 German officers and engineers to come to Russia in order to expand trade relations with Europe, construct this new capital, and reshape the government bureaucracy.[3] The influx of Germans under his reign led in 1703 to the construction of a wooden Lutheran church in St. Petersburg. These and other German immigrations into Russia up until 1750 largely constituted what Karl Stumpp has termed the "Urban German element" solicited by the crown from 1550 to 1750.[4]

Another policy initiated by Peter and perpetuated by his successors, which would later be associated with German migrations to Russia, was the calculated intermarriage of the Romanov family with German princely houses. Peter the Great's son Alexis married the princess of Brunswick-Wolfenbüttel in 1711, and in 1725 his daughter Anne married the Duke of Holstein.[5] The result was such that the Russian royal family was almost entirely German by blood at the time Catherine II became tsarina in 1762.

Catherine II was born in Stettin, Germany, in 1729, the daughter of the Prince of Anhalt-Zerbst, a minor principality in Saxony. Named Sophie Auguste Fredericka, she was brought to St. Petersburg at the age of 16 by Empress Elisabeth Petrovna to marry the heir apparent to the throne, later Peter III. Following the palace revolt that unseated him in 1762, Catherine capably assumed the responsibilities of head of state and began to implement plans to reform her backward country in the spirit of Peter the Great. On ascending to the throne Catherine declared that her chief task would be "to devote care and attention to the peace and prosperity of the Empire's wide expanses of territory, which God had entrusted to her, and to the increase of its inhabitants."[6] An intelligent and clever woman, she mastered the Russian language and became devoted to Russia's growth and prosperity. A key element of her program involved the colonization of the fertile lower Volga region, which for centuries had stood idle near the unstable Turkish border, virtually "a happy hunting ground for adventurers, vagrants, bands of marauders and river pirates."[7] Both the eastern plains side (*Wiesenseite*)

Tsarina Catherine the
Great (1762). *Richard
Scheuerman collection*

of the lower Volga and the hilly western side (*Bergseite*) were inhabited by a variety of nomadic peoples of Turkic and Mongolian descent
including the Tatars, Bashkirs, Kirghiz, and Kalmyks.[8]

Since a prerequisite to the continuation of her ambitious policies
was the cooperation of the Russian aristocracy, Catherine found it both
unwise and impractical to suggest that the institution of serfdom be
altered in order to provide the Russian peasantry with the opportunity
to colonize the frontiers. While not only challenging the order of the
nobility on whose support she depended, Catherine realized that the
peasants themselves were incapable of effective colonization. Writing
to the new commission investigating the subject Catherine wrote:

> Russia not only does not have enough inhabitants but it also has such
> vast expanses of land which are neither populated or cultivated. So
> enough incentive cannot be found for the state population to increase...
> To restore an Empire, denuded of inhabitants, it is useless to expect
> help from the children who in the future may be born. Such a hope is in
> any case untimely; people living in these open spaces of theirs have no
> zeal or incentive. Fields which could feed a whole people hardly provide
> enough food for one household.[9]

The logical solution to the dilemma was to summon capable foreign colonists to Russia in order that they "might by their acquired arts, handicrafts, industry, and various machinery as yet unknown in Russia, reveal to Russian citizens the easiest and most efficient ways of tilling the ground, breeding domestic animals, nurturing forests, making the fullest use of all products, establishing their own factories, and regulating the entire peasant economy."[10] Central to this eighteenth-century philosophy was the idea that agriculture was the basic form of productive labor, and that only through its ties to trade and industry could the national wealth increase.[11] This policy was in contrast to mercantilist conceptions of economic growth dominant in Western Europe and pursued previously by the Empress Elisabeth, who sought to extend the financial base of the economy by employing new methods of manufacturing, principally through the silk and fur industries.

However, Catherine did in part resurrect the framework of Elisabeth's earlier scheme to bring French Protestants into Russia. She was particularly impressed with the manner in which the French farmers had transformed the "marshy, sandy, and infertile domains of the King of Prussia" into a region of great productivity.[12] In a decree written personally by the empress and delivered to the Russian Senate on October 14, 1762, Catherine ordered immediate cooperation with the Foreign Office to facilitate the entry of all foreigners wishing to enter Russia.[13] Her manifesto of December 4, 1762, gave the program further impetus and more active measures were taken to inform European peoples of settlement opportunities in Russia as the senate was ordered to publish the manifest "in all languages and in all foreign newspapers."[14] A decree on December 29 directed the Russian Foreign Office to distribute hundreds of copies of the manifesto in various languages to their diplomatic representatives. Furthermore, the Russian ambassadors and representatives were ordered to "not only make known the Manifesto by publishing it in the usual trade periodicals, but also to make every effort to see that it has an effect."[15]

The appeal brought little response. The conflict on the continent brought on by the Seven Years War had still not been resolved and the general feeling of the Russian diplomats was that Catherine's pledge of "imperial kindness and benevolence"[16] in the manifesto was hardly sufficient to attract a significant number of colonists. Writing from London to his uncle the Russian chancellor, Count Vorontsov stated that, "A mere promise to accept those who apply will not attract a large number of settlers, for in that case they will be leaving a situation where they have some hope of security in order to enter a completely unknown situation."[17]

After considering these observations, the Foreign Office submitted a report to the senate recommending payment for each settler's travel expenses since it was assumed it was largely the poor who desired to emigrate, and asked for clarification of such issues as which areas would be open to foreign colonist settlement, what benefits and facilities would be available to them, and how their transport would be arranged once in Russia. In addition the Senate was reminded of Elisabeth's earlier scheme negotiated with de la Fonte and these proposals were attached in order to help resolve the question.

The program may well have succumbed to the same fate as other long pending legislation in the bureaucratic committee of the senate had not Catherine personally intervened in the matter. At her insistence, a list of privileges and conditions were drafted under the supervision of the procurator general, A. I. Glebov, to form the July 22, 1763, Manifesto of the Empress Catherine II.[18] As the foundation of Russia's new colonization policy, it became the instrument through which thousands of impoverished Europeans, primarily Germans, were enabled to begin new lives in Russia between 1763 and 1766.[19]

Variously termed a "masterpiece of immigration propaganda" and the "Magna Carta"[20] of the German colonists in Russia, the manifesto enumerated the conditions of settlement summarized as follows:

1. All foreigners received permission to settle in any Russian province by declaring their desire to do so to the Chancery for the Guardianship of Foreigners (*Tutel-Kanzlei für Ausländer/Kantselyariya Opekunstva Inostrantsev*) in St. Petersburg or to the proper authorities of Russian border towns. Prospective colonists who lacked the means to settle elsewhere need only to apply to the Russian diplomatic representative who would, at the expense of the crown, supply them with the money for travel expenses.

2. On arrival in Russia the settlers had to declare whether they wanted to register as merchants, industrialists, or if they desired to form farming settlements in appropriate areas. In accordance with their response they received assignments after taking the oath of allegiance in accordance with their faith.

3. In addition other rights and privileges were granted:
   a) Freedom of religion was guaranteed with the right to construct churches and belfries and to maintain pastors and other church officials. Proselyting Christians of other faiths in Russia was strictly forbidden although converting Moslems was permitted.
   b) The colonists were to be immune from all taxes, military, and government service; both "ordinary and extraordinary" for those who settled in colonies in uninhabited territories, this to last thirty years, after which they would be under the same obligation as native Russians to pay taxes and carry out local government service. However, they were freed "for eternal time" from military service.
   c) Settlers were to receive sufficient land well-suited to growing grain as well as for building factories and other new industries for which special subsidies and exemption would be allowed.
   d) Foreign industrialists who built factories in Russia at their own expense could purchase the necessary serfs and peasants.
   e) Ten-year, interest-free loans were given for building, to obtain livestock, and agricultural implements.
   f) Permission was granted to import specified amounts of personal property and settlers were guaranteed freedom to return to their countries of origin, though a portion of their property would be relinquished to the state.
   g) Colonists had the right of local self-government within the limits of Russian state law.
   h) Settlers were allowed to organize duty-free markets and fairs in the colonies they established.
   i) Upon arrival in Russia, settlers were allotted money for their sustenance and transport to the assigned areas of settlement.
   j) Any settler wishing to discuss other privileges would be allowed to address his request to the government.[21]

Section II of an attached register of vacant lands specified a vast area up and down the Volga River from Saratov in the province of Astrakhan. It was to this region in particular that the colonists were directed.

In July of 1763, on the same day that the manifesto was promulgated, a second decree established a special government department to administer the anticipated flood of foreign settlement. The Chancery for the Guardianship of Foreigners (*Tutel-Kanzlei*) was responsible only to the empress and given far-reaching authority. As the equivalent of a government ministry, its central functions were to supervise the Russian representatives of the program throughout Europe and arrange for colonist transportation and payments. Appointed as president of the department was a personal favorite of the empress, Count Gregory Orlov. Orlov supervised operations in what was destined to become a ponderous bureaucracy that often led to disastrous incidents during settlement.[22] With an enormous annual budget of 200,000 rubles, the *Tutel-Kanzlei* consisted of several counselors appointed by the president, a "special secretary with a knowledge of foreign languages" to adjudicate diplomatic problems, lesser bureaucrats, translators,[23] and later, immigrant agents in Europe.

Despite the favorable intentions of the Russian diplomats in Europe, it became increasingly difficult to execute their normal responsibilities while directing immigration activities. In 1764 only about four hundred families arrived in Russia,[24] most from Westphalia with others from Scandinavia. Mismanagement was widespread as scores of disreputable individuals received financial support initially, only to refuse to emigrate at the appointed time.[25] Opposition to the program extended

Catherine the Great's 1763 Manifesto. *Engels Museum, Saratov, Russia. Photo by John Clement*

throughout Europe and only in England, Holland, and southwestern Germany did the activities of the recruiting agents initially meet little opposition. Religious conflicts, abject poverty caused by the wars, and the corrupt rule of the princes made this area of Germany particularly receptive to Catherine's invitation. Centers for departure to Russia during this early stage were established in Regensburg, Freiburg, Roslau, Worms, and elsewhere.

Great response in the two Hessian states of Cassel and Darmstadt and in the Rhineland led to the concentration of a major effort of the colonization campaign there under the authority of the Russian ambassador to the Reichstag at Regensburg, Johann Simolin. In an effort to alleviate the deceptive practices of some prospective emigrants, the program underwent two important revisions in Germany at Simolin's recommendation. Since previous experience demonstrated the difficulties of transportation and regular payment of expenses during overland treks to Russia, the procedure was systematized by selecting Lübeck in December, 1763, as the central gathering and dispersal point to Russia. A reliable merchant there, Heinrich Schmidt, was appointed special commissioner in May 1764, to supervise the operations.[26] From Lübeck, Hanseatic or English vessels shipped the emigrants to Kronstadt near St. Petersburg.[27]

The *Tutel-Kanzlei* offered proprietorships to individuals capable of organizing scores of emigrants for settlement in Russia. Several French immigration recruiters responded, most of whom acted with numerous independent agents through unscrupulous tactics to entice people to emigrate.[28] The fraudulent methods they utilized to fill various transport quotas led to their characterization as *Menschenfänger* (people catchers) and *Seelenverkäufer* (soul sellers).[29] While they succeeded in attracting thousands to Russia, their approach was condemned by Simolin, whose more orderly program involved as much as possible the sanction of local authorities.[30] As the combined effect of these efforts grew, particularly in Germany, the ruling families realized that their labor force and tax base were steadily eroding and responded with legislation restricting emigration. In 1764 action was taken in the German states of Bavaria, Saxony, Hamburg, and Würzburg to forbid further emigration to Russia and in the following year Frederick II of Prussia took steps to remove the foreign agents from his county.[31]

By 1766 it had become clear to Simolin and the various French recruiters that concentrated work in areas of southern Germany, where the ruinous effects of the Seven Years War were still widespread, would continue to be advantageous. Simolin was assisted in his endeavors by two German special commissioners, Friedrich Meixner in Ulm and Johann Facius, headquartered in Frankfurt am Main, beneath whom functioned a number of German agents at various assembly points. Facius' achievements in Hesse became particularly noteworthy to Simolin while at the same time attracting the suspicions of the local magistrates.

In a letter to the government of Hesse-Darmstadt on February 7, 1766, the Counsellor-President of Mainz, Friedrich Karl Joseph von Erthal, wrote:

> According to reliable reports, emissaries…are busily recruiting many of our country's subjects to go to foreign colonies. They are successful by picturing untrue advantages, in gaining large crowds of colonists…who soon go to ruin…Since, however, the country is in danger because of this disadvantageous depopulation; we deem it necessary for the preservation of our country's welfare…that the harmful recruiters be prevented from carrying out their intentions as soon as possible.[32]

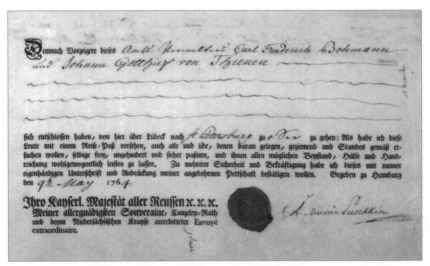

German immigrant travel pass to Russia, 1764. *Engels Museum, Saratov, Russia. Photo by John Clement*

The Hessian government concurred in a letter of reply on February 24, 1766, adding that it would "instruct each and every official to meet this evil with great care and diligently further recruitment."[33] Accordingly, edicts forbidding emigration and threatening emigrants with the expropriation of the possessions were issued in Mainz on February 18, by the Prince of Nassau-Weilburg on April 12, and by the Mayor and Council of the Free City of Frankfurt am Main on April 21. Concerted action was taken similarly by the princes of the Lower Rhine and in the province of the Palatinate and on April 28 by the landgrave of Hesse.[34]

In such pronouncements the activities of the agents for settlement in Russia were variously labelled *das verderbliche Unheil* (the pernicious disaster), *einer Menschen Handel* (a slave trade), and a trade dealing with people *wie mit dem Viehe* (as though they were cattle).[35] In some cases advocating the arrest and execution of the offenders, Simolin sought to arbitrate the matter through the proper diplomatic channels while suggesting to Facius in Frankfurt that he "quietly and well ahead of time" find a more secure place to reside in the area.[36]

Various court-appointed investigators made journeys throughout Hesse to ascertain the nature of the problem, finding much of the citizenry still resolved to emigrate due to the pressing economic situation; particularly distressing conditions prevailed from the Odenwald to Vogelsberg areas. Official recommendations to eliminate servile tributes, establish food repositories, and reduce interest rates on loans were disdained by government officials who chose to advocate a less costly and inadequate solution of "honest work and diligence."[37]

After considerable effort following his expulsion from Frankfurt, Facius succeeded in relocating his operations to Büdingen, the capital of the small Duchy of Isenburg located northeast of Frankfurt am Main near the hilly Vogelsberg area.[38] In this relatively isolated area Facius received an overwhelming response at a time when a Hamburg official of the *Tutel-Kanzlei* ordered him to "halt the sending of more colonists for the year entirely."[39] Simolin immediately filed a vehement objection to Catherine II herself upon learning of Facius' embarrassing position in Büdingen, where scores of Germans were preparing to leave and were living in the city on crown subsidies.[40] The entire issue of curtailing the program at this point was contrary to Simolin's personal plans to establish a continuing ordered flow of European colonists to develop the Russian's vast agricultural and industrial potential. However, bureaucratic difficulties in the *Tutel-Kanzlei* with the settlement program for the vast empire were becoming increasingly apparent and heavy foreign diplomatic pressure was now being exerted in St. Petersburg.

Though Simolin's intervention allowed Facius to continue his operations in Isenburg throughout the summer of 1766,[41] the Russian government arranged for the publication of a decree in German newspapers that September, warning that "in the year following 1766, settlers would no longer be accepted" and they were exhorted not to be deceived into "making agreements with persons independently assembling settlers." Simolin had received the previous June a dispatch from the Russian vice-chancellor, Nikita Panin,[42] directing him to "limit himself to sending only the settlers who have already been accepted and who cannot be decently discharged."[43] The significance of this action is evident in that most of the Volga German colonists in Russia that ultimately immigrated to America's Pacific Northwest descended from those recruited by Facius in Büdingen in the summer of 1766.

Lübeck, Germany, c. 1750. *Richard Scheuerman collection*

When promised a subsidy for the use of his capital as Facius' new *Sammelplatz* (assembly point) for organizing emigrant caravans, the Duke of Isenburg in Büdingen reciprocated by promising to "afford every assistance" to him.[44] A guarantee was secured against inflated prices under such conditions for food, provisions, wood, straw, and other supplies. Simolin was soon reporting that "Commissioner Facius, having now changed his place of residence from Frankfurt to Büdingen, cannot find words to adequately praise the goodwill and friendliness which the ruling family there has shown, both to him personally and in the matter of the settlers, on the recommendation of my letter." He further stated that in order to "accommodate the colonists, he was given the use of the local town-hall and another large public building, and if they found these too crowded, he was allowed to quarter the settlers in the house of any citizen. Bakers, butchers, and brewers were ordered to provide sufficient edible provisions and to sell these for a fair price." The general public was ordered not "to lend anything to a settler, and if he did, no complaints would be dealt with." According to Simolin, the "ruling Duke of Isenburg-Büdingen himself made it clear to the commissioner that if he experienced any difficulties, he was to apply directly to him."[45]

Facius sent the first group of settlers from Büdingen to Lübeck between February 25 and March 6, 1766. The Germans moved overland through Schlitz, Cassel, and Hildesheim to the port city of Lübeck, a journey involving approximately five hundred people per trek.[46] As the parties moved through the towns, it was not uncommon to attract the interest of others who joined the groups of immigrants bound for the Volga region. In Lübeck they boarded ships and began their long, arduous journey to their new home in Russia. Once on Russian soil, the Germans acquired wagons, which they loaded with their goods and their families. Thus they began their lives in their adopted country of Russia. A typical column departing Büdingen in the summer of 1766 consisted of eighty families from some thirty-seven villages in Vogelsberg and neighboring areas who would ultimately found the Volga colony of Yagodnaya Polyana (Beerenfeld) the following year.[47]

These renewed activities elicited two divergent responses in the surrounding provinces where the emigration had been officially curtailed. Such appeals as the following addressed to the landgrave of Hesse-Darmstadt drew the sympathies of some and the condemnation of others:

> We the following people are as a whole all so reduced in circumstances that we for that reason are prepared to take a beggar's staff, because even our few possessions have debts and we can not support ourselves. For that reason we have decided to travel to the Russian Empire with others. Most esteemed landgrave, most gracious prince and master, I Johann Hofmann, myself and family, Johannes Bechtold with wife and

children have been arrested and put in a state of serfdom to you lord-
ship and because of this and to be permitted to leave the country we
need your gracious dispensation. We, therefore, ask your princely serene
Highness that you graciously grant our most subservient, humble and
prostrate request to leave your princely lands. We comfort ourselves
with the thought of a most gracious favorable hearing, etc.

> Johann Hofmann with wife and 5 children
> Johannes Bechtold with wife and 3 children
> George Michel Müller with wife and 2 children
> Johann Tobias Lentz with wife and 4 children
> Johannes Alten, widower with 5 children
>
> Von Eckhardsborn
> District Lissberg Superior
> Baliwick Nidda[48]

Such pleas were not isolated and evoked the sympathies of many
officials. On March 7, 1766, the Hessian government in Giessen
advised the landgrave in a report that it would not be harmful to the
state to allow emigration in such cases where debt and poverty were the
motivating circumstances as their efforts to mitigate these situations
had been admittedly fruitless.[49]

Coupled with additional recommendations by other magistrates,
principally the Elector of Mainz, who demanded a strict enforcement
of the earlier legislation forbidding emigration altogether, the Hessian
government sought a compromise. It released to its courts a statement
dated April 11, 1766, ordering that permission to emigrate could only
be given to those "indolent" persons who had paid all outstanding taxes
and fulfilled their civil obligations, realizing that they would not be
extended acceptance in the future should they ever desire to return.
Likewise, anyone immigrating without permission from the government was in danger of having all of their property and any remunera-
tion for previously sold personal items confiscated by the government.
Furthermore, the borders would be carefully watched to prevent anyone
from leaving without proper authority, and anyone who observed and
reported a Russian agent operating in Hesse-Darmstadt would receive
a reward of twelve florins.[50]

Inevitably authorities in areas neighboring Isenburg began calling
upon the government at Büdingen to expel Facius since their decrees,

by nature difficult to adequately enforce, had not resulted in stemming the steady flow of their subjects to refuge in Isenburg. Throngs of people converged on the town and made preparations to depart, with 375 marriages taking place in the small village between February 24 and July 8, 1766.[51] Particularly incensed were officials in Hanau and Mainz who learned that twenty-five and twenty-two citizens from their cities respectively had been illegally accepted into one of Facius' transports. Simolin attempted to arbitrate the dispute by ordering these forty-seven persons be excluded from the group en route to Lübeck while Facius promised to add a special Isenburg government official to his staff in order to check the backgrounds of prospective emigrants.[52]

Nevertheless, in accordance with the instructions from the Empress, Simolin ordered Facius to attenuate recruitment and by the close of 1766 operations throughout Germany had virtually ended. It was, however, the culmination of one of the most successful efforts ever in a programmed migration with approximately 27,000 people immigrating to Russia's Volga region alone between 1763 and 1766.[53] Three thousand families of "crown" settlers were largely recruited by Facius alone, the remainder under the authority of proprietors.[54]

Although Catherine's original manifestos regarding colonization indicated settlers would "be assigned to their destination according to their wishes and desires," she modified this clause through the Ukase (decree) of March 19, 1764, in which she appropriated lands in the Saratov province for their occupation, extending between the Volga and Medveditza Rivers from Volsk to Tsaritsyn. Later that year and in 1765 she arranged proprietory grants on the east side of the Volga in the province of Samara. It was to these regions that the majority of the German colonists were directed and by the end of 1767 they had founded 104 colonies,[55] forty-four on the western *Bergseite* and sixty on the eastern *Wiesenseite*.

In Germany final action was taken to curb emigration as German princes prevailed upon Emperor Joseph II to issue an edict on July 7, 1768, prohibiting all such foreign activity in the remaining free cities of the Empire that harbored agents.[56] As the Russian government had already begun curtailing transport subsidies, only 604 persons managed to emigrate between 1767 and 1773.[57] These did so voluntarily and some founded the Volga colony of Pobochnaya in 1772 while others were settled in colonies previously established on the Volga.[58]

2

Colonial Development on the Volga

Wir verliessen unser Vaterland,
Und zogen in das Russenland.
Die Russen war'n u ns sehr beneidt,
Und weil wir war'n so lan befreit.

And so we left our fatherland,
To Russia then we moved, as planned.
But jealous the Russians turned out to be,
Because so long we had been free.

—*"Das Manifest,"* verse 2

Migration and Settlement

The nine-hundred-mile voyage from Germany to Russia could normally be made in nine days although events often prolonged it to weeks and in one instance to nearly three months. For the most part the delays were unavoidable due to inclement weather or unfavorable winds, but often ship captains wanted to wait and sell their provisions at inflated prices as supplies diminished.[1] According to one German passenger:

> The majority of us had never been upon a ship, it was hard for people to stand up because of the natural swaying of the boat. They tumbled against each other; fear and trembling mastered every mind; one cried, another swore, the majority prayed, yet in such a varied mixture that out of it all arose a strange and woeful cry.[2]

Reports on food and accommodations vary, some offering only praise for their treatment while others stated the only food available was salt, moldy bread, and water.[3]

After arrival in Kronstadt, the Russian naval port on an island in the Gulf of Finland, the colonists were taken to the city of Oranienbaum

19

(Lomonosov) on the mainland, the site of one of Catherine's royal residences. The German pastor of the Lutheran Church there would often
lead them in the oath of allegiance to the Russian crown. Catherine
herself sometimes went there personally to welcome the colonists in
their native tongue. Many of them had intended to pursue their trades
near St. Petersburg but most were compelled by Guardianship Chancery officials to join the others in developing the agricultural districts
on the lower Volga. The colonists often remained in Oranienbaum
from two to six weeks while preparations were made for their trek to
the Volga, which could take place over various routes. Some crowded
again into ships which took them up the Neva River past St. Petersburg
to Schlüsselburg and down Lake Lagoda to Novgorod via the Volkov
River. From there they traveled overland to Torshok on the Volga where
ships transported them to Saratov. From there the groups dispersed to
the sites of proposed settlements.[4]

A second major route led entirely overland from Oranienbaum, the
men on foot escorting wagons loaded with women, children, and provisions as they traveled southeast through Novgorod, Waldai, and Tver. At
this point some traveled on barges down the Volga to Saratov while others continued overland through Moscow, Ryazan, Penza, and Petrovsk
to Saratov. Guided by Russian officers, the caravans traveled deep into
the interior on primitive roads that became nearly impassable in the fall
and spring; heavy Russian snows prevented travel by both river and land

Kronstadt Harbor near St. Petersburg, c. 1765. *Richard Scheuerman collection*

during the harsh winter months. While the advertisements had indicated such an excursion from St. Petersburg to Saratov could be accomplished in two to three weeks by land or from five to six weeks *zu Wasser auf dem Wolga* (by water on the Volga), in actuality it often took from nine to eighteen months for the settlers to complete the entire trip.[5]

During the coldest winter months the immigrants were quartered in the homes of Russian peasants in villages such as Torschok and Kostroma,[6] where they had to adapt to the peasant diet consisting largely of cabbage soup, millet porridge, and *kvas* (a fermented grain beverage).[7]

Great distances remained to be covered after travel recommenced in the spring; many colonists finally reached their destinations on the Volga too late to plant their crops and many were compelled to eat the seed grain to avoid starvation.

The first contingent of German colonists arrived in the Volga settlement area to establish the village of Dobrinka, located near Kamyshin, on June 29, 1764. By the fall of the year additional expeditions founded Beideck, Shilling, Galka, and Anton. The steady stream of German settlers peaked in 1767 when sixty-eight colonies were established, including several that would contribute heavily to nineteenth-century emigration from Russia to America's Pacific Northwest, most notably Kolb, Yagodnaya Polyana, Norka, Frank, Walter, Warenburg, and Hussenbach.[8] All were located on the *Bergseite*, and two other villages there would also be involved in this later movement: Balzer, founded in 1765, and Messer in 1766.

Since many had expected to find available materials and buildings constructed in anticipation of their arrival, the sudden termination of their journey on the broad unbroken steppe instilled in many a sense of utter abandonment. One of the colonists who established Kratzke in 1767[9] recalled the scene:

> Our guides call "Halt!" at which we were very much surprised because it was early to put up for the night; our surprise soon changed to astonishment and terror when they told us that we were at the end of our journey. We looked at each other, astonished to see ourselves here in a wilderness; as far as the eye could see, nothing was visible except a small bit of woods of grass, mostly withered and about three shoes high. Not one of us made a start to climb down from his horse or wagon, and when the first general dismay had been somewhat dissipated, you could

read the desire in every face to turn back. This, however, was not possible. With a sigh, one after another climbed down, and the announcement by the lieutenant, given with a certain degree of importance, that everything we saw here was presented to us with the compliments of the Empress, did not produce in one of us the slightest pleasure. How could such a feeling have been possible, with a gift which was useless in its present condition and had not a particle of value; a gift that must first be created by us with great toil and which gave no certain assurance that it would repay the labor and time spent upon it.

"This is truly the paradise which the Russian emissaries promised us in Lübeck," said one of my fellow sufferers with a sad face.

"It is the 'lost paradise,' good friend," I assured.[10]

The column of eighty families that departed Büdingen in the summer of 1766 abruptly arrived at their destination forty miles northwest of Saratov on August 28, 1767.[11] Again the colonists were dumbfounded when they were commanded "Here you will stay!"[12] Without proper tools and implements it was impossible to cut lumber from the forest to the north or turn the virgin sod. Moreover, no one believed that the spring there could support an entire colony.

> So a few men took some arms and went north (about two miles)... and heard a strong roaring of water in a deep gorge, like a small waterfall. They worked their way through in numerable obstacles until they found it. Nobody had ever found this spring before them. Everybody agreed this was the place for their new colony...Yagodnaya Polyana (Berry Meadow).[13]

As with other groups immigrating to start new colonies, the problem of shelter became acute in a land where early winters strike with great severity. The settlers learned from the native Russians how to construct *zemlyanki*, or earth houses, which consisted of excavated pits roofed with wagon planks, limbs, and twigs, then covered with a mixture of dry grass and mud. Most dugouts, particularly those constructed in low-lying areas or on river banks, were threatened by heavy spring runoffs. Marauding packs of wolves were a constant threat to livestock, and winter trips across the glistening steppes in troikas were sometimes interrupted by the descending predators. For this reason an extra horse or colt was often tied to the sleigh and released if necessary to deter their attacks.[14] The difficult plight of the German settlers, suffering from constant dampness in their earthen homes, led to an alarmingly mortality rate, particularly among the infants.

One of the original colonists, Anton Schneider, described the conditions: "Throughout the winter we lived miserably and in greatest need. The dark winter days and the eternally long nights seemed to last forever. We were separate from all other human beings, and in many cases did not even have enough to eat."[15]

The number of German colonist families on the Volga decreased from 6,433 in 1769 to 4,858 in 1775 and stability was not established until 1785.[16] Russian German historians came to term the period between 1765 and 1775 *Die Jahre der Not* (the Years of Want). In many cases it took several years before the townsites could be platted and the blocks sectioned off into homesites. Some homes were built with bricks formed from loam mixed with straw and covered with pole-framed, thatched roofs. Rectangular wood dwellings were later constructed parallel to the street as the building materials became available. These homes were typified by an enclosed central entryway opposite the street side leading into a summer kitchen. Two nearly identical rooms flanked the entryway serving as living quarters for the extended family. Furnished simply, each room usually held two or three beds, a table and benches for eating, and a wall cabinet holding wooden spoons, bowls, the family Bible, and other necessary items. Farmyards were arranged six to a block, usually about 125 feet wide and nearly twice as long, and divided into front and rear portions (*Fehderhof* and *Hinnerhof*). The former was a fenced compound enclosing the family home, barns, equipment sheds, root cellar, and a fireproof hut to protect valuables. In the *Hinnerhof* the family maintained a large vegetable garden and several fruit trees. Wooden granaries were also often built there to escape damage in case of a house fire.[17]

Most Volga German villages had a single main street and several parallel and cross streets with the church and school at the center of the community. Certain streams, wells, stone quarries, sand pits, and hardpan deposits for whitewash were held for use by all residents of the colony. Woodlands were protected, though certain areas were periodically opened for cutting. Apiaries were established in some colonies with the hives often formed out of hollowed tree trunks. Families farmed their eighty-acre allotments in the outlying areas but rarely lived apart from the colony. In later years, it often became necessary for some to lease or extend operations to lands located on the periphery of the colony's domain. In such instances a *khutor*, or self-sustaining settlement, often composed of a dozen or more families, was established.

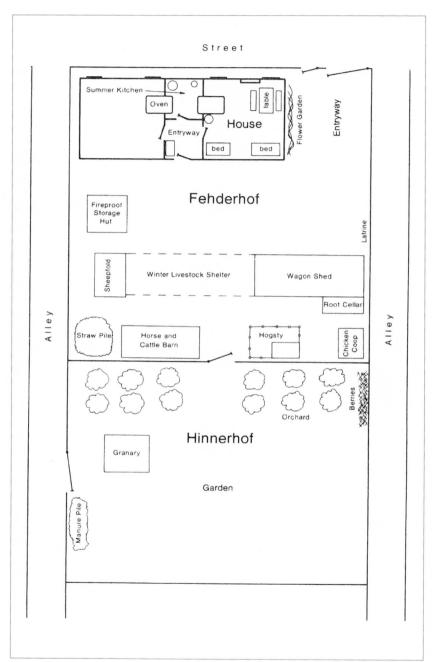

Volga German farmstead.

In addition to the natural calamities associated with their early settlement, conflicts with the indigenous peoples of the Volga also stalled colonial development. Bands of escaped Russian serfs and fugitives stalked the region, attacking and robbing the German colonists. The nomadic Mongol tribes of Kirghiz and Buddhist Kalmyks looked with suspicion upon the encroaching settlers. As early as 1764, the German colonists were assailed by marauders who sought money, provisions, livestock, and in some cases enslaved their captives. The Kirghiz became particularly adept at horse raiding and wreaked devastation on a wide scale on the *Wiesenseite* beginning in 1771, particularly in villages along the Great and Little Karaman Rivers. Such depredations continued for over a century, and as late as 1882 nearly 10,000 horses were reported stolen during the previous eight-year period on the east side as well as innumerable cattle and sheep.[18]

Insight into the gradually improving conditions on the *Bergseite* is reflected in the following letter, one of the few to survive the primitive postal services that severely restricted communication with the German homeland. Written in January 1774 by Johann Heinrich Kühn of Beideck, the letter was sent to his relatives in Hesse describing his journey and conditions of settlement. After praising God, "who has shown me and my loved ones so much grace," he thanked his "dear Saviour" who had "torn us out of earthly poverty and transformed us to a land and climate where we have nothing more to complain about than our physical needs." Kühn reported: "we have a climate suitable for growing and the soil is fertile. We can write this in truth—everything can be raised here, corn, wheat, barley, oats, peas, lentils, millet, potatoes, tobacco…watermelons, melons and cherries." Not only was he encouraged by the possibilities of production, but he was likewise excited about the marketing possibilities of these and other crops, including hay, cabbage, cucumbers, and other vegetables. Kühn was convinced that livestock thrived in the natural habitat along the Volga, and in particular he felt that hogs, horses, cows, oxen, chickens, and geese did well in the region. He believed that the Germans who had moved to Russia had made the correct decision, and he wrote:

> When we, dear friends, think back to our fatherland, what a great change now has taken place in the meantime, how we were burdened down with work and ate our bread in tears but now have been set in material and mental security—for which I and my dear wife and

children want to give thanks our whole life. Our great monarch cared for us at our arrival with a real mother's heart. Our great Empress as long as we can breathe, that our dear Savior will bless her to the thousandth generation and grant all inhabitants peace and tranquility.[19]

Revolt

By the following summer, however, whatever tranquility existed in the Volga German colonies was shattered by one of the greatest peasant revolts in Russian history. Beginning in the autumn of 1773, the Don Cossack, Emelian Pugachev, led the insurrection, posing as the escaped and still reigning true Tsar of Russia, Peter III, who intended to punish his wife Catherine II. He promised freedom from serfdom and taxation and called for the extermination of civil officials and landlords. Within months the rebellion attracted thousands of serfs, factory workers, and miners, Old Believers, Tatars, Bashkirs, and others who descended in a massive campaign southeast from Petrovsk toward Saratov in the first week of August 1774. On August 5, Yagodnaya Polyana was attacked, three men were captured and later whipped to death.[20] The following day Saratov was taken and the rebels ransacked the city, opening prisons, government storehouses and executing captured aristocrats and officials whose bodies Pugachev ordered left unburied.[21] After three days he led his forces down along the west bank of the Volga through the German villages, which he left ravaged and in ashes.

Many settlers fled to hide in the countryside, burying what few valuables they possessed while others remained in the villages. One such individual, Johann Wilhelm Stärkel, great-grandfather of Reverend Wilhelm Stärkel, a leading figure in the later pietistic movement, was seized by Pugachev's men when they entered the colony of Norka. Along with others he was forced to drive the rebels' stolen wagons to a point near Kamyshin and later miraculously escaped.[22] Continuing to sweep southward, the main force under Pugachev passed through Dönhof and approached Kratzke where "cellars, and clay pits and even wells were filled with all kinds of property and strewn with earth. The cattle were driven into the forests and canyons or tied among the reeds and rushes of the river."[23]

A young man, hiding with others in the garret of the Kratzke schoolhouse, later related how Pugachev arrived in front of the school in a heavily escorted carriage and promptly had a gallows erected from two long poles and a crossbeam. Four bound prisoners on horseback were led in and beaten, then hung in pairs on two ropes thrown over the crossbeam.[24] The grim scene was repeated many times as surviving colonists recalled the times when at night the horizon was bright with the lurid flames of destruction in the villages. Pugachev was finally defeated by Government forces south of Sarepta and was later captured following his betrayal by fellow rebels. He was taken to Moscow where after a trial, he was executed.

Such violent episodes were rare in the isolated Volga colonies and their location prevented any direct involvement in the European wars of the period. However, following the debacle of Napoleon's invasion of Russia in the Franco-Russian War of 1812, many German-speaking prisoners of war from Lorraine, Switzerland, Mainz, Brunswick, and other powers allied with Napoleon were sent to the Volga colonies for internment. Weary of the endless wars being waged on the continent, many chose to marry into local families and begin new lives among the secluded colonists.

Economic Prosperity

Following the difficult period of adjustment and drought, economic prosperity steadily developed in the Volga colonies, especially in the realm of agricultural production. This was particularly evident on the *Bergseite* where the black chernozem soil was highly organic and often three to five feet deep. This region is among the most fertile in Europe although the soil becomes more chestnut-brown in color further south on both sides of the river, deteriorating into the semidesert conditions of the upper Caspian depression.[25]

Apart from Saratov, the old center of trade and industry for the Volga colonies, the village of Sarepta, founded on September 3, 1765, developed into an important industrial center. Settling over 150 miles below the original colonial enclave's southern boundary, Moravian Brethren in Sarepta introduced the manufacture of *sarpinka*, a choice cotton material, to the region.[26] The economic achievements of this industry gained the attention of the Guardianship Chancery, where the authorities were quick to point out their success to other Russian officials. The production of the cloth soon expanded to Norka, Messer, Balzer, Katharinenstadt, and elsewhere and was exported throughout the empire, making Sarepta a showplace for visiting government bureaucrats and delegations.

Virtually every German colony constructed a flour mill for local consumption, most on the western side and initially powered by water from the abundant streams. Settlers on the eastern plains side fashioned Dutch-type windmills. Management of the mills, which were technically owned by the colony, was awarded on a bid basis; resulting funds were used to operate the school system and other public services in the village. Oil mills were also widespread in the colonies; tall sunflowers grew well in the area and the crushed seeds from their broad yellow heads yielded a high-quality cooking oil and the refuse was fed to the livestock.[27] Tanning and tobacco industries also developed. The hilly prairies of the *Bergseite* were well-suited to cattle production while tobacco growing and pipe manufacturing were largely confined to the *Wiesenseite*.

Balzer became an important commercial center for the Volga colonies, its fabric dyeing establishments, founded in 1840, contributing to the prosperity of its textile mills.[28] At one point the city boasted of two oil mills, a foundry and machine factory, two clothing factories, seventy-two *sarpinka* factories with fourteen thousand looms, fifteen dyeing houses, seventeen tanneries, twelve pelt factories, twelve smitheries, and numerous other enterprises.[29]

Colonial Agriculture

The vast majority of colonists, as many as 97 percent, remained farmers. The first decade of despairing crop yields ended in 1775 when adequate rains fell throughout the region, ending the period of drought. In addition the virgin acreage could be brought under greater cultivation as colonial smiths replaced the crude Russian *sokhi* or iron-tipped wooden plows. The settlers introduced German moldboard plowshares which, when used singly or joined in pairs, could penetrate deeper and turn larger tracts of the heavy sod. Cultivation improved with iron harrow teeth and other implements and many colonists became adept at breeding quality draft horses to pull tillage equipment.

The colonies found it impractical to farm intensively since large areas were opened for them to cultivate. Commercial fertilizing techniques were unknown but they did practice three and four-year crop rotation.

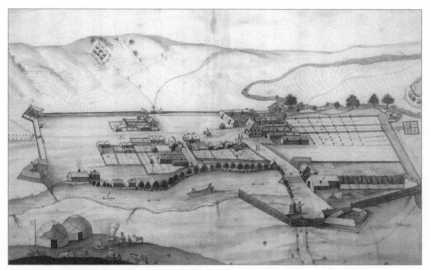

Plat view of Sarepta, Russia, c. 1780. *Concordia Center for Volga German Studies, Portland*

A typical field cycle might rotate from rye one year to sunflowers and potatoes the next. This land was summer-fallowed during the third year until sown back to rye. Several vast fields were maintained surrounding each colony to insure that adequate supplies of each commodity would be produced annually.[30]

Farm work began every spring as the melting snows revealed a lush growth of winter rye covering at least one of the large colony fields. The Volga German preference for rye flour made it the most important cereal grain raised in the colonies. Generally the colonists planted rye in late August following summer rains, and planted crops more susceptible to winter kill—sunflowers, spring grains, and potatoes— in late March and April. They raised both soft and hard varieties of spring wheat. Demand for hard wheat increased due to its high protein and gluten content, and the settlers commonly grew it as a cash export crop.[31] They sowed millet, the third major grain raised in the colonies, in the spring and used it to make *Hirsche*, a coarse porridge. Oats and barley, both used chiefly as animal fodder, were also spring crops.[32]

The farmers carefully prepared seed grain to ensure that it was free of weed seed and uncracked. They accomplished this by running bulk grain from the previous harvest through both a fanning mill and a

Volga German granaries, c. 1890. *Concordia Center for Volga German Studies, Portland*

special sieve. They often prepared the seedbed by breaking the previously plowed ground with a crude triangular-shaped cultivator pulled by a team of horses. This was followed by a ten- to fifteen-foot-long roller that crushed the clods and packed the ground to conserve moisture.[33] Sowing was by hand-broadcast, which was sometimes followed by a light harrowing. Sunflowers were planted by hand in alternate furrows during spring plowing, the successive rounds with the single or double share plow covering the preceding planting. Potatoes were planted in the same manner. It was exhausting labor that demanded skillful handling of the draft horses and careful measuring of the distance between seeds. Colonists also planted large communal melon and cabbage gardens, and smaller vegetable gardens in the *Hinnerhof*.[34]

In late spring the settlers turned their attention to the manufacture of *Mistholz* (manure wood), an economical fuel developed by the Volga Germans which prevented the destruction of their dwindling wood lands. Barnyards were usually cleaned weekly and the refuse deposited in one corner of the yard or, more commonly, at one of several places on the outskirts of the colony near a stream. Families gathered to prepare the *Mistholz*, adding water and straw to a layer of manure, which was spread out over a hard flat surface. Horses were then led around several times to mix the mass with their hooves. The mixture was then allowed to dry in the hot sun in large rectangular molds or cut into blocks with a spade and piled for use in winter as an odorless, slow-burning fuel.[35]

In May the colonists busied themselves repairing their homes, mills, and farmyard buildings. Most houses received an annual coat of white-wash mixed from chalky soil near the village. This was also the time to augment the winter hay supply by cutting the wild grasses that grew in the communal meadows. Next, it was time to hoe the vegetable crops in the fields and gardens while the livestock was turned out to graze on the volunteer grain growing in the fallow fields. In June spring plowing commenced on lands that would remain idle until sown to rye.

It was not unusual for the colonists to find that their stores of rye were entirely depleted by early summer. It was often necessary, there-fore, to cut a few bundles of rye ripening in the fields in late June or early July. These bundles were allowed to dry for at least two weeks and then flailed to get several bushels of the grain. Rye was the first grain to mature and was usually ready for harvesting in mid-July. Prior to the introduction of mechanical binders early in the twentieth century, the rye was cut with sickles the government had distributed in the colonies soon after their settlement. However, pioneer ingenuity led them to fashion larger scythes equipped with cradles in order to cut and wind-row in one movement.

Great dexterity was demonstrated by the women who followed the men to gather the cuttings into bundles tied together with several lengths of skillfully twisted and knotted rye stalks. The bundles were then collected into shocks for aeration and carefully arranged into long rows. A patter of thousands of shocks (*Kopitzen*) was soon visible on the hills dotting the landscape around the colony. At the same time the vast expanse of bright yellow sunflowers came in to full bloom as they followed the sun's path during the warm daylight hours.[36]

The next stage of the harvesting process required the preparation of a threshing floor (*Den* or *Tenne*). The *Den* was usually located near the outskirts of town at a designated area where each family had a small area to stack their bundles for threshing. A team of horses was led around an area about fifty feet in diameter to flatten the surface. The area was then watered down and sprinkled with straw to form a hard surface, and left to dry for two to three weeks. Once the floor was ready, families hauled the bundles of grain to the threshing site by wagon. Several bundles at a time were arranged side by side in a short row then flailed by four or six adults standing on either side of the row. In large scale operations, dozens of bundles were spread out in a circular pattern to be threshed in a manner similar to that done with wheat later in the summer.[37]

The workers often sang rhythmic folk songs to set a tempo for swinging the long wooden flails. A narrow leather strap bolted on the end of the flail handle connected to a cylindrical piece of wood about a foot long. The bundles were turned over, and struck again, then opened for a final beating. Other workers lifted the stalks with wooden forks and stacked them for horse and cattle fodder. Until the middle of the nineteenth century, the colonists had to clean the threshings by tossing them into a crosswind by hand or with special wooden scoops to separate the slender brown kernels from the chaff in the ancient manner.[38] This technique continued until about 1840 when fanning mills were introduced in the colonies. This made it more practical for the farmers to thresh the grain as it was needed, especially for those who did not have their own granaries. It was not uncommon to see families busy in winter flailing rye on a hard layer of ice in the *Fehderhof* (farmyard). Families with granaries could store all their rye during the winter but, since these were built off the ground to prevent mice infestation and moisture damage, they also risked the loss of some grain by theft as holes could easily be drilled through the wooden flooring.

The first spring crops to mature, oats and barley, were usually harvested in late July. Both were cut and stacked in the barnyard for the animals. This was followed by the threshing of millet. The production of hemp and flax, gathered in late summer, had been introduced by the *Tutel-Kanzlei* to fill the domestic needs of the colonists. After the heads were cut and beaten into a silken mass, they could be spun on a wheel into large balls, providing the women with material to fashion clothes during the long winter months.

By August the wheat fields were sufficiently ripened under the hot sun of the Volga summer for harvest to begin. The grain had to be threshed as soon as possible to avoid hail or fire damage. The farmers also dreaded the withering effects of a *Höhenrauch*, a searing hot dry wind from the southeastern desert region that could drastically reduce yield by shriveling the kernels and parching the ground.[39]

Сарратовъ. — Saratoff. № 51.
Мельница Реннеке.

Roenicke (Rennecke) flour mills, Saratov, c. 1890. *Courtesy Jean Roth*

All able-bodied members of the family took part in the harvest work, which began as early as two o'clock in the morning with the move out to the fields in the countryside. Wheat was principally an export crop although some white flour was used in making fruit pastries (*kuchen*) and other foods. Wheat was often raised on acreages distant from the village on lands rented from wealthy Russian landlords on a 50 percent commission basis. The family would sometimes remain *in dem Khutor* (on the settlement) for the entire week, living in tents if houses were not built, and returning to the village only on Saturday evening to prepare for worship on Sunday when all but the most essential labor ceased.[40]

A circular threshing floor was again prepared, though as wide as 150 feet, at a central location on the family's plot. Again the brittle stalks were cut and bundled, but then brought directly by wagons to the threshing site. As many as two hundred bundles were then arranged into a circle along the perimeter of the *Den* and opened. A team of horses was led over the grain to "ride it out" of the heads. As with rye, the stalks were turned several times with wooden forks then vigorously shaken, raked aside, and stacked. Meanwhile, others would scrape the golden particles and chaff into a pile in the center of the ring. By late afternoon as many as three hundred bushels of wheat had accumulated to be winnowed and sacked in a process that often lasted until ten o'clock at night. Adequate supplies of grain were stored for seeding and domestic use, and an amount proportional to the size of the family was deposited in the local *Grossambar*, a communal grain reserve, for emergency use. For this reason the Volga Germans were able to avoid famine until the Soviet period despite periodic crop failure.[41]

About the same time that winnowing mills were introduced to the colonies (circa 1840), "threshing stones" also came into use. Much more efficient than merely leading horses through the pilings, these were long sandstone rollers with canted grooves that revolved in a wooden frame as they were pulled by a team of horses. Mechanical reapers and binders were not introduced until late in the nineteenth century, and the revolutionary steam-powered stationary threshing machines appeared about 1910.[42]

Harvesting operations in August were often interrupted by summer rains, which enabled the farmers to plant their winter rye while the standing grain dried. Planting took place on lands that had been spring plowed. Broadcasting continued to be the principal method of seeding in the colonies until American-made mechanical drills were made available just before the First World War. The farmers also began to turn the stubble on the recently harvested rye fields since these would later rotate to support spring crops.

The sunflower harvest usually began in early September. The four-foot high stalks were cut two rows at a time before the plump seeds became too brittle and were arranged in long rows with all the heads lying in the same direction. They were allowed to dry for about two weeks, during which time fall plowing continued. The stalks were then carefully placed on both sides of a wagon drawn between the rows. For this work the farmers sought oddly shaped branches in the timber which could be fashioned into four-pronged wooden forks. These resembled pairs of open claws on the end so that the stalk piles could be speared and placed with the heads in the middle of the wagon.

The wagons were then taken to the prepared threshing floor and the loads dumped so that the heads remained in the middle of the pile. The pile was extended into a row about a foot high and the heads either flailed or pounded with a wooden paddle. The stalks were turned three or four times, shaken and then raked away on both sides into a large stack. This was then hauled home and used as a secondary fuel source. Some stalks were saved for extracting a type of baking soda. The seeds were run through a fanning mill and the chaff and leaves saved to feed the sheep.

Sunflower seed generally commanded a high price on the Volga since it yielded a high quality cooking oil that was processed in the *Oehlemüle* (oil mills) located throughout the region. Sold by weight, the farmer's crop could be docked if it was too damp. Late harvesting sometimes resulted in a high moisture content so a drying process was devised in which hundreds of pounds of seeds were spread out on a large canvas. Old men and children would walk barefoot through the mass to keep it stirred and aerated. A penalty could be imposed at sale if the sample taken indicated that too much dirt had "accidently" been sacked with the seed during the threshing operation.[43]

Potatoes were the last major crop to be taken in and these formed a major part of the Volga Germans' diet. Dug with steel-tined forks and tossed into wagons in an arduous operation that continued for days, the potatoes were dumped in small piles behind the houses to dry, then put in a root cellar where they would be stored through the winter. Irregular blocks of ice insulated with straw and chaff usually lined portions of the large cellars so that dairy products and fresh meat could be stored there during the hot summer months. These ice chunks were collected early in the year along the banks of rivers and mill ponds after the spring thaw.

Loading barges on the Volga, c. 1905. *Courtesy Jean Roth*

After digging potatoes, the families began gathering the cabbages, melons, and pumpkins that grew in the large communal gardens located on choice lands adjacent to the village. Sauerkraut, another staple food for the Volga Germans, was prepared immediately after the fall cabbage harvest. Melons were often packed in grain bins for storage. Women made a sweet syrup from ripe watermelons, and pickled small ones in brine. Pumpkins provided a minor food source; the large seeds were often roasted to create a nut-like treat, discarded shells were fed to the hogs. Garden vegetables commonly grown in the *Hinnerhof* included carrots, onions, and sugar beets, which could be buried in a sanded corner of the root cellar for winter use. Tomatoes clinging to pulled vines often lasted through fall when hung in the cellars, while cucumbers were crocked with dill or sweetened.

Apple, pear, and cherry trees were planted in both family gardens and in large communal orchards. Most fruits were preserved simply by sun-drying although apples were sometimes pickled for consumption later in the year. Wild pear trees were common and wild strawberries and other berry varieties ripened as early as June. August showers sprouted succulent mushrooms.[44] Licorice root gathered in the fall was used to make the preferred Volga German drink—hot *Steppetee*. Volga German dinners typically consisted of nutritious combinations such as *Schnitzel Suppe und Kartoffel Wurst* (fruit soup and potato sausage), *Kraut und Brei* (sauerkraut and pork ribs) or *Klees und Arbuza* (fried eggs and dough with watermelon).[45]

The large numbers of animals maintained by the colonists provided an adequate supply of fresh meat, milk products, and eggs. Grazing areas were set aside in close proximity to the village, but wolves were a constant threat to the livestock. Separate herders (*Hirten*) were often appointed to safeguard the villagers' cattle, sheep, and swine that fed on nearby fallow land in the spring. Every evening the herders returned the milk cows to the edge of town, where they were collected by their owners.[46] When the fallow land was planted, the animals were moved to the forest where they foraged through the summer until fall, then turned out to the recently harvested fields. The livestock wintered in the protected confines of the *Fehderhof*, where large temporary shelters were often built for the cattle and horses. Grain straw and hay for winter feed was stored in the spacious lofts of these structures.[47]

Several families often joined together for the annual butchering bee in November or early December. Fruit tree cuttings were slowly burned to smoke sausage and other meat products. These were hung on racks placed in the summer kitchen chimney for smoking and then stored in the granary or other dry place. One of the last tasks undertaken by the farmers before the heavy snows curtailed outside activity was the gathering of old timber in the forests to supplement the winter fuel supply.[48]

With the long harvest season over, fall plantings completed, and produce sold or stored, the villagers gathered to celebrate their bounty in an exuberant festival, the *Kerb*.[49] This event signaled an end to the field season as the people prepared for the long Russian winter. Isolated on the steppe, the Volga German villages quieted to self-sufficient passivity. Courtship began among young couples considering matrimony and this custom often culminated in a mass marriage ceremony conducted in the gaily decorated church at Christmastime.

Distribution of Land

Following the period of sharp population decline between 1765 and 1775, when the number of families decreased from an estimated 8,000 to 5,502, the population began to steadily increase, reaching 31,000 by 1788 and 39,193 in 1798.[50] The crown's plan of family allotments became increasingly complicated with each new generation. This required reapportionment within the limits of the colony's boundaries and in 1797 a new government survey was mandated which yielded a reduced allocation the following year of about forty-two acres per male. Colonist grievances evoked a promise from the government to increase the total to twenty dessiantines, as had been the case after the 1788 revision. This was not fully accomplished, however, until 1835 when any benefits were virtually cancelled, since by then the prolific Germans' shares averaged only about fifteen acres. This diminished even further to a scant 10.3 acres in 1850[51] and the population was still increasing, reaching 238,000 in 1865,[52] tenfold the number that settled on the Volga a century earlier.

Problems arising from land tenure plagued colonial administration and because the 1763 manifesto's tax exemption period had expired, the colonists gradually adopted the native Russian institution of the *mir* (from *mirskoi skhod*, the "village assembly" of the Russian peasant commune), as a means of equitably resolving these matters and for orderly self-government. On March 12, 1812, they were officially given identical tax status as landed Russian peasants, which required a tax levied equally on all the male "souls" (*dushi*) but remitted collectively from the village *mir*. It became convenient, therefore, to adapt land distribution in accordance with the *mir* system of repartitional tenure (*obshchinnoe pof'zovanie*) in which the land was divided among the male population in regular revisions and could not be sold or mortgaged. By 1816 the system was in general use throughout the colonies and usually incorporated into the administration of the daughter colonies.[53]

Great care was taken during the periodic revisions to ensure an equitable distribution of land. At these times a specified number of males, usually about twenty and invariably related to one another, joined together to form an economic unit. Each of the main colony fields was surveyed, divided, and marked into lots to be farmed by the groups. The size of the lots was sometimes proportional to the fertility of the soil, which was usually divided into three classifications: good (fertile lowlands), medial (or steep), and poor (sandy or rocky areas). This guaranteed that each family would be provided with spring crops and rye on variable soils and would have to maintain some summer fallow.[54]

A public lottery, attended by at least one representative from every unit, was held to determine who would receive which land parcels. Each male within a unit was delegated a specific number of shares in their lands. The procedure was as complicated as it was judicious since each individual held title to as many as sixteen or more small plots. The communal garden properties were similarly apportioned. The basic problem of inadequate land supply, however, was not alleviated and new difficulties involving changing lines of demarcation, family size and composition, and varying soil quality compounded matters for the growing Volga German populace.

The government's solution to the dilemma of a regressive land supply was simply to expand Volga German settlement to other crown domains, and between 1848 and 1863, the colonists founded sixty-eight daughter colonies (*Tochter Kolonien*). Most were located on the *Wiesenseite* where approximately 675,000 acres were appropriated in the Novousensk district in 1840. Of these colonies, over one-third were located along the Yeruslan River, where residents of Yagodnaya Polyana founded Neu-Yagodnaya (1855) and Schöntal (1857), while others from Pobochnaya established Schöndorf (1855) and Schönfeld (1858). Rosenfeld, a daughter colony of Norka, was established in this area in 1859 while others there included Neu-Beideck (1858) and Neu-Bauer (1859). Neu-Balzer, Neu-Messer, and Neu-Dönhof were founded in 1863 in an area between the Medveditza and Karamysh Rivers on the *Bergseite* close to their mother colonies. Neu-Frank and Neu-Walter were built on land grants near the Shchlkan River on the *Bergseite*, and Neu-Norka was founded further south near Kamyshin in 1855.[55]

Life in the daughter colonies strewn along the upper Yeruslan River was difficult for the early settlers. They traveled to the distant lands in large caravans of livestock and wagons laden with seed grains, farm tools, and domestic items. Crossing the broad Volga River was hazardous on primitive wooden ferries. The families had been compensated for the loss of their property rights in the mother colonies and had volunteered to colonize the newly opened areas. However, they found the soil on the eastern rim of the *Wiesenseite* to be less fertile and the climate more arid. Many feared the nomadic Kirghiz horsemen who frequented the treeless plain and the distance from the mother colonies and major Russian trade centers effectively isolated them. Lands surrounding these daughter colonies were divided according to the *mir* system and the communities were governed in the same manner as the mother colonies.

United States Immigration

It is significant that at least two Volga Germans chose to immigrate to the United States while others were moving to the daughter colonies on the *Wiesenseite*. Possibly the first two Volga Germans to live in America, Johann Adam and Matthias Repp, brothers from their native Yagodnaya Polyana, journeyed to America about 1855 and homesteaded southeast of Humboldt, Kansas. Soon after the outbreak of the Civil War, however, they decided to escape the panic and return to Russia to join their families who had since relocated to Neu-Yagodnaya. In 1876, Johann Adam Repp returned to Kansas with his family, other relatives, and over two hundred others aboard the SS *Mosel*, most from Neu-Yagodnaya and Schöntal.[56]

Like their ancestors who had come from Germany several generations earlier, the settlers first lived in dugouts or tents until permanent
homes could be constructed. The basic building material in this area
was adobe brick. To prepare the bricks, a wide pit was dug to a depth
of about three feet down to a dense layer of clay. Water was poured into
the pit and a horse was led around to soften the clay with its hooves.
Next, straw was added for resiliency and the mixture was poured into
wooden forms approximately sixteen inches square and eight inches
high. Both houses and barns were built out of this brick and covered
with pole-frame roofs thatched with reeds. The interiors remained
remarkably warm in the winter and cool in the summer. Near the center of each house, a massive adobe oven protruded from a separate fuel
storage room and was fired with *Mistholz* (dried manure and straw).[57]

Civil Authority

Civil authority in the colonies had been defined by the decree of April
28, 1776, which established the Saratov Office of the Guardianship
Chancery (*Vormundschafts Kantor*). The Kantor consisted of a "chief
judge" (*Oberrichter*), two assistants, a secretary, translator, bookkeeper,
and later, various other bureaucrats. Besieged by the initial problems
of settlement and drought relief, its first chief executive General I. G.
Rezanov staffed the office largely with Baltic Germans who looked
upon the Low German colonists with some condescension. In 1769 the
Guardianship Chancery introduced a detailed directive, "The Instruction," which defined the role of the Kantor as arbitrator in criminal
and civil disputes, regulator of the agriculture economy, and responsible
for the collection of crown taxes—a provision that led to widespread
graft among the bureaucrats. In addition, six district commissars were
appointed to supervise the transition of the colonists to Russian society,
increased in 1775 to thirteen to provide one for each colonial district.[58]
Government on the local level was to be administered by an elected
major (*Vorsteher* or *Schulze*) and two assistants (*Beisitzer*) who oversaw
public propriety and enforced legislation.

Intended to be only temporary institutions, the Guardianship Chancery in St. Petersburg and Saratov Kantor closed in April 1782, and
colonist affairs were transferred to the regional bureau of the State Eco-

nomic Directorate in Saratov. The move proved to be premature. While the German colonists had become an integral part of Catherine's plan for exploiting and securing that region of the Empire, language difficulties and jurisdictional problems associated with the change exacerbated tensions between the Germans and the aloof officials in the directorate. The tsarina personally intervened again by appointing Privy Councillor K. I. Hablitz to investigate the situation. Not only had she already extended the ten-year moratorium on the repayment of government loans specified in the manifesto by an additional decade, but in 1782 Catherine reduced their total liability of over 5,000,000 rubles by nearly 46 percent.[59] However, the ambitious monarch suffered a stroke and died on November 17, 1796, without having time to act on Hablitz's recommendations for reform.

Paul I, Catherine's son and successor to the Romanov throne, followed tradition by marrying a German princess, and throughout his short reign (1796–1801) maintained great admiration for the colonists' character and ability, often to the chagrin of the Russian bureaucrats and intelligentsia. Following Hablitz's advice, the tsar reopened the Saratov Kontor on July 31, 1797, under the Jurisdiction of the Department of National Economy, Guardianship for Foreigners and Rural Husbandry,

Saratov, Russia, with St. Mary's Lutheran Cathedral left of dome, c. 1905.
Courtesy Jean Roth

a ponderous organization evolving in 1802 into the Ministry of the Interior which became in 1866 the Ministry of Royal Domains. The subsequent reigns of Alexander I (1801–25) and Nicholas I (1825–55) were both characterized by continued benevolence toward the German *kolonisty*, a term denoting their distinct legal status as landed state peasants which continued on officially until the Ukase of 1871, which abolished the privileges granted through Catherine's manifesto although its usage prevailed in general use until the Communist Revolution.

A series of directives known as the "Uniform Instructions for the Internal Organization and Administration" of the colonies was promulgated between 1801 and 1803 in an attempt to allow more effective self-government in the colonies and restore confidence to the newly reinstituted *Kontor* at the community, district, and provincial levels. Locally, a village assembly (*Gemeinde/mirskoi skhod*) was formed, composed of one adult male representative from each household.[60] Additional provisions were made for an executive committee (*Kleingemeinde*) consisting of the Schulz and two assistants, elected by majority vote for two year terms, and a clerk (*Schreiber*), a qualified hired official who maintained communication with officials in the next administrative level, the district (*Kreis*), which functioned as the intermediary between the Kantor in Saratov and the local Gemeinden.

Under the terms of the new legislation, however, the offices of appointed district commissars were abolished and substituted by an elected *Oberschulz* (*okruzhnoi golova*), one for each of the ten newly created Volga colony districts. Two or more elected assistants and an appointed district secretary (*Kreis Schreiber*) also served at this level, the chairman holding a three-year term and the assistants for two years. The district office was charged with the supervision of colonial farm management; it collected taxes and crown loan repayments and also served as a higher court for colonist litigation not resolved by the *Kleingemeide*.[61]

It was on the village level that civil responsibility and authority were particularly broadened as the functions of the *Gemeide* were enlarged and constables (*desiatski* or *sotniki*) were also elected to enforce the laws. At the village assembly, voting was done *viva voce* on such issues as the election of public officials, financial disbursements and local tax levies, distribution of surplus land and individual farmer assignments, crop rotation plans, the expulsion of citizens for immoral conduct, and confirmed the selection of teachers, pastors, fire inspectors, and village livestock herders.[62]

The pivotal figure in the administrative network was the mayor, a position that combined both civil and religious functions. His presence was required at the district meetings and he was responsible for seeing to it that taxes were paid promptly, buildings and homes were inspected to ensure cleanliness and safety, everyone was diligent in church attendance, public morality was maintained by forbidding the sale of liquor to those "addicted to drunkedness, laziness and dissipation...(and that) every farmer began the day's work at sunrise."[63] Such indications of German industriousness and thrift coupled with the growing markets for grain in the mid nineteenth century led to growing prosperity in the colonies. At that time, several western European nations, notably England, Belgium, and Holland, lowered and in some cases abolished tariffs on grain imports. Due to subsequent revisions in internal excise regulations, Russian markets substantially increased after 1860 commensurate with expansion in world demand.[64] During this same period, the activities of the Kantor at Saratov were gradually restricted and transferred to other provincial departments; by 1866 its functions were limited primarily to supervising the churches and schools in the colonies,[65] both of which faced serious difficulties.

Religion

Organizational problems had long been associated with the Lutheran Church in Russia, the inception of which can be traced back to the construction of a Lutheran Church in the German suburb of Moscow under the reign of Ivan the Terrible in 1576. The early expansion of the church was largely confined to urban areas in Russia where German artisans and technocrats were brought in by the tsars in efforts toward modernization. It was not until 1711 that Peter the Great appointed the first Superintendent of the Lutheran Church in Russia, Reverend Berthold Vagetius of Moscow, to preside over the activities of the ten parishes in Russia. The office was discontinued, however, following his retirement in 1718.[66]

New impetus was given to Protestantism in the predominantly Orthodox empire after 1763 when German Lutherans, Reformed, and pietistic Moravian Brethren colonized the Volga region. Under the terms of the manifesto the colonists were allowed freedom of religion and were settled in villages according to their denomination. A principal reason for establishing the Moravian outpost at Sarepta was to proselyte among the Mongol tribes inhabiting that region and the Astrakhan steppe. Of the other Volga colonies, thirty-two were Catholic and seventy-two were Protestant with the majority (80 percent) being Lutheran; only seven Reformed villages were founded on the *Bergseite* where their two parish centers were at Norka and Messer while a number of Reformed villages were located on the *Wiesenseite* where a minister was placed in Katharinenstadt, ministering at twenty-two locations.

Despite the great preponderance of Protestants, few pastors came or stayed with the colonists. With the meager salaries provided to clergy faced with ministering to scattered parishes often numbering over two thousand souls, a lack of pastors became an acute problem. By 1805 there were only fifteen Protestant pastors in the entire colonial enclave, these living in Messer, Grimm, Beideck, Galka, Dietel, Frank, Norka, Stephan, Yagodnaya Polyana, Saratov, Rosenheim, Warenburg, Bettinger, and two in Katharinenstadt.[67] The University of Dorpat (Tartu) in Estonia was the nearest theological school but the great distance and expense virtually prevented enrollment by eligible Volga German men.[68]

The shortage of clergy led to two significant developments in colonial Protestantism. Laymen of the congregations were increasingly compelled to handle spiritual matters themselves, and between 1764 and 1825 the colonies witnessed an influx of Moravian Brethren missionaries from Sarepta.[69] Language problems and other difficulties with the Moravian missions to the Buddhist Kalmyks diverted their zeal to the Volga colonists in an attempt to justify the existence of their *Brüdergemeinde* (brotherhood meeting). The Swiss Pietist Johann Janet began the work following a visit to Sarepta in 1766 when he enlisted the support of Johann H. Langerfeld for his church in Anton. Janet had been installed in the Reformed Church in Anton in 1765 after responding in Germany to their appeal sent the previous year soon after the colony was founded, many settlers having been acquainted with the work of the Brethren in Isenburg and other areas of Hesse and the Palatinate.[70]

Additional problems ensued as disputes arose between the growing pietistic Reformed movement and the rationalistic Lutheran leadership that rejected certain tenets of Calvinistic theology. They also differed in methods of distributing the elements at communion services and some Lutherans looked with suspicion upon local revivals, lay prayer meetings, and the personal lifestyle of piety. Nevertheless, the efforts of the Moravian missionaries met with a great response in many areas, particularly in Anton, Dietel, Balzer, and Dönhof.[71]

Antagonisms between the two groups reached such proportions between 1818 and 1819 that government authorities in St. Petersburg decided to intervene. A decree was issued on October 25, 1819, establishing the Protestant Consistory for Inner Russia with headquarters to be in Saratov, from where a superintendent and staff would handle matters in all Protestant parishes throughout the entire empire.[72] The tsar appointed Ignatius Fessler head of the new Consistory. Fessler, formerly a Capuchin priest and language professor, proved to be an effective organizer and sought to reconcile differences in Protestant Volga German clergy.

Fessler began by subdividing several parishes and personally recruiting new pastors from Germany—six in 1820 alone. At the same time he forbade missionary activity by the Moravians who withdrew their last evangelist, C. F. Lessing, in 1821.[73] He also fought tirelessly to obtain needed salary increases for the clergy and organized synod meetings for each side of the Volga and convened an annual general synod conference to discuss any problems confronting the churches. Further accommodation was reached through the publication of a common hymnal, the *Wolga Gesangbuch*,[74] and liturgical manuals acceptable to both Reformed and Lutherans, while preserving certain confessional variations. With the assimilation of the *Wiesenseite* Reformed parish into the larger Lutheran body in 1832 and the administrative union of the Norka and Messer Reformed parishes on the *Bergseite*, the title of the Protestant Consistory was altered to "Lutheran."

Among Fessler's most important contributions was organizing the struggling parochial school system of the colonies. Educational standards had severely declined due to financial problems and following the deaths of the original immigrant teachers as the colonies lacked teacher training institutes to prepare qualified educators despite numerous pleas by the colonists to the government. The situation in Norka was indicative of the eventual crises since at one time a single teacher supervised 1,100 pupils and was able to use only one large school room.[75]

Fessler responded by raising the issue of school reform at the meeting of the first general synod in January 1822. Proposals were later enacted systematizing curriculums to include regular instruction in Bible history, Catechism, reading, writing, arithmetic, and music,[76] class time usually amounting to three hours six days a week. Shifting frequently occurred in the morning and afternoon to accommodate a larger number of students. Maintaining the strict discipline characteristic of the system under the difficult circumstances required the services of an often stern and usually highly respected individual, the village *Schulmeister*. One of the few well educated members of the colony, he functioned—as had been the case in Germany also—as church sextant (*Küster*) and registrar, all of these responsibilities being considered a single position. As the colony's pastor frequently ministered to other churches in the parish, he performed the necessary ecclesiastical duties and liturgical readings although only ordained men could preach from the pulpit.

In the congregation each woman, her head reverently covered with an embroidered or lace shawl (*Halstuck*), sat with the smallest children on the left side of the church while the men and older boys sat on the right. The Küster also could not administer the Sacraments or baptize infants, unless in case of emergency.[77] He was authorized to conduct funeral services, usually held in the courtyard of the home of the deceased following a two or three day wake (*Totewacht*) held in the home by the family. He also officiated at the internment rites which always concluded with the singing of "*Wo findet die Seel die Heimat der Ruh*" (where the soul finds rest in the homeland).[78]

Fessler succeeded in convincing the government that it should permit the selection of schoolmasters by the parish pastor instead of the village assembly. This brought some ire from the colonists as did his attempts to obtain additional tax monies to remedy the deficiency in instructional materials, the number of teachers and their salaries, but these efforts were largely fruitless. Additional administrative reform coordinated terms of instruction in the Volga German *Volksschule* which had been largely confined to the winter months. School commenced in October and was extended usually until about Easter when all laborers were needed at home and in the fields. Instruction generally began at age seven and continued eight years until at fifteen, following a detailed examination, the students were confirmed into full church membership in a grand and inspiring service held either on Palm Sunday (*Palmsonntag*) with communion on Good Friday (*Karfreitag*) or at Pentecost (*Pfingsten*).[79] Other festivals were celebrated in accordance with the liturgical church calendar including Easter (*Ostern*), Ascension Sunday (*Himmelfahrt*), Memorial Day (*Totenfest*), Thanksgiving

(*Danksagenfest*), and Christmas (*Weinachten*); in some colonies their original founders were honored in an annual *Herkommenstag.*

In 1832 the Lutheran Consistory was reorganized throughout the empire resulting in the interruption of Fessler's ambitious reforms. The main office in Saratov was suddenly shifted to Moscow, which now became headquarters for the huge Moscow Consistory, one of eight major consistorial districts established by Nicholas I. These were all under the direction of a lay president of the General Consistory of the Lutheran Church in Russia, based in St. Petersburg. Each district was to have its own general superintendent and staff. The largest of the eight was the Moscow Consistory, serving scattered congregations stretching from Eastern Europe to Asiatic Russia, and it became necessary for effective organization to establish two sub-districts (*Propsteien*) for the Germans on the *Bergseite* and *Wiesenseite* of the Volga, each headed by a chief pastor (*Pröpste*). With minor alterations this structure remained intact throughout the Tsarist period. However, the authority in religious matters had now been transferred to distant Moscow and the division of the colonies into separate entities further complicated efforts to solve mutual problems. Attempts to establish normal schools that could lead to adequate staffing in the parochial system failed and the lack of manpower continued to plague the clergy with pastors serving parishes averaging 6,592 people in 1861, swelling to nearly 13,000 in 1905.[80]

The appearance of two Moravian Brethren evangelists from Germany in 1868 in the Volga colonies marked the reemergence of pietistic fervor. Actually the activities of those influenced earlier by the missionaries from Sarepta had not been suspended despite Fessler's official termination of their efforts in 1820. On the contrary, a movement of the Brotherhood (*Brüderschaft*), largely confined to the laity, continued to persist in the form of regular prayer meetings (*Versammlungen*) attended by many who objected to the liturgical formalism of the Lutheran Church. These sessions were often held secretly as they violated the Church Law of 1857 which decreed "that religious meetings which exceed the bounds of family devotions may hereafter not be conducted by laymen without previously notifying the civil authorities and obtaining permission from the Consistory."[81] The activities of the missionaries in 1868 were centered in the Reformed districts of Balzer and Messer where they gave new impetus to the movement, traveling widely in their trade as cobblers at the risk of public corporal punishment. Interest was kindled again in neighboring villages on both sides of the Volga and as far south as Dönhof.[82] Expansion northward reached Pobochnaya, Yagodnaya Polyana, and Katharinenstadt so that by 1872 the entire region was engulfed in a great revival that continued until the early 1890s.

It has been suggested that the official demurral expressed by the church against the pietists was due to its fear of the sectarianism that was being propagated by various cults on the Volga.[83] In order to disassociate themselves from such groups, the organization in 1871 of a non-sectarian Brotherhood Conference was effected in the village of Brunnental by the leaders of the movement. This was done in order to "consolidate the strength of the Brethren, to give them official recognition, to protect them against persecution, to provide a bulwark against Separatism and other sects, to clarify the doctrinal position of the converts, to set up rules for the individual prayer meetings, and to provide opportunity for mutual counsel and fellowship."[84]

The motivation force behind the Brotherhood's organization was the Reformed pastor from Norka, Wilhelm Stärkel, who had himself been converted in a revival meeting on the Volga. A brilliant organizer and inspiring preacher, he had traveled to Missouri, Kansas, and Wisconsin in the 1860s on a missionary journey. He returned in 1868 to serve a number of daughter colonies on the *Wiesenseite* until 1877 when he accepted a call to Norka.[85]

Religion played an extremely significant role in the lives of the Volga Germans, and religion would remain a central component of their social and cultural makeup throughout their history both in the Old and New Worlds. The roots of a separate denominational movement which characterized the lives of the Volga Germans in the Pacific Northwest emerged in Russia. Members of the Brotherhood expressed their theology in terms of a living dynamic expression of faith. While embracing traditional evangelical doctrines of the Trinity, universal priesthood of all believers, Biblical infallibility, and the Sacraments, they emphasized salvation by grace through the regenerative new birth experience. They taught that the Holy Spirit would then manifest itself in the believer's life through nonconformity to the world, involving a personal lifestyle of piety, prayers, study, and devotion to God. In addition, the Brethren were predominantly pre-Millennial, believing in the possibility of Christ's immediate bodily return to earth when he would gather His church to Himself. Their resolve to maintain church membership was equally evident. It was expressed on numerous occasions by one of their leading spokesmen, H. P. Ehlers, with the words *"Brüder, bleibt bei der Kirche"* (brother, stay with the church).[86] Ehlers and Johannes Koch were elected evangelists for the organization at the 1871 Conference.

Koch would later be instrumental in transplanting the movement to America's Pacific Northwest where the separate denominational movement arose—German Congregationalism. It has been suggested that one of the principal reasons for the burgeoning emigration of Volga Germans from Russia in the mid-1870s was the intolerant attitude of many toward the brethren.[87] One of the first Volga Germans to settle in the Pacific Northwest, George H. Green, was once flogged for protesting the punishment of a *Bruder* while others sympathetic to the movement were often made objects of ridicule and persecution.[88] It is significant that the first two groups of Volga Germans to the Pacific Northwest left Russia during this period and founded the first German Congregational Churches in the American West.

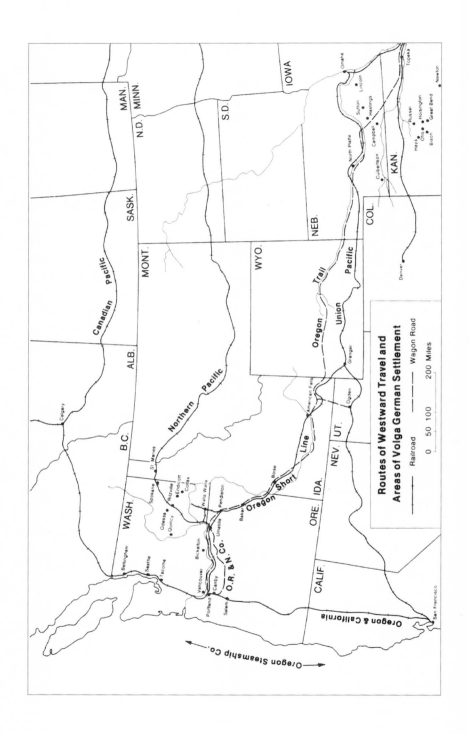

Routes of Westward Travel and Areas of Volga German Settlement

Railroad ———— Wagon Road ————

0   50 100   200 Miles

3

Immigration to the United States

Hier in Russland ist nicht zu leben,
Weil wir müssen Soldaten geben,
Und als Ratnik müssen wir stehen—
Drum wollen wir aus Russland gehn.

Here in Russia it's no good to live,
We must our men as soldiers give.
And now as soldiers we must stand,
That's why we leave the Russian land.

—*"Auswandererlied,"* verse 1

Ethnic German identity in the Volga colonies was increasingly threatened with the rise of the Slavophile movement in the 1840s and Pan-Slavism after 1870. Conceived among a group of romantic intellectuals during the reign of Nicholas I (1825–55), Slavophilism came to embrace a vision of the superior nature of the Orthodox Church and Slavic people. It held that they were on a supreme historical mission which would lead to peace and fraternity among all men. The traditional peasant commune was viewed as reflective of the Slavic people's primordial union with freedom and social harmony. While the rightist Official Nationality policy of Nicholas I tended to conflict with the liberal notions of the Slavophiles, his disastrous involvement in the debacle of the Crimean War (1854–55) led his son, Tsar Alexander II (1855–81), to inaugurate the Era of the Great Reforms in Russia to modernize the nation and abolish the onerous state of serfdom.

As early as 1840, Count Paul Kiselev, as head of the Ministry of Imperial Domains, was commissioned to study the implication of a general emancipation of the serfs. His investigations led to little constructive change under Nicholas although Kiselev's study of the rural

51

populace revealed the conspicuous isolation of the German colonies. His finding were essentially confirmed by an earlier report by a Kontor official who related that "there are only a few of the colonists who enlighten themselves as much as they should concerning the Russian language, wherefore they do not know the Russian laws...and evidently take pains to avoid every intercourse with Russia."[1] A contributing factor to this situation was their special status as *kolonisty*, which guaranteed certain advantages not available to the general public. Accordingly, legislation altering their judicial and political systems was introduced in the 1860s. In 1861 Russia's twenty-five million serfs were freed from serfdom and in 1861 *zemstvo* reform established district and provincial assemblies among all classes through an indirect electoral process. Within a decade these were functioning in the Volga, uniting Germans and Russians in common assemblies. Local colonial autonomy was now replaced by the integrated zemstvos, which had jurisdiction over education, public finance, and other matters.

In most areas of colonial settlement the Germans remained the predominant ethnic group, and they generally acquiesced to these changes. It was not until 1871 that these developments culminated in a decree perceived by thousands of Volga Germans as unacceptably minacious. By that time the flourishing colonies also attracted an element of suspicion due to their comparative prosperity. One scholar noted, "One hundred years after Catherine had called the Germans to the Volga, they had progressed to a level of farming leadership in Russia. Their farms were models of productivity to all the native Russians."[2]

The Ukase of June 4, 1871, was promulgated by the Council of Ministers just as routinely as other policies of the day. It was to have, however, far-reaching effects on the Germans in Russia. The senate decree repealed all privileges originally granted "for eternal time" under the terms of Catherine's 1763 manifesto, including military exemption. Attempts by a sympathetic tsar and his foreign minister, Prince Alexander Gorchakov, to modify the military exemption clause succeeded only in allowing a ten-year grace period in which colonists would have the option to legally emigrate although few of these landed people seemed eager to do so. Grievances expressed to the authorities brought no redress and even Alexander II remarked with reference to the sudden abrogation that "a hundred years is an eternity!"[3]

The temporary exemption did, however, serve to quell domestic agitation among the Germans, who had never exhibited violent political temperament. Furthermore, the most significant changes in the law involved their administrative and legal status, issues that were typically remote to the isolated colonists. In terms of their status, the term *kolonist* was replaced with *poselianin-sobstvennik* (settler-owner) which denoted a "foreign rural resident who owned land and who was legally equal to rural residents of Russian nationality (*selskeya-obitatelye*)."[4] Other changes in terminology mandated to the Russian such terms as *selo* (village), *volost* (a group of villages), *uyezd* (several *volosti*) and *gubernia* (province). While German officials generally continued as village elder (*sel'skii starotsa*) and volost elder (*volostnoi starshina*), their records now had to be kept in Russian and control at the upper levels of government jurisdiction shifted away from the German minority.[5] The Russians now dominated the civil administration of the region, since the Saratov *Kontor* of the Guardianship Committee was also abolished in 1871, and the affairs of these former colonies were now assigned to the Ministry of the Interior.

A decisive preemption of the ordered transition toward assimilation with the Russian populace occurred with the unexpectedly early issuance of the law of universal military conscription and corresponding annulment of the grace period on January 1, 1874. The dread of serving in the Russian army was widespread among the males in the nation and especially the Germans, many of whom had a poor command of the Russian language and were often looked upon with disdain in the predominantly native Russian regiments. Discipline was cruel with minimum chance for advancement and terms of service lasted up to six years. Wages were pitifully low and the eligible draft age began at twenty. Lotteries were held to fill the ranks of the standing army.[6] The threat of conscription became the chief motivating factor for the initial emigration of Germans from Russia to North and South America and in 1874 over six thousand Germans, predominately Mennonites, immigrated to the United States. A tragic drought struck the Volga region in 1878 along with cattle diseases and epidemics of typhus and smallpox among the people. The resulting economic decline prompted continued German emigration from Russia as did events during the reactionary reigns of Alexander II (1881–94) and Nicholas II (1894–1917).[7]

Large-scale German emigration from Russia to the Americas
at this time began in the Black Sea region in response to favorable
reports communicated by some of their number who had located in
the Midwest as early as 1849.[8] The encouraging news of opportunity abroad coupled with their growing political consternation led a
group of twenty-one families from Johannestal, Worms, and Rohrbach to emigrate in the fall of 1872, most settling in Ohio and the
Territory of Dakota near Yankton. Some Mennonite colonists from
the Black Sea region also sought refuge elsewhere at this time as the
military terms of the 1871 Ukase were in conflict with their religious
beliefs. In 1872 a group petitioned the American consulate in Odessa
requesting the position of the United States government regarding
the possibilities of their special settlement in that country. The consul
advised them favorably, indicating that not only would their religious
views be respected but that the Northern Pacific Railroad and others
could assist them in finding desirable lands to purchase as well as offer
reduced transportation rates and temporary employment on line construction. In the summer of 1873, a delegation of twelve Mennonite
elders was sent to explore areas of Canada and the United States and
an exodus began the following year.[9]

Although the Volga Germans were generally more secluded from
the political affairs of the nation, they too became alarmed at the trend
toward Russification evidenced by repeal of the original manifesto and
subsequent legislation. In addition, antagonism was still being directed
against the pietistic Brethren in many Volga colonies. By contrast, there
was strong attraction to North America brought about by reports from
early immigrants to the United States about the many opportunities of
the New World. Promotional literature was sent to Europe expounding
upon the wealth of the country and the rich soil that was yet to be turned.

In the spring of 1874, mass meetings were held to discuss the situation among Catholic colonists on the *Wiesenseite* at Herzog, and in
Balzer on the *Bergseite* by the Protestants. A prime mover in the drive
to emigrate was Rev. Wilhelm Stärkel, the Reformed pastor in Norka
who, having done mission work in Kansas and Missouri in the 1860s,
extolled the virtues of that land and related the liberal provisions of the
Homestead Act of 1862.[10] Accordingly, a total of fourteen scouts were
selected to explore potential areas of settlement in the United States.

Sailing from Hamburg on July 1, 1874, on the SS *Schiller*, the *Kundschafter* (scouting party) included the following individuals:

(Catholic)
Peter Leiker, Ober-Monjou
Jacob Ritter, Luzern
Nicholas Schamne, Graf
Peter Stöcklein, Zug
Anton Wasinger, Schönchen
Anton Kaberlein, Pfeifer

(Protestant)
Johannes Krieger, Norka
Johannes Nolde, Norka
Georg Kähm, Balzer
Heinrich Schwabauer, Balzer
Christoph Meisinger, Messer
Johann Benzel, Kolb
Franz Scheibel, Kolb
Georg Stieben, (unknown)[11]

Upon arrival in the United States, the party divided into several units to explore areas in Nebraska, Kansas, Iowa, and possibly Arkansas. Prairie grass and soil samples were retrieved to support their optimistic report upon their return to the Volga, as was technical information regarding the various modes of transportation and settlement. In the fall and winter of 1874, a small group departed for Nebraska, Kansas, and Arkansas. One year later, on August 23, 1875, emigrants from Balzer, Dietel, and Mohr went to Red Oak, Iowa, under the leadership of Heinrich Schwabauer. Part of this group followed Jacob Bender to Sutton, Nebraska, where they had heard Black Sea Germans had settled, while others went to Kansas. In November of that year, Catholics from the Volga reached Topeka, Kansas, moving on to Ellis and Rush Counties. Both Topeka and Lincoln became central distribution points for Volga German settlement in the region which began en masse in the summer of 1876.[12] A number of Protestant families arriving that year formed the basis of two separate groups that would almost simultaneously leave Kansas and Nebraska for the Pacific Northwest.

During these years many Germans in Russia were also induced to explore settlement possibilities in Brazil, Argentina, and Canada. Large

Franz Scheibel, shown here with his wife, was part of the 1874 scouting party. The Scheibel family traveled from Kolb to Nebraska in 1876. *Courtesy Harland Eastwood*

scale immigration to South America began in 1877, while in western Canada the lack of railroad service and the colder climate delayed significant immigration until after 1896. Nevertheless the movement of Russian Germans to the Americas grew to massive proportions in the period from 1874 to 1914. The flood of immigration from Europe in general was interrupted after 1914 as a result of World War I. Prior to the war's outbreak, however, approximately 300,000 Russian Germans immigrated to the Americas as their plight in Russia went from bad to worse.

Following the assassination of the reforming Tsar Alexander II in 1881, his reactionary son, Alexander III (1881–94), countered in a reign characterized by further attempts directed, in the words of Peter Durnovo, chief of the state police, "toward the complete liberation of Russia from the foreign element."[13] Such sentiment at higher levels of government led to anti-German policy in both the foreign and domestic realm, continued under Nicholas II (1894–1917). A ukase issued on March 26, 1892, prohibited the private ownership of land by foreign residents in Russia—the status of the Volga Germans—and forbade the leasing of land by foreigners. Immunity from these stipulations was contingent upon application for naturalization and membership in the Russian Orthodox Church, an unlikely prospect to most Volga Germans.[14]

Their school systems also came increasingly under the scrutiny of the authorities and in 1890 legislation was introduced requiring a Russian teacher in every German school, followed by a decree in 1897 requiring Russian as the principal language of instruction. In 1905 certain restrictions on the private ownership of land and use of German were rescinded, but the status of German ethnicity in Russia continued to be precarious. Finally, per capita land supply continued to regress with the growing population while tragic crop failures struck the Volga region in 1884, 1889, 1892, and 1897.[15] The developments continued in great contrast to revelations of prosperity and security in America.

In some respects, Russia and the United States were undergoing similar changes in the late nineteenth century. Both were becoming more aware of their great natural wealth and had recently met the problems of servile emancipation and looked forward to growth in transportation and industry. Relations between the two countries were good and while William F. "Buffalo Bill" Cody supervised a spirited buffalo hunt on Grand Duke Alexis' United States tour in 1872, both nations' diplomats often referred to mutual "manifest destinies." However, the United States, though not always oblivious to ethnic distinctions, molded a new order in the nineteenth century through unprecedented achievements in transportation, agriculture, and education.[16] Revision of the Homestead Act of 1862 led to grants of available land to foreigners who simply declared their intentions of becoming United States citizens, allowing them to secure a deed to a 160-acre tract after cultivating a portion of it for five years. Preemptions could be obtained under the same qualifications but after only six months of residence at $1.25 per acre. Supplementary federal legislation such as the Timber Culture Act of 1873 and Desert Land Act of 1877 eventually succeeded in filling what Abraham Lincoln had earlier termed a labor deficiency in agriculture.[17]

The completion of the first transcontinental railroad in May 1869 sparked a new era of settlement in the American West. Not only were new areas now made readily accessible to settlers, but the scheme to subsidize the construction of over one thousand miles of Union Pacific track was to grant lands adjacent to the lines, the sale of which would then become a profitable enterprise for the railroad. Through this arrangement Congress mandated grants totaling millions of acres to the Union Pacific as well as other railroad companies operating lines west of the Mississippi River. By 1872 the Kansas Pacific and the Atchison, Topeka

Kansas Colony homestead in Rush County, c. 1880. *Courtesy Ramon Huntley*

and Santa Fe were given the claim to seven million acres in Kansas Territory alone, consisting of alternate sections along the right of way for twenty miles on both sides.

Carl B. Schmidt, a native of Saxony who had settled in Lawrence, Kansas, was selected in 1873 to head the immigration office of the Atchison, Topeka and Santa Fe. His contacts with German ethnic groups throughout the country led him to seek communication with dissatisfied Germans in Russia in order to arrange their settlement in America. He supervised the inspection of property near Great Bend, Kansas, by leaders of a contingent of Volga Germans, mostly Catholics from the *Wiesenseite*, who arrived in Baltimore on the SS *Ohio* on November 23, 1875, and went to Topeka, Kansas, five days later.

Most of the group under the tutelage of Schmidt deemed the price of land near Great Bend, five dollars per acre, too expensive and later formed Catholic communities in Ellis County. Here they either homesteaded or purchased lands offered there for less by the Kansas Pacific Railroad with the first families arriving in Hays and Victoria in February 1876.[18] A contemporary reporter described the scene of their arrival:

> The whole outfit, wagons, horses, dogs, cows, women, and children of the men folks of the Russians, who had taken claims in this (Ellis) county, arrived last Wednesday night and a queer looking set they are. Most of them came fully supplied with stock, wagons, household furniture, etc.
>
> They are strong looking animals, and seem capable of any work, especially the women, who seem to perform as much menial labor as the children, which are numerous.[19]

Subsequent statements also noted another interesting quality of Volga German life: "One of the pleasing features of the Russian presence in our town is their singing. All have good voices, and none have any hesitancy in displaying their vocal accomplishments."[20]

Among the few Protestants on board the November SS *Ohio* transport were the following family heads (most locating near Great Bend, Kansas): George Brach, Peter Ochs, Henry Scheuermann, and two Conrad Scheuermanns.[21] They were soon joined in Kansas by the families of George H. Green, Henry Rothe, and Conrad Aschenbrenner, who had arrived in New York on January 6, 1876, on the SS *City of Montreal*.[22] These families began forming the nucleus from which Russian German immigration to the Pacific Northwest would be first undertaken in 1881.

Songs of lament grew in intensity on the Volga as more Germans tore the bonds of family and homeland to emigrate to America. The news of local *V'shteyeroongen* (auctions) became more frequent as families sold off most household wares to pay travel expenses. They took little more than the physical necessities of food and clothing along with

Conrad and Catherine Schierman (Scheuermann) were among those who traveled on the SS *Ohio* and settled first in Kansas. *Courtesy Gayle Schoeflin*

the *Wolga Gesangbuch* and family Bible, all carefully packed in a large wooden-ribbed trunk. Travel from the Volga region was facilitated by the linking of Saratov in 1871 by railroad with southern and northern points. This also opened the region to foreign contact through visits by American railroad immigration agents with literature extolling the virtues of life in the Midwest.[23]

The general pattern of travel began upon receipt of a passport from the provincial capitals of Saratov or Pokrovsk. Since the authorities often denied requests for permanent residence abroad, some applicants registered for temporary certification while intending to flee induction into the army. Railroad service from Saratov made connections for travel to Bremen, Hamburg, or other European port cities, where enormous passenger vessels crossed the Atlantic to Baltimore, Philadelphia, or Castle Gardens, New York in about two weeks. Like so many other immigrants to the United States, many Russian Germans had their first experiences in dealing with the New World at unpleasant receiving stations, particularly New York's Castle Gardens, which was the largest in all of North America prior to the opening of Ellis Island in 1892. The principal passenger lines used by the Volga Germans included the Hamburg American Line, the Inman Line of Liverpool, and North German Lloyd (of Bremen).

Other Volga Germans who were among the first to settle in the Pacific Northwest traveled aboard the SS *Mosel*, which arrived in New York on October 24, 1876, carrying more than two hundred Volga Germans, largely from the *Wiesenseite* where most had lived in the daughter colonies along the Yeruslan River of Neu-Yagodnaya, Schöntal, Schönfeld, and Schöndorf. Villages there had been established in the 1850s principally by residents of Yagodnaya Polyana and Pobochnaya on the *Bergseite*, but unfavorable conditions along the Yeruslan prompted another move. Having brethren who had settled in Kansas in 1875 (those noted previously on the SS *Ohio* and SS *City of Montreal*), these Volga Germans also chose to emigrate and eventually formed the basis of a "Kansas colony" that would be the first group of Russian Germans to move to the Pacific Northwest. They settled in Portland, Oregon, in 1881 and in Whitman County, Washington Territory, the following year.[24]

Families aboard the October transport of the SS *Mosel* included those of Conrad Appel; Mrs. Henry Brach; Christian, John, and Phil-

lip Kleweno; Henry Litzenberger; Conrad, Henry, Phillip, John, John
Phillip, and two Peter Ochses; Adam and Henry Repp; Adam Ruhl;
John, Henry, Peter, and two George and Adam Scheuermans (Schier-
mans); and Henry Scheuermann.[25] This group traveled to Lawrence,
Kansas, where they stayed for about a month in the fall of 1876 while
it was determined where they would settle, eventually moving to Great
Bend and Pawnee Rock where some established small businesses or
worked for the railroad. Most, however, selected lands to farm and
many settled in areas along the border of Barton and Rush Counties.[26]

Intermarriage solidified relationships between the various pioneer
families to form a close-knit ethnic group that would soon immigrate
westward. These early pioneers of the Northwest often lived in isolated
areas where the bond of the groups of families was extremely important
for their physical survival and their social well-being. This was certainly
true for Henry Rothe, a native of Frank and former resident of Schönfeld on the *Wiesenseite*, who migrated to the United States with his family and settled in Bison, Kansas. Through his daughter's marriage with
Phillip Green in 1878, the Rothe family formed a formal bond with the
Green family. Phillip's father, George Henry Green, who originally was
from the Volga colony of Norka but moved to Rosenfeld, had traveled
with the Rothe family to America and settled in Otis, Kansas. Thus
the two families had known each other for some time, but were firmly
united as a result of the marriage of Phillip and Anna Margaret. This
example of a marital relationship developing into family bonds occurred
often and strengthened the ethnic identity of the Volga Germans.[27]

Like the Rothe and Green families, there were others who ventured
to the Great Plains seeking prosperity. Mrs. Henry Brach, for example,
settled with her sons near Otis where they later became prominent in
business and farming. Her son Peter's wife, Sophie (née Kniss), was the
sister-in-law of one of the Ochs cousins, John Peter, who remained in
Great Bend, Kansas, with others seeking employment on the Atchison,
Topeka and Santa Fe Railroad. They were all from the colony of Schönfeld. Many Volga Germans were compelled to live in old railroad cars
due to their lack of finances and the lack of suitable housing in central
Kansas. One of the Schierman brothers, John, was a skilled carpenter
and butcher, opening a small grocery store in Great Bend.[28] John and
Anna Marie's daughter, Mary, married one of the Ochs cousins, Peter.

Henry Litzenberger and Henry Repp were brothers-in-law as their wives, Anna Elizabeth and Mary (née Baht) respectively, were sisters and all of these people were from Neu-Yagodnaya.[29]

The Volga Germans who migrated to the Great Plains did not experience the extreme forms of discrimination that other ethnic and religious groups experienced. This was due in part to the character of the Russian Germans. Besides being recognized as an industrious people, they were known for their willingness to learn the English language and to participate in the educational opportunities of the American frontier. Many Volga Germans deemed the American system of public education superior to the educational institutions of Russia. One Kansas newspaper, the *Russell Record*, noted in 1876 that "what pleases us the best is to see them (the Russian Germans) sending their children to public school. We will risk any people's becoming Americanized, who patronize free schools." The accomplishments of the Kansas colony were equaled by those of the Nebraska colony. In Nebraska, the Volga and Black Sea Germans busied themselves with the essential elements of settlement and survival.[30]

Russian Germans who formed the Nebraska colony were eventually to become the first individuals from the Volga to settle in Adams and Lincoln Counties of eastern Washington. Most of the Volga Germans of the Nebraska colony were from the same general area of *Bergseite*, and they moved to Nebraska because of the influence of Black Sea Germans. The Black Sea people who had settled near Sutton served to confirm for many Volga Germans that the sod in Nebraska was very productive. The Black Sea group originally consisted of fifty-five families from Worms and Rohrbach who emigrated in the summer of 1873 and were directed to Lincoln. After a brief foray to Dakota Territory that ended because of a cholera epidemic, the group returned to Nebraska and settled in the Sutton area.[31]

The Volga German scouts who had visited Nebraska in 1874 were favorably impressed and their testimony was enhanced by the extensive foreign advertising of the State Board of Immigration in Nebraska. It depicted the unbroken plains as a virtual Paradise—reminiscent of an earlier period in Volga German history. Ten thousand pamphlets in German and 21,000 maps of Nebraska were distributed among the Mennonites by Fritz Hedde, a state official. An immigrant settlement house was constructed in Sutton, Nebraska, and the Union Pacific,

Burlington, and Missouri Pacific Railroads spent an estimated one million dollars to entice European settlers to the state.[32] The Union Pacific had been awarded twelve million acres of land along its tracks from Omaha to Promontory Point, Utah, and together with other railroads, it opened vast areas in Nebraska for sale and development.[33]

Booming grain production in the Midwest contributed to a 100 percent increase in the export of farm commodities from the United States between 1871 and 1874. This agricultural development was brought about by the advancement of American technology, and these new changes severely reduced Russia's traditional hold on the European market because its production declined during the same period.[34] Many Germans from Russia first settled in the Midwest where agriculture was rapidly becoming an important national source of wealth and pride. Indeed, the word "bunchgrass" became synonymous with untapped soil fertility in America's Midwest, and one published account by a trading firm in Odessa, Russia, ventured to suggest a significant development resulting from the expansion of American agriculture: "The mind is positively lost in painful thought when considering the quantity of corn (grain) America will soon be able to export. America will absolutely command the English market, and reduce prices to a minimum, with which it will be utterly impossible for us to compete."[35]

In 1875 a number of Volga German families from Balzer settled near Sutton after an unfavorable reception in Iowa. They were joined the following year by a number of families from Norka.[36] On August 5, 1876, the SS *Donau* docked in New York carrying a large number of Volga Germans who had departed Kolb and Dietel on June 25. Among the Kolb group were several families who would later compose a portion of the Nebraska colony that moved to Washington Territory in 1882. Among the families who arrived on the SS *Donau* in 1876 were Henry Bauer, Henry Kanzler, Henry Rehn, and Franz Scheibel, a member of the earlier scouting party who had been the schoolteacher in Kolb.[37] Scheibel and his group endured a difficult, circuitous journey to Nebraska, directed at first to Dorchester in Clark County, Wisconsin. The forested terrain was hardly suited for farming, and after several days, during which the Henry Bauer infant died, the group decided to seek a more promising site in Nebraska. When they reached Chicago, they were given employment as laborers for the Burlington Railroad which arranged for their free passage to Hastings, Nebraska. Accordingly, the

George and Maria Kanzler arrived on the SS *Donau* in 1876, and eventually moved to eastern Washington. *Courtesy Harland Eastwood*

party arrived there in August 1876. After a week, some members of the group were induced to purchase lands in Franklin County, southwest of Hastings; their transportation again furnished by the railroad. They wintered in a settlement house on the Little Blue River and later established St. Paul's Church under Scheibel in the small village of Wilhelmsruhe.[38]

For several years the Volga German settlers farmed there, living in sod houses and marketing their grain in nearby Hastings. The group was joined in 1878 by a number of families from villages on the *Bergseite* who arrived on June 5 in New York on the SS *Wieland*. Many passengers on this voyage were from Kolb, and they formed the other major segment of the Nebraska colony: The families of J. Frederick Rosenoff and Jacob Thiel with his sons George and John and their families and, from Frank, the Conrad Kiehns and Henry Amen, both of whom had immigrated with their parents. Other families on the same trip included Heimbigners (Norka and Frank), Schosslers (Walter), Hoffs (Frank), Müllers (Kolb), Dewalds (Hussenbach), and others.[39]

Members of the colony decided in 1878 that prospects for expansion would be greater in the southwest portion of the state even though the area was semiarid.[40] In September they filed on homesteads in Hitchcock County near Culbertson, Nebraska, and moved in May, living in "soddies" along Blackwood Creek. They made their livelihood by raising livestock and harvesting crops there as well as on their acreage in Franklin County. Large gardens provided the settlers with a variety of vegetables and melons while wild fruits grew abundantly along the river.[41] Unfortunately, their contentment was again short-lived. They soon learned that their settlement was located near the Great Western Cattle Trail, a major thoroughfare for the long drives of Texas long-horns to the northern markets. Their fields and gardens were overrun by cattle and their miseries were compounded by a disastrous drought on the Great Plains during the early 1880s. This led many to consider moving to a region that would become their ultimate destination. The same move was being contemplated simultaneously by members of the Kansas colony. Both groups were looking toward America's northern frontier—the Pacific Northwest.

The Kansas colony suffered considerably from the effects of the grasshopper plagues in the late 1870s. Particularly from 1875 to 1877, massive hordes of the insects left the Germans with little seed to replant. A dismal gloom hung over the land as swarms of the pests darkened the midday sky. The subsequent drought also adversely affected them and some remarked of the terror they felt during the frightening electrical storms. The Germans were not accustomed to such storms in Russia, and they dreaded the devastation of the plains tornados.[42] One infor-mant humorously related an Oz-like fantasy: after a cyclone his father emerged from a storm cellar to find that a small lake and team of horses had been swept from his Rush County homestead. En route to town he came upon the relocated lake and nearby stood the two horses—still harnessed and unharmed.[43]

Conditions on the plains compelled many disgruntled immigrant groups in the Midwest to consider settling in the Pacific Northwest. The settlers learned from men who had worked in the Oregon Country on railway surveys that the land was fertile and beautiful. Their inter-est was further stimulated by the favorable descriptions provided by transportation companies that advertised the lush regions of the inland Northwest as the "Great Columbia Plain." Not only were companies that owned land interested in selling acreage, but they also wanted to tap an unskilled labor source for the construction of their railroads. In order to fill this need, company officials turned to immigrants. Various railroad companies formed associations offering reduced rates to those who would travel westward to settle while guaranteeing employment until such arrangements were possible. The Union Pacific, Northern Pacific, Oregon Steamship Company, and others were particularly interested in encouraging the development of the West in order to profit not only from passenger service but the anticipated shipments of industrial and agricultural commodities.

One man's name in particular became synonymous with the growth and development of the Northwest—Henry Villard—who by 1876 had shrewdly wrested control of Northwestern transportation systems from railroad magnate Ben Holladay of Overland Stage and Pony Express fame. In the centennial year, Villard assumed the presidency of several companies that were heavily in debt, including the Oregon and California Railroad and the Oregon Central Railroad, both far from completion. In addition, Villard gained control of the Oregon Steamship Company, which operated regularly between San Francisco and Portland.[44] Within six years Henry Villard's position in Northwest transportation was clearly paramount as his holdings appeared secure and were among the largest of any individual in the entire nation. Villard's companies, principally the Oregon Railway and Navigation Company and the Northern Pacific Railroad, were instrumental in bringing the first Volga German settlers to the Pacific Northwest.

4

Arrival in the Pacific Northwest

Wenn wir auf dem Wasser fahren,
Schickt uns Gott einen Engel dar,
Gott, streck aus deine milde Hand,
Dass wir kommen an das Land.

When we upon the water sail,
God sends an angel without fail.
Stretch out then, God, Thy gentle hand,
That we can safely come on land!

—*"Auswandererlied,"* verse 5

The ultimate fate of many Volga Germans was linked very closely to the life of Henry Villard, a native of Bavaria. He came to the United States in 1853 and labored for several years in various occupations. Well educated in Germany, he studied law in Carlisle, Illinois, and worked in the offices of several influential United States senators from the Midwest. Finding a talent in journalism, he reported on various political campaigns for several newspapers, and he was on hand to cover the Lincoln-Douglas debates in 1859. His experiences led to personal acquaintanceships with Abraham Lincoln, Horace Greeley, and other people in influential circles of American business and politics. He became increasingly interested in the subject of railroad securities and finance, although for reasons of health he was compelled to return to Germany for recuperation in 1870 and again in 1871. He remained in Germany until 1873.

Villard's growing reputation in American journalism, combined with his coverage of the European Prussian wars, enabled him to establish many business contacts on the continent. This was a significant development because of the business link it would provide him in the future

Volga German Settlement in the Pacific Northwest.

as he promoted economic growth in the Pacific Northwest. Villard was keenly aware that several European finance houses, chiefly the firm of Sulzbach Brothers, had invested heavily in Ben Holladay's Oregon and California Railroad bonds, the value of which were steadily declining. The young entrepreneur hoped to use his business associates to develop the economic potentials of the American West. Aware of Villard's experience in America and his expertise in economic and political matters, a group of bondholders approached Villard in 1873 while he was convalescing in Heidelberg, and asked him to advise a protective committee based in Frankfurt. Villard was invited to join the committee, which he formally did in the spring of 1873. The chief problem, however, remained a lack of detailed information about the committee's investments on the distant Pacific Coast of North America. To correct the problem, the committee sent an inspection team to Oregon in April that soon returned to Germany with a very discouraging report.[1]

Villard's proficiency in English led to his appointment, along with Richard Köhler, to a team sent to the United States to execute a financial settlement with Holladay's troubled enterprise. Departing in April of 1874, Villard first attended a meeting in New York with Holladay, which provided the German an opportunity to comment on Holladay's "illiteracy, coarseness, presumption, mendacity, and unscrupulousness."[2] These impressions would lead to an intense rivalry between the two. Villard was not satisfied with the interview with Holladay and decided to see for himself the conditions in the Pacific Northwest. He set out for Oregon in May of 1874, arriving in San Francisco in June. There Villard and his associates boarded the California and Oregon Railroad and traveled by an alternate rail and wagon route to Portland.

Villard was awed by the scenery of the Pacific Coast and the Willamette Valley. He reported that "the beautiful landscapes unrolled to us one after another and framed the east by the green clad Cascades, overtopped by its isolated snowcovered peaks, and to the west by the picturesque Coast Range." Moreover, he was impressed, too, with the evidence of agricultural wealth in the "broad wheat fields that greeted the eye." Villard felt that he "had reached a chosen land, certain of great prosperity and seemingly holding out better promise to my constituents than I had hoped for."[3]

The talented entrepreneur became thoroughly imbued with a determination to capitalize on the great potentials of the region. Realizing that settlers would be needed to transform the virgin lands into acres of productivity, Villard began efforts to promote immigration to Oregon in November 1874. Supplied with the distinction of "Oregon Commissioner of Immigration," he opened an office in the heart of Boston's financial district and named it the "Eastern Bureau of the Oregon State Board of Immigration."[4] In the following year, he established agencies in Omaha and Topeka that cooperated with the main Northwest Immigration Bureau in Portland. The major purpose of these agencies was to encourage immigrants to settle in the Pacific Northwest by offering them reduced travel rates over the lines of the Union Pacific Railroad and the Oregon Steamship Company. It was the duty of railroad officials in the Northwest to provide them with employment on construction crews or sell them land to develop.

Both of these schemes led to the further development and use of the railroads. Both made sound economic sense, for the immigrants would use the railroad to ship their livestock and grain. The immigration bureaus used various methods to promote migration to the region. They circulated lavish displays of Oregon grains, fruits, and vegetables; placed large format advertisements in English, Scandinavian, and German language newspapers throughout the country; and distributed thousands of circulars and pamphlets. All of these were used as promotional materials to foster an interest in settlement of the Pacific Northwest.

Villard observed that geographically the central artery of transportation throughout the entire Pacific Northwest was the Columbia River. He assumed that whoever navigated the great waterway and controlled the railways along its course virtually monopolized transportation east of the Cascades. He would embark on a grand scheme of uniting both water and rail routes and placing these under his personal control. Although traveling extensively in both the United States and Europe, he skillfully managed the affairs of the European financiers whom he represented while formulating his plans.

He journeyed up the Columbia to The Dalles for the first time in May 1876.[5] Impressed by the great natural beauty of the area and imposing basaltic formations, he noted the natural outlet of the vast fertile and untouched regions drained by the Columbia and Snake Rivers, the control of which "influenced my thoughts with enticing visions of the empire that could be built upon such resources and of the share I might secure in founding and developing it." According to Villard, "it was at that early date that a plan arose distinctly in my mind which remained ever present with me until it was carried out through the organization of the Oregon Railway and Navigation Company."[6]

Within a year Villard's manipulation of several heavily indebted concerns led him to the presidency of three companies: the Oregon and California Railroad, the Oregon Central Railroad, and the Oregon Steamship Company, the latter of which operated a regular schedule between San Francisco and Portland.[7] An important component in the migration of immigrants to the Pacific Northwest was the northern transcontinental railroad. President Lincoln had signed the Northern Pacific Act on July 4, 1864, but construction was delayed because of the Civil War. Extensive land grants amounting to 25,000 acres of adjacent land per mile of track had been granted to the company to encourage construction,[8] but no progress was made until the summer of 1870 when work commenced at Thompson Junction Mission on Lake Superior in Minnesota. On the Pacific side, grading began at Kalama, Washington Territory, north up the Cowlitz Valley toward Puget Sound in December of the same year. However, the financial panic of 1873 led to the bankruptcy of the Northern Pacific Railway Company in 1875, and the Northern Pacific lost control of the Oregon Steam Navigation Company, the integral link in the system between Ainsworth and Portland. Villard realized this was a major opportunity to gain a foothold in the transcontinental traffic and subsequently purchased the Oregon Steam Navigation Company with their portage roads at the Cascades, The Dalles, and Celilo Falls. With the election of the energetic Frederick Billings to the presidency of the Northern Pacific Railroad in 1879, work was resumed at both ends of the beleaguered line and the prospects of final completion brightened.

Materials were needed on the construction of the Northern Pacific's Pend Oreille division, which stretched from Ainsworth, Washington, northeasterly through Spokane to Lake Pend Oreille. It was a massive undertaking employing thousands and provided a strong local market for agricultural produce. Villard was now in the position to provide the needed supply services through his river route. Accordingly, he entered into traffic agreements in 1880 with Billings through which Villard's Oregon Railway and Navigation Company carried materials to Ainsworth while contracting to build a line down the left bank of the Columbia River with feeder lines extending into eastern Oregon and

Washington Territory. For this purpose he had organized with eastern capital the Oregon Railway and Navigation Company in June 1879, which assumed control of the Oregon Steam Navigation Company and the Oregon Steamship Company. After the purchase of Dr. D. S. Baker's narrow gauge line from Wallula[9] to Walla Walla, Villard gained complete control of transportation from Wallula to Portland and from there by steamer to San Francisco.[10]

The agreement reached with the Northern Pacific further stipulated a division of interest between the two lines with the Columbia and Snake Rivers forming the boundary line. An exception was made in deference to Villard's insistence on a detached Palouse line, construction of which was being planned from Palouse Junction (Connell) eastward through the heart of the fertile Palouse Hills to Endicott and Colfax, leading eventually to the Coeur d'Alene mining district. It was in this central Palouse region that many Volga Germans were led to settle.

Improvements in transportation and agricultural mechanization led to increased agricultural production east of the Cascades. Only half of the crop of 1879 could be exported before navigation of the rivers ended in December for the winter.[11] Transportation however, was not completely halted, for up to 1,800 settlers were moving to the Columbia Plain each month. They came by wagon up the south bank of the Columbia en route to fertile lands in the Walla Walla area, Big Bend country, and the Palouse Hills.[12]

To facilitate the orderly settlement and exploitation of their holdings in this region, Villard incorporated the Oregon Improvement Company on October 21, 1880, with capital stock of $5,000,000 provided by American financial associates. The Oregon Improvement Company purchased the Seattle Coal and Transportation Company and the Seattle and Walla Walla Railroad, the forerunner of the Pacific Coast Railway. In addition to other land acquisition, the new company bought nearly 150,000 acres (alternate sections in fourteen townships) from the Northern Pacific in the heart of the Palouse country, these being carefully selected and varying in price from five to ten dollars per acre, selling on a six year installment plan at 7 percent interest.[13] Many of the early Volga German arrivals in the area, however, found that land was more easily obtained by homesteading.

Villard appointed General Thomas R. Tannatt of Manchester, Massachusetts, to handle the affairs of the Oregon Improvement Company.

Tannatt was a prominent New England figure and retired brigadier general who had commanded Union forces south of the Potomac in 1862. During his command in defense of the capitol, he became personally acquainted with President Lincoln. He was later reassigned to the Second Army Corps. In 1864 he was severely wounded in action at Petersburg. For reasons of health he moved to Colorado after the Civil War where he managed the mining interests of several New York investors before relocating to McMinnville, Tennessee, in 1870. In 1876 he returned to Massachusetts and became increasingly interested in developing railroad land grants in the Pacific Northwest.[14] This prompted him to write a letter to Villard in 1877 in which he offered several suggestions which would aid in the westward settlement of immigrants. Impressed with the advice, Villard appointed him the eastern agent for the Oregon Steamship Company in 1877, and in the following year Tannatt began directing the immigration program for Villard's other Northwest transportation companies.

After the formation of the Oregon Improvement Company in 1878, Villard elevated Tannatt as its general agent and his office was transferred to Portland. S. G. Reed of that city was the Oregon Improvement Company's first president and the other directors were William Endicott Jr., Boston; George M. Pullman, Chicago; Artemas Holmes, New York; and C. H. Lewis, Henry Failing, C. J. Smith, J. N. Dolf, and C. H. Prescott, all of Portland.[15] Tannatt embarked on his new responsibilities with a vigor that characterized his entire career. He was instrumental in persuading the Oregon railroads and the Oregon Steam Navigation Company to issue reduced travel certificates to immigrants and he personally supervised the settlement of numerous immigrant groups from New England and the Midwest. He cooperated with Union Pacific ticket agencies throughout the East in order to arrange transportation to the Northwest where an intensive campaign was under way to popularize settlement in the Inland Empire. In 1882 Villard's Northern Pacific Railroad employed over nine hundred agents in Europe who distributed thousands of pamphlets in several languages extolling the Pacific Northwest as the "best wheat, farming and grazing lands in the world."[16]

Unknown even to his closest associates at this time, the implications of Villard's ambitious plans of railroad ownership were not only regional but national in scope.[17] He came to the realization that direct railway connections to the East were imperative if the Pacific

Northwest was ever to be actively involved in the commerce of the nation and the influx of European immigrants. With this in mind, he embarked in December 1880 on the unprecedented scheme of secretly collecting $8,000,000 from his financial supporters, which formed his famous "blind pool." Reflecting their confidence in Villard, his request was actually oversubscribed, enabling him to purchase the controlling interest in Billings' Northern Pacific Railroad, work on which had again been stalemated. With Villard's election to its presidency on September 15, 1881, and work on both ends resumed, his dream of a northern transcontinental rapidly approached reality.

Work on the Oregon Railway and Navigation Company line from Portland to Wallula continued at brisk pace and although the earlier agreement with Billings specified its completion by October 31, 1883, the energetic crews of the company finished it on October 20, 1882, with the first through passenger train leaving Portland on November 20, 1882.[18] By July of that year a number of branch lines had begun fanning out in the Walla Walla country, one extending north from Walla

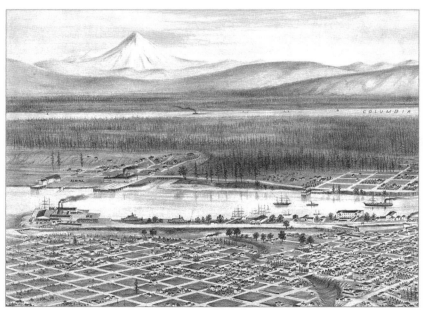

Portland Albina District, 1879, from an E. S. Glover lithograph of Portland, Oregon. *Courtesy Richard Scheuerman*

Walla to the Snake River at Texas Ferry and the Columbia and Palouse, incorporated in 1883 by Villard, continued construction eastward from Palouse Junction to Endicott.

The program launched by Villard and Tannatt to induce settlement east of the Cascades bore fruit among many immigrants in the Midwest, including the Volga Germans. In the case of the Kansas colony in Rush and Barton Counties, and the Nebraska colony in Hitchcock County, frustration was particularly evident for reasons enumerated in Chapter III. In both places a segment of these groups elected to emigrate, the former in 1881 and the latter in 1882 (See table, p. 80). The Kansas party took advantage of reduced fares over the Union Pacific line and traveled to San Francisco where steamers of Villard's Oregon Steamship Company transported them to Portland.[19] In Portland some of the immigrants labored on the construction of the enormous Albina fill earth-moving project while others worked at a local lumber mill.[20]

Their intention to settle on prime farmland remained foremost in their minds, however, and finding the surrounding forested areas unsuitable for this purpose, they were directed to officials of the Portland Oregon Improvement Company office to explore the possibilities of settlement east of the Cascades. Having just completed the purchase from the Northern Pacific of the odd sections in fourteen townships in the Palouse country totaling 150,000 acres, a scouting party was selected to view the area. Both Phillip Green and Peter Ochs were fluent in English, and thus they were selected to go with others on the tour. The *Walla Walla Weekly Statesman* noted their activities through a letter of May 11, 1881, received from Agent R. W. Mitchell of the Oregon Improvement Company's Colfax Office of the Land Department:

> Five locating agents of the Kansas colony, composed of about seventy families, passed through here Thursday on their way to inspect lands of the Oregon Improvement Company. Col. Tustin is in charge of the party. They look like solid, progressive farmers, such as we are willing to welcome to our broad acres. One of them remarked, "If the land is anything like what we've seen around Dayton, I guess we can be suited. We are surprised and delighted at what we have seen." Mr. Mitchell of the Oregon Improvement Company will meet this party in the Palouse Country next week.[21]

Writing from Dayton to Villard's office, Tannatt relayed his intentions for dealing with the group in a note on May 10. Tannatt wanted

Phillip Green, shown here with his wife Anna, was a member of the Kansas colony contingent surveying lands in the Pacific Northwest. *Courtesy Janice Enos*

"to sell them a township and will on Mr. Oakes' return if there is any trade with them."[22] Indeed, the vanguard returned favorably impressed with the area, and Tannatt planned to meet them in Portland in order to arrange the sale.[23] However, he found them reluctant to enter into such a massive bargain on behalf of the others in Kansas without consulting them first. The negotiations took time, and it was not until the fall of 1882 that members of the Portland group moved on company lands in Whitman County. Having endured the struggle of a journey halfway around the globe to this remote area, they soon discovered brethren who had also come from the Volga. A contingent of the Nebraska colony had decided to relocate, and they too arrived in Washington in 1882.

Some Volga Germans of the Nebraska colony had considered moving to the Pacific Northwest as early as 1880. In that year the Nebraska group at Culbertson wrote J. E. Shepherd, the immigration agent of the Oregon Railway and Navigation Company in San Francisco, expressing their interest. The letter was forwarded to Villard himself who must have been pleased to see that many immigrants could be lured to the Pacific Northwest. In the letter the farmers indicated their discontent with conditions in the Midwest. The Volga Germans wrote the company to inquire "about the country of Washington Territory." They explained that they were 160 families strong and that their major reason for seeking a new home was "that the wheat crop has failed here for three years past." The immigrants feared another drought was imminent. Their cattle were in deplorable condition because of the lack of range. In addition, they lived on the "open prairies" where "the heavy winds that prevail here are unendurable." The Volga Germans wrote:

> Our houses consist of "Dugouts" and "Sod houses." Our people are all discouraged and homesick, but too far to go back to Russia, and we want to see…the Territory we have heard so much of its great yielding wheat fields and wonderful Fruit Country. We understand the Navigation Company has Rail Road land for sale. There are 160 families here, and 70 families in Clay Co. this state, and 100 families coming from Russia this Fall. I think we can locate 230 families there this fall and winter. We are desirous of seeing this country first, and our minister Mr. Kansler and myself wish to go out and see the country. And we wish to know whether you can furnish passes for two persons out and one to come back and head the colony. We are a good, honest, straightforward, hard working class of people, and the colony also instructs me to state that the two passes will be paid back to the Company after they are located, so as to be sure of our honesty of intention.[24]

The Volga Germans of the Nebraska colony received a favorable response from the railroad officials but it was not until 1882 that they decided to immigrate to the Pacific Northwest. In the spring of 1882, a number of these families boarded a train at North Platte, Nebraska, en route to Ogden, Utah, on the Union Pacific Railroad.[25] The value of having its own direct connections to the Oregon country had become increasingly evident to the Union Pacific with the developing economy of the region. For this reason it had incorporated the Oregon Short Line in 1879 to run from Granger, Wyoming, roughly along the route of the old Oregon Trail to a connection with Villard's Oregon Railroad and Navigation Company on the Columbia at Umatilla. The line was not completed until 1884, and the enterprising men of the Nebraska colony were given temporary employment constructing this stretch of the railroad from American Falls, Idaho, to Pendleton, Oregon. They first formed a train of forty wagons at Ogden and lumbered north on the California Trail until they reached the Oregon Trail near the headwaters of the Snake River.

The group chose Frederick Rosenoff to be the wagonmaster and they traveled from American Falls through Boise and Baker en route to Walla Walla.[26] Memories of the Custer massacre of 1871 and the Bannock Indian War of 1878 were still fresh in the minds of many residents as well as the immigrants. They feared Indian attack and therefore they appointed Henry Oestreich and George H. Kanzler as scouts for the party. The Volga Germans made detailed plans for their overland journey and they proved to be a resourceful people who made do with what they had to make the trip. For example, Conrad Wolsborn, a shoemaker, did not have a pair of oxen to pull his wagon. He could not afford to purchase another animal, so he fashioned a special harness uniting his horse and his one ox. The women sewed garden seeds into clothing to ensure good plantings in their new home.

The caravan encountered the usual hazards associated with pioneer travel, enduring intense heat on dusty trails that often led through areas infested with rattlesnakes. Marie Thiel, wife of John, went into confinement in Baker, giving birth to twins on April 10, 1882; only one, Jacob, survived. The group entrusted their earnings from work on the railroad to a former Nebraskan sheriff who accompanied them but near the end of the journey he absconded with the funds. However, they maintained a strong attachment to their cultural traditions despite the rigors of the journey. They were devout Christians and remained steadfast in their faith, never traveling on Sundays. Instead they gathered their wagons into a large circle and held worship services each Sunday with an elder reading the lessons in German. Upon arrival in Pendleton some members of the party decided to go on to Portland although most continued north to Walla Walla. The first Volga Germans drove their wagons into Walla Walla late in the summer of 1882.[27] Because they were exhausted and the weather was changing rapidly, they decided to winter in Walla Walla while investigating the various possibilities of settlement in the region.

This was not an idle time for the Volga Germans. As the bunchgrass surrounding Walla Walla turned brown, the tired immigrants ventured out to find jobs. Some of the men found employment on farms in the area, while others contracted to haul rock for the construction of the territorial penitentiary. One of the Thiels was hired by Phillip Ritz, a successful Walla Walla farmer and businessman, to dig fence-post holes on his property near Ritzville. In addition to other extensive holdings in the territory, Ritz had acquired 5,000 acres near Ritzville from the railroad in 1878. Finding that Ritz paid well for his labor, Thiel decided to continue working at Ritzville and Ritz encouraged him and his companions to settle on lands nearby.[28] Ritz was an intelligent businessman who recognized the worth of the immigrants and thus began a massive migration of Germans from Russia to Adams and Lincoln Counties.

J. Frederick Sr. and Maria Rosenoff. *Courtesy Harland Eastwood*

Table: Pacific Northwest Germans from Russia
Immigrant Roster of Families, 1881-1883*

Kansas Colony 1881–82 Train and Trail Group	Native Volga Villages
Conrad Appel	Schoental†
Phillip and Catherine (Ochs) Aschenbrenner	Brunnental
Phillip and Anna (Rothe) Green	Rosenfeld
John and Mary (Kleweno) Helm	Schoental
Adam and Anna Marie (Voelker) Hergert†	Schoental
J. Phillip and A. Margaretha (Brecht) Hergert†	Schoental
Henry and Anna Elisabeth (Scheuerman) Kleweno	†
John and Catherine Kleweno	Schoental
Phillip Kleweno	Schoental
Henry and Anna (Barth) Litzenberger	New Yagodnaya
Henry and Catherine Ochs	Schoenfeld
Peter and Mary (Scheuerman) Ochs	Schoenfeld
John Peter Ochs	Schoenfeld
Henry and Mary (Barth) Repp	Schoental
Henry ("Palouse") and Maria (Kleweno) Repp	†
Adam Ruhl	Schoental†
John and Maria (Hergert) Scheuerman	Yagodnaya Polyana†
(Johann) Conrad and Catherine (Holstein) Schierman	Schoental
Henry and Anna (Ochs) Schierman	Schoental
John and Anna Marie (Koch) Schierman	Schoental
George and Mary (Repp) Schierman	Schoental
John and Elisabeth (Scheuerman) Schreiber	†
Johann Heinrich and Maria K. (Bafus) Yoelker	†
Adam and Catherine (Luft) Weitz	†

*This list is based on available records and includes families believed to have arrived in the region before the completion of the Northern Pacific Railroad in the fall of 1883.
†Volga colony of origin uncertain.

Nebraska Colony 1882 Wagon Train Family Heads	Native Volga Villages
Konrad and Anna (Brungardt) Amen(d)	Frank/Frank
Heinrich and Maria Katherine (Kiehn) Amen	Frank
Jacob and Katherina (Heimbigner) Bastron	Frank/†
Henry and Barbara (Benzel) Bauer	Kolb
Joh. Jacob and Marie Elis. (Koch) Bauer	Kolb/Kolb
Christina Marg. (Engelmann) Bauer	Kolb
G. Jacob and Katherine (Rodenberger) Dewald*	Hussenbach/†
Conrad and Anna Marie (Kühn) Heimbigner*	Frank
Henry and Katherine Marg. (Koch) Kanzler	Kolb
George and Maria (Oestreich) Kanzler	Kolb/Alt Messer
John Jacob and Maria Elisabeth (Koch) Kanzler	Kolb
Fred and Dorothea Elis. (Dewald) Kembel	Kolb/Hussenbach
Conrad and Maria Kath. (Barth) Kiehn	Frank/Frank
Susanna (Getman) Kiehn	Frank†
Henry and Anna Katherine (Amen) Kiehn	Frank/Frank
Rev. Henry F. and Mary (Oestreich) Michel	Alt Messer
Henry and Katherine (Kanzler) Miller	Kolb
Joh. Christian and Katherina (Leichner) Oestreich	Alt Messer
Joh. Kasper and Katherine (Leichner) Oestreich	Alt Messer
J. Frederich and Maria (Achzinger) Rosenoff, Sr.	Kolb
J. Frederich and Suzanna (Kanzler) Rosenoff, Jr.	Kolb
J. Conrad and Barbara (Hill) Schaefer	Frank/Walter
George and Margaret (Weiderman) Schaefer	Frank
Conrad and Anna (Dewald) Schaefer	Frank/Hussenbach
Jacob and Maria (Stumpf) Schaefer	Frank/Warenburg
Jacob and Elisabeth (Walter) Schoessler	Walter
Carl and Susan (Krauser) Stumpf*	Warenburg/†
Conrad and Katherina (?) Stumpf	Warenburg
Philip and Anna (?) Stumpf	Warenburg

Continued on page 82.

Nebraska Colony 1882
Wagon Train Family Heads (continued)   Native Volga Villages

Heinrich G. & Anna Marie (Reiber or Propp) Thiel	Kolb/†
John and Marie Elisabeth (Meier) Thiel	Kolb
Jacob and Eva Elis. (Thorn) Thiel	Kolb
Joh. Jacob and Maria Elis. (Stromberger) Thiel	Kolb/†
Henry and Anna Elis. (Bauer) Thiel	Kolb
Johann Jacob Wagner	Frank
Conrad and Katherine (Thiel) Wolsborn	Frank/†

This list was is based on research by Pauline Dudek, Harland Eastwood, Joan Oestreich Schwisow, Jean Roth, Brent Mai, and Richard Hergert. The roster does not include accompanying family members. Maria Elizabeth (Koch) Kanzler died on the Oregon Train journey in Baker City on September 6, 1882, eight days after the birth of her son. Anna (Bauer) Thiel gave birth to twins in Pleasant Valley, Oregon, only one survived.

*Some evidence indicates these families may have preceded the main group.
†Volga colony of origin uncertain.

5

Regional Settlement and Expansion

Wir sind ja all recht gut emphangen,
Und können jo nichts mehr verlangen
Wie glickich sein jo wir,
Dass wir sind alle hier,
Jetzt fallen wir auf der Knie
und danken Gott dafuer.

We were welcomed with open arms.
Now we're free from want and harms.
Sorrow's turned to jubilee
We've come safe o'er the sea.
And we fall to our knees
To praise God thankfully.

—*"Die Reis' Die War Erzogen,"* verse 4
(Translated by Nancy B. Holland)

Volga German settlement in the inland Northwest took place at the beginning of a pivotal decade in regional development. As early as the 1860s, the range cattle industry had been dominant east of the Cascades as stockmen capitalized on the vast unfenced grazing lands of the region. In the 1880s, however, their presence was challenged by the growing number of colonist farmers who were clustering in the area's fertile valleys and prairie districts.

The bitter winter of 1880–81 resulted in the financial ruin of many cattlemen, with some herd losses reaching fifty percent. Grain marketing problems had long stalled agricultural development but the completion of the Northern Pacific Railroad in 1883 facilitated farm exports to both coastal and eastern markets. At the same time, farmers began fencing their properties with barbed wire and joining together to enact "herd laws" in order to prevent cattlemen from freely ranging their stock on the recently claimed lands.

North of the Snake River in Washington was a geographic region often called the Palouse Country. With continued settlement there it was organized in November 1871 into Whitman County. Pioneers from the Walla Walla Valley had first settled in the Palouse along Union Flat Creek during the previous decade. In 1870, settlement began at present Colfax and Farmington and during the next two years pioneers located along Rebel Flat Creek, Pine Creek, Four Mile Creek, near present Genesee and Moscow, and at the foot of Rock Lake.[1] By 1872 the population of the area totaled about two hundred whites, increasing to about one thousand the following year.[2] In the summer of 1873, surveys began to extend the existing Territorial Road from Walla Walla to Penawawa northward to the forks of the Palouse River at Colfax and north to Spokane Falls. Other main roads intersecting the region led from Walla Walla to Spokane and Colville country, including the Texas Road, which crossed the Snake at Texas Ferry (Riparia), and the Mullan (Colville) Road, which crossed the Snake at Lyon's Ferry and paralleled the Palouse River and Cow Creek, leading near the future sites of Ritzville and Sprague. A portion of this route was later followed by the Northern Pacific Railroad, which greatly enhanced immigration to the area.

In 1876 a federal land office was opened in Colfax and within a year the immigration thrust began with Almota becoming the chief entry port. Additional landings were built to carry busy ferry traffic at Penawawa and Wawawai. These sites were regularly serviced by the steamboats of the Oregon Railway and Navigation Company including the *Yakima, Nez Perces Chief, Owyhee, Tenino,* and *Spray.* By 1880 the population of Whitman County had risen to over 7,000 as settlers discovered the fertility of the Palouse's loess soils.[3]

Separated to the west of these rolling hills by the channeled scablands was the Big Bend country, a vast undulating plain lying in the Columbia River crescent. Because the southern part was characterized by a treeless sandy expanse, the rich loam of its northern sector was largely overlooked by settlers until the 1880s. Few individuals were more convinced than Phillip Ritz of the great agricultural potential of the region and he became enamored with the idea of its development.

Ritz accompanied representatives of the Northern Pacific on tours of the area as early as 1873, urging their commercial efforts in the region. He traveled the breadth of the nation on numerous occasions to meet with various government and railroad officials and encouraged them to promote settlement in the Big Bend.[4] At the same time he was awarded contracts by the Northern Pacific to plant maple, chestnut, locust, and other trees along its tracks from Ainsworth to Ritzville, a project Ritz embarked on as much from an experimental standpoint as financial. The *Walla Walla Statesman* optimistically predicted the results based on Ritz's earlier experience stating, "those planted last year are thrifty…The experiment gave emphatic denial to the theory that the sandy soil was unproductive."[5] For his efforts, the town of Ritzville was named in his honor, platted in 1881 with other towns on that section of the Northern Pacific line.

Ritz was making great progress promoting the settlement of the plateau, and his efforts were matched by those of General Thomas R. Tannatt. Already the Kansas colony was entering the region. According to colony spokesman Phillip Green, the Volga Germans from Kansas were rapidly approaching the Palouse Country and "would be at Texas Ferry in a day or so, and asking for several four-horse teams to convey them to Plainville," a point between Endicott and Colfax, Washington. Green commented that the immigrants were looking forward to their new home because "the land, climate and general outlook of this country, was all that could be desired." He reported that three separate colonies from Kansas had sent inspectors to the Pacific Northwest to examine the land, and all were convinced that the region would make an excellent choice for a new home. Several of the early Volga Germans from the Kansas colony located "land for other coming immigrants" and they encouraged their families and friends to move to the inland Northwest. The response was so great that one account reported: "There is to be an exodus from Kansas this fall."[6] Members of this group were determined to locate on suitable farm land. Their previous expedition to the Palouse Hills reminded them of the terrain on the Volga *Bergseite*, and they were convinced that the Palouse had soil as rich as they had ever known. Tannatt's Oregon Improvement Company provided their fares over the Oregon Railway and Navigation Company as far as Texas Ferry, where some arrived on October 17. Some of the men then walked over twenty miles to Endicott, enlisting the aid of Henry D. Smith and J. T. Person to procure wagons, and returned the following day to transport the families and belongings.[7]

Carrying the pioneer necessities, the Phillip Green family traveled from Portland in a covered wagon drawn by very stubborn mules. Leaving on a warm morning late in September, they followed the Emigrant Road and soon began ascending the Cascades. On the other side of the pass it began snowing and raining with such intensity that the wagon and occupants were soon drenched. The Green's infant, Magdalena, celebrated her first birthday on October 3 under miserable circumstances. Despite the weather, they made their way to Walla Walla. After traveling north for a time out of Walla Walla, the weary settlers finally reached their destination, on October 12, 1882. They were to build their home and a new life for themselves four miles east of Endicott, Washington Territory.[8]

The arrival of the Kansas colony in Walla Walla sparked great interest in a local newspaper. The editors were impressed that the immigrants were traveling to the regions surrounding Endicott and Plainville, "where they will settle, having already secured places for location." By wagon trails and iron rails the colonists came to the region: "A part of the colony go by wagon from Portland, the others by rail." When they arrived at Texas Ferry, Tannatt's agents helped them to cross the river and complete their journey to their new home. Indeed Tannatt was instrumental in aiding the Volga Germans, and it was reported that "every help possible will be given these people by General Tannatt and his subordinates."[9] The interaction between Tannatt and the Germans was close and extremely significant to the successful settlement of the Palouse Country by the immigrants. The editor of the *Walla Walla Statesman* wrote about the immigrants' first visit to the office of the Oregon Improvement Company:

> Calling at the office of the Oregon Improvement Company on Monday to introduce gentlemen from the East we found quite a delegation to whom General Tannatt was explaining the Palouse Country and arranging for settlement. Some weeks since a portion of this Kansas Colony was met by the Oregon Improvement Company's teams at Texas Ferry and are now building on lands purchased of the Com. The portion of the Colony now here, with their own teams will be met by additional teams at Texas Ferry, to carry out household goods sent by train. Gen. Tannatt will meet them in Endicott, to complete contracts and outer houses built for their use. This organized method of handling immigrants is doing much for the Palouse Country, directly and indirectly for all of eastern Washington. The ample capital of the Oregon

Improvement Company and their simple method of dealing promptly with newcomers, upon an easily understood plan, is most proper—a Mr. Greene who is with those who left on Saturday says twenty-four families are on the way hither and those now at Endicott are much pleased with the country and their reception.[10]

Large tents were staked out for the newcomers in the bustling young community of Endicott, which had grown rapidly since it had been platted by the Oregon Improvement Company early in 1882. The town was named for one of its directors, William Endicott Jr., and an ambitious building campaign was launched through the resident Oregon Improvement Company agent, John Courtright.[11] Phillip Green was one of the first immigrants to arrive in the area and his first experiences there are indicative of other immigrants who settled the Palouse Country. One of Green's first activities was to fashion an earthen home in a hillside on his farm, similar to the *zemlyanki* dug by the first German colonists on the Volga. Some blamed Indians for stealing Green's horses shortly after their arrival.[12] After enduring a difficult winter, he

Zemlyanka cellar near Endicott. *R. R. Hutchison Collection, Manuscripts, Archives, and Special Collections, Washington State University Libraries*

hauled lumber from Colfax the following spring and built a four-room house.[13] To supplement his income, Green, like many others, went to work on the construction of the Palouse line of the Northern Pacific Railroad. Some of the men were accompanied by their families who lived in tents. The rails reached Colfax in 1883 and grading continued toward Pullman and Moscow.[14]

Tannatt further reported that the settlers were learning a great deal about their new home and how to tend the land. In a graphic description of the early farming, Tannatt said:

> Seeding in the Palouse Country as late as June 1 with certainty of crops. This season being measurably backward we can seed as late as June and continue plowing for fall sowing much later. The policy of buying but a limited number of teams has proven itself correct. Our teams have been fully employed up to plowing season in hauling lumber and fencing. The Co. have now erected Boarding house, Company Building, Smith Shop, tool shed and three cottages (in Endicott).
>
> Grain for feed. Spring and fall sowing was brought in early fall at an extreme low figure is well cleaned and sacked. Seven acres are just in garden which will supply us with potatoes and in ample quality. Temporarily our lands are isolated. The advancement of line from Snake River to Willow Springs have left our lands in a position where immigration cannot reach them except when entering Washington Territory from the East with their own teams.[15]

Adding new impetus to regional development was the completion of the Northern Pacific Railroad on September 8, 1883, when the gap was closed on the transcontinental line at Gold Greek, Montana. More Volga Germans came to the area, and in the fall of 1883, Mrs. Green's father, Henry Rothe, arrived with his daughter, but died within two weeks. Other Volga Germans who came to the region were Henry Repp, his wife Mary, and Mary's sister, Anna Litzenberger, and the families of John Helm, John and George Schreiber, Conrad Wilhelm, and John Peter Ochs. Within five years of the completion of the Northern Pacific line, other Volga German families who immigrated to Whitman County included those of Conrad and Peter Aschenbrenner, Henry Fisher, Christian Hagen, Conrad Kammerzell, Christian and Henry Kleweno, George P. Litzenberger, Conrad Machleit, and Adam Weitz.[16] As one family settled in the Palouse Country, they wrote their friends and families still living in other parts of the world and encouraged them to migrate to the Pacific Northwest. In its widely distributed 1883 guidebook, the Northern Pacific hailed the area as:

> One of the most fertile and extensive agricultural regions on the Pacific Coast. The Palouse country extends from the base of the Coeur d'Alene Mountains westward sixty miles, so is partly in Idaho, and it reaches northwardly from Snake River seventy-five to 100 miles. The railroad will push east to the mountains nearly 100 miles, with branches to Moscow, Idaho, and Farmington, W.T. West of the Palouse there is very little arable land, but east of that stream is a fertile country of the best description. Endicott is a new town that the road will develop. It is in the midst of a farming country not yet settled and cultivated. The chief town in this region is *Colfax*, which has hitherto been the centre of business. *Moscow* is the terminus of the southeast branch of the road. It has the mountains for its eastern background, and a rich surrounding country that will build up its prosperity.
> The same is true of *Farmington*, twenty-five miles to the northward, to which another branch will extend. The Palouse region consists of a rolling surface of country, with rich soil even on the highest hilltops. There is no timber on its prairies, but abundance of it along the streams and on the mountains.[17]

Villard's empire fell victim to increasing financial pressures, and in December 1883 he was forced to relinquish control of the Oregon Railway and Navigation Company as well as the Northern Pacific, both of which reverted to separate private control. Under new management the Palouse branch of the Northern Pacific pushed on in April 1885 from Colfax to Pullman, Washington, and Moscow, Idaho. In the following year, the railroad reached the budding farm communities of Garfield, Tekoa, and Farmington, where General Tannatt moved in 1888, to live on a large farmstead. Through his recommendation, many Volga Germans found temporary employment with the railroad or at his Farmington ranch.[18]

Their exposure to these other areas led many to homestead throughout Whitman County. Volga German settlement expanded to many of the towns serviced by the railroad including Farmington, Garfield, Steptoe, and Colfax, which later harbored its own "Russian Town" in the city's northeast section along First Street. In the summer of 1888 an immense railroad bridge was built at Riparia spanning the Snake River which allowed the Oregon Railway and Navigation Company to reach its Columbia and Palouse line at Lacrosse. Spokane was reached in 1889 from Tekoa, and the Palouse Country was totally encircled that year when a feeder line from Winona to Farmington by way of Oakesdale and St. John was completed.[19] The Volga Germans were greatly influenced by the railroad. Many traveled to their new homes by rail, many were first employed by the railroad, many settled in towns serviced by the trains, and all of them depended on the railroad to transport their crops to markets.

Endicott, Washington, 1901. *Richard Scheuerman collection*

One million acres of potential crop land were said to be within the revised 1883 boundary of Whitman County which conformed then to its present shape. The Volga German settlers from Kansas were anxious to establish a colony within Whitman County and they set out to find a suitable site. Shortly after Conrad Schierman arrived in the Palouse, he rode horseback north from Endicott to explore the surrounding countryside.[20] Waves of knee-high tawny bunchgrass blew in the breeze across the broad hills. After riding about five miles, he came to the crest of a massive basaltic bluff overlooking the Palouse River Valley. Finding it too steep to descend, he followed the river's course upstream until he came to a more gentle slope near its northernmost point in that area. Descending here and riding back a short distance to the expanse spied earlier, he found a beautiful tableland bordered on the west by the river and sheltered on the east by the steep rock bluffs. He returned to the railroad camp and shared the news of his discovery with the other families who proceeded to investigate the site together. They were taken by the beauty and fertility of the site, and traveled to the federal land office in Colfax to arrange for a somewhat unorthodox purchase of the land. Perhaps because Henry Litzenberger was among the oldest of the group and had greater savings, he purchased the entire quarter-section tract (160 acres) from the Oregon Improvement Company in 1889, but immediately subdivided it into long, narrow *Langstreifen* parcels ranging in size from twenty to over forty acres. These tracts were arranged to provide each Palouse Colony family with river access and fertile bottomland. Residents organized a functional commons (*Almenden*) by working together in field operations, sharing pastureland, and raising enormous gardens.[21]

The colony consisted of the Peter and Henry Ochs families together with those of Conrad, Henry, George, and John Schierman. John Schierman became the group's treasurer and chief carpenter. Other Volga Germans joined these families in the small collective, including John Schreiber and Phillip Aschenbrenner.[22] Daily life in the commune was busy for both parents and children, as everyone assisted in the building of the first eight homes, all simple yet adequate three-room structures.

Palouse River homestead of Henry and Mary Repp and Henry and Anna Litzenberger, c. 1885 (oldest known photograph of Palouse Country Volga Germans). *Courtesy Lee McGuire*

With the abundance of prime farmland and mechanized methods of cultivation, individuals could acquire and manage larger estates in relative self-sufficiency. In later years, this led members of the Palouse Colony to move away from the colony and to purchase their own farms. Others, however, chose to pursue business ventures in neighboring towns that served the interests of the agrarian populace. The original colony soon became a way station for newly arriving Volga Germans, serving as a temporary residence until they located nearby. One immigrant who settled in the Palouse Country was John Peter Ochs who had remained in Kansas but migrated to the colony in 1883 only after his cousins had done so. He added greatly to the colorful history of the Palouse Colony. His melodic whistle filled the air of the colony as he worked in the fields, and in the evenings his voice echoed throughout the valley as he sang the familiar German hymns.[23]

It was a difficult task for adults and children alike to leave their homes on the Volga and migrate to a foreign land. Naturally they had some fears and anxieties about the far-off lands of America, but parents were convinced that their move to the United States would benefit the family significantly. To convince their children and perhaps themselves

Palouse Colony homes and fields, c. 1910. *Richard Scheuerman collection*

that the overseas move was in their best interest, mothers and fathers, grandmothers and grandfathers, told the children fascinating tales of America—"the land where milk and honey flows." Shortly after their arrival in the area, the children would steal the wild honey from hollow trees along the Palouse River and herd the cows home each evening, their udders bulging with milk after grazing in the thick green pastures. Then the parents reminded them, "Look—see, you have the milk flowing from the cows and the honey flowing from the trees, just like we said it would be like here when we were in Russia."[24]

A large spring and brook provided all the water needed for the colony, and farming was confined at first to large gardens of potatoes, corn, and melons. The settlers soon found that wheat and barley, sown by hand broadcasting, grew particularly well on the chestnut brown soil as well as oats which were planted on the areas bordering the bluffs. Well acquainted with the cultivation of these grains in Russia, the colonists learned a great deal from other farmers they met through their dealings with the Oregon Improvement Company. They gained much practical information on their trips to Colfax or Walla Walla where they purchased food, hardware, and clothing.

The colony expanded as they planted an orchard of fruit trees and started a small herd of cattle. The pasture land was thick with wild grasses in the spring and summer and the herd prospered. A watchful eye was ever focused on the livestock as they grazed along the river since large packs of coyotes roamed the hills and cougars were a common sight on the rocky precipices. Phillip Schierman was made quite aware of their presence when one boldly attacked him while he was riding horseback one evening. Luckily, he escaped with only minor cuts and a clawed rifle stock to verify his ordeal.

One of the greatest threats to the cattle proved to be the huge flocks of sheep that grazed along the river. As on several American frontiers, problems arose when these animals grazed in the same area. Indeed, as many as five thousand sheep moved through the valley at a time and clipped the grass almost to the root. The *Palouse Gazette* reported on livestock numbers in 1885:

> General Tannatt as general agent of the Oregon Railway and Navigation Company has collected the following figures, not counting small farmers owning from 10 to 15 head of cattle: Taking Endicott as a center there are within a radius of twelve miles, 75,250 sheep, 3,562

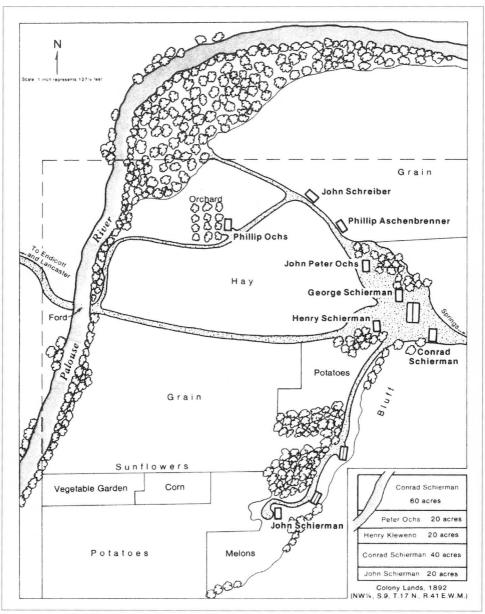

N

Scale 1 inch represents 127½ feet

Grain

Orchard

John Schreiber

Phillip Aschenbrenner

Phillip Ochs

River

To Endicott and Lancaster

John Peter Ochs

Hay

George Schierman

Henry Schierman

Springs

Ford

Conrad Schierman

Palouse

Potatoes

Bluff

Grain

Sunflowers

Vegetable Garden   Corn

Conrad Schierman
60 acres

Peter Ochs   20 acres

Henry Kleweno   20 acres

Potatoes

Melons

John Schierman

Conrad Schierman 40 acres

John Schierman 20 acres

Colony Lands, 1892
(N.W.¼, S.9, T.17 N., R.41 E.W.M.)

Palouse Colony, Washington, 1884.

head of cattle, 5,395 horses, 8,176 acres of land under cultivation and 1,510 acres in improved hay lands.[25]

Many Indians of the Palouse bands often passed the settlement en route to the ranches of Steve Cutler and the McCrosky brothers, several miles upstream, where they traded salmon for fruits and meat. Particularly fond of Mrs. Aschenbrenner's biscuits, they often stopped to barter but often succeeded only in frightening the women. In a minor incident in the 1880s, the J. H. Lairds, a pioneer family of 1872, was compelled to flee their home near the river and seek refuge in the colony when several Indians forced their way in to their house. Laird returned with several members of the colony to his farm a short distance downstream to find the house abandoned but in complete disarray.[26]

The chief task of the Russian German settlers was always farming. The warm weather brought on by spring marked the time to begin plowing, and the first turning of the sod was extremely difficult because of the fibrous root system of the native vegetation. The men used as many as six horses to pull the single shear of the walking plow which constantly had to be cleared of the roots that collected on it. It took days to plow a few acres of ground. Next they sowed the seed by hand from horseback or on foot. Harrowing the field with a crude wooden implement completed the process until the summer harvest.

Adam Kanzler threshing crew near Ritzville, c. 1910. *Courtesy Harland Eastwood*

Improvements in equipment enabled farmers in the Pacific Northwest to increase productivity and manage larger acreages. Mechanical broadcasters and self-rake reapers were introduced to the region about 1884, both of which allowed the operator to cover a significantly larger area in the long work day.[27] Seeding by broadcast and harrowing was not an effective method in the drier areas of the inland Northwest since the seed often laid for weeks in the dry *chernozem* (fertile, black soil) before seasonal rains induced germination. The appearance of the mechanical shoe drill by 1890 and the later disc drill marked important advancements in agricultural mechanization as the seed could then be deposited in uniform rows below the surface nearer to the moisture level.

At harvest time, the colonists gathered the grain stalks in the field, forked them into wagons, and took them to a centralized location. Before the introduction of the reaper, which cut and tied the grain into bundles, farmers used a cradle for cutting. As in Russia, the families gathered to flail the piles of grain, or placed them on the ground and let the work horses trample the golden particles out of the heads. The farmers would then wait for a moderate wind and toss the trampled grain into the air to blow away the chaff.[28]

Early varieties of wheat raised by the pioneers on the Columbia Plateau were two spring strains, Little Club and Pacific Bluestem, followed by the winter varieties, Red Russian and Turkey Red. A crop of forty-five bushels per acre was a typical yield, and often as much as twenty bushels per acre could be gleaned from a crop volunteer.[29] One of the major problems faced by these early farmers was working the steep slopes of the Palouse hills. This was extremely difficult with the primitive equipment but it was soon found that the grain grew just as well on the hilltops and that the hills had the advantage of having less risk of frost than the lowlands.

Settlers continued flocking to the region by the thousands during these years, and population growth led to the new jurisdictional changes. In 1883, Whitman and Spokane Counties were detached from the Big Bend, forming the counties of Adams, Lincoln, Franklin, and Douglas. The town of Sprague was the principal shipping and receiving station for the area and the town maintained its importance until the Northern Pacific Railroad began construction on its trunk line into the fertile upper Big Bend near the end of the decade.

Members of the Nebraska colony, who had wintered in Walla Walla after their arrival in 1882, investigated various options for collective settlement in the area. Some of the Volga Germans of the colony including Dewalds, Schoesslers, Schaefers, Heimbigners, and others, decided to remain in Walla Walla, which was blossoming into a major trade center for the region. They recognized the potential of the community which grew to a population of 3,588 by 1888. A visitor that year reported that the people of Walla Walla were "bright, intelligent and pleasant to meet, but not without the ambitious and progressive natures of other places we had visited. The feeling of self satisfaction, possessing the thought that Walla Walla was the hub of the universe, was like the old feeling of the Bostonian for his beloved Boston."[30]

In the final stage of their quest for land, a large segment of the Nebraska colony was induced to settle near Ritzville, the community Phillip Ritz had developed. In the spring of 1883 the Nebraska colony of Volga Germans left Walla Walla in wagons and traveled on the Colville Road to Ritzville. The party included the families of Henry Amen Sr., Hemrich Bauer, Henry Kanzler Sr., Conrad Kiehn, Henry Miller, Frederick Rosenoff, Jacob Thiel Sr., and Conrad Wolsborn.[31] These immigrants were just a few of the many who were moving into

Ritzville Flouring Mill, 1905. *Courtesy Harland Eastwood*

the region. The April 1882 issue of *The West Shore*, an early regional magazine, noted that the land around Ritzville "is rapidly being settled upon now, though the general opinion until last fall was that it was of little value for agriculture. Mr. Ritz and a few others have practically demonstrated that the idea was erroneous…The roads leading into the Big Bend are dotted with emigrant wagons."[32]

The Volga German families located on half sections about five miles northwest of Ritzville, but the men had to make a three-day journey to Colfax to file their claims. Most immigrants homesteaded while others purchased railroad land or filed timber culture claims on the treeless prairies. The loam was dark and rich in the area, but without lumber they had to live in sod houses or dugouts and use sagebrush and cow dung for fuel. Through efficient methods of tillage and fallowing, the industrious farmers achieved remarkable success. "Good houses, orchards, wind breaks, and windmills already made them a distinctive island in the semi-arid pioneer landscapes of Adams County."[33]

Of those remaining in Walla Walla, a small group led by John C. Oestreich moved in 1884 to the Horse Heaven country near Bickleton, Washington, in Klickitat County. Again traveling by wagons, this party included the families of Jacob Bastrom, George Jacob Dewald, John F. Kembel, Henry F. Michel, and Conrad Schaefer. Most of the men filed on homesteads and many raised livestock. Wild horses ranged in large herds throughout the area, and the settlers often traded them with the neighboring Klickitat Indians. Some of the early Volga Germans settlers who raised livestock and began the first farming in the area were the Schoesslers, Heimbigners, and Ekhardts. Many of these people told their relatives of the Northwest and were joined by them as a result. Some who went to Klickitat County, including the John F. Kembels and Henry Oestreichs, relocated to Ritzville about 1890 as Volga German settlement there was rapidly expanding into the Marcellus district and southeast of Odessa.[34]

Communication between the settlers and their families in the Midwest and Russia facilitated immigration as many forwarded to relatives the necessary funds for travel and were then paid off in labor or cash. Furthermore, with the completion of the Northern Pacific transcontinental line in 1883, the company intensified its advertising campaign to attract immigrants to the area. The guide distributed by the Northern Pacific Railroad, Oregon Railway and Navigation Company, and Oregon and California Railroad contained the following description of a portion of the lower Pend Oreille division along which many Germans from Russia settled:

> Sprague—(148 miles from Heron; population, 1,100.)—This is a place of importance, being the headquarters of the Pend d'Oreille Division of the railroad. Here the railroad company has a large building for its offices, workshops and a roundhouse, and employs several hundreds of workmen in car building, repairing, etc. Sprague is also within easy reach of good agricultural country in all directions, and does a flourishing trade. The place almost rivals Jonah's gourd, that came up in a night. It was a vacant space in the autumn of 1881, but now it is a favorite resort of immigrants, being situated centrally to the fertile regions north of the Snake River and along the railroad...
>
> Ritzville—(117 miles from Heron.)—This is the starting point of what is likely to be a town of importance in the course of time. As yet immigration goes further north, and shuns the dry hills and plains below Sprague. The future will show that much of this soil is fertile, and well worth cultivation.[35]

Recurrent waves of immigrants responded to newly opened regions, and by 1888 the town of Ritzville had sufficiently developed for its residents to seek incorporation. In the same year a post office and store were opened in Lind. In the late 1880s, Walla Walla experienced the continued influx of immigrants from Walter, Walter-Khutor, Frank, and Hussenbach. In time many of them congregated in that section of Walla Walla that became appropriately known as "*die russische Ecke*" (the Russian Corner) or "Little St. Petersburg," extending between Chase and Second Streets from Willard to Chestnut. Another enclave in the city was near the German Congregational Church by Ninth and Birch Streets.[36]

Portland Settlement

Phillip Green's father, George Henry, remained in Portland with his wife and others in 1883 while the rest of the colony journeyed to Endicott. Between 1888 and 1890 Portland witnessed a considerable movement of Volga Germans from the Volga colonies of Balzer and Frank to Portland. This was followed by an even larger influx of those from Norka between 1890 and 1895.[37] Many joined the earlier arrivals living in Albina, which was incorporated into Portland in 1891.

The ward around Northeast 7th Avenue and along Union Avenue from Freemont to Shaver Streets in Portland became a "Little Russia." This area of Portland was filled by the enterprising Volga Germans who began such business establishments as Repp Brothers' Meat and Groceries, Hildermann's Groceries, Hergerts' Meat Market, Geist Shoe and Department Store, Trupp Shoe Repair, and Weimer's Hardware and Furniture. Among the earliest Volga German immigrants to the district were Conrad Schwartz, George and John Betz, Adam, Conrad and Constantine Brill, Frank and Henry Meier, Adam and David Schwind, the Repps, Popps, and Millers.[38] As forests were cleared around the city, some of these people moved south to Canby. In 1892 Catholic Volga Germans from Semenovka and Kohler began settling in Portland while others located in Toppenish, Washington.[39]

• • •

It was not until 1888 that the Northern Pacific Railroad began efforts for the construction of its upper Big Bend branch which was dubbed the "Washington Central." When completed, the line ran westward from Cheney through Davenport, Wilbur, Almira, Hartline, and on to Coulee City. This line facilitated immigration into the area known to be rich and desirable farmland. The average annual rainfall was greater in this higher country and the soil was correspondingly richer. It is understandable, then, that the entire area from Davenport to the Grand Coulee had been settled prior to the construction of the Washington Central branch.[40] The completion of James J. Hill's Great Northern transcontinental railroad into the Big Bend country in 1892 virtually bisected the Northern Pacific's service lines in the area, facilitating new settlement along the Great Northern's Crab Creek route at such newly platted sites as Harrington, Mohler, Odessa, Krupp (Marlin), and Wilson Creek.[41] Odessa's name reflected the great number of Russian Germans who were locating in that vicinity, while other names indicative of Russian immigrant presence in the area included Batum, Schrag, Tiflis, and Moscow (Bluestem).[42] In the drier areas of the western Big Bend, the climate combined with the imperiled national economy of the 1890s to inhibit settlement until the turn of the century. In Grant County, Ephrata was platted in 1901 as was Quincy in the following year.

The Weber family pioneered Volga German settlement near Quincy in 1902. Adam Weber had emigrated from Walter-Khutor, Russia, to

Jacob Wacker farm near Odessa, 1914. *Courtesy Harland Eastwood*

Walla Walla in 1889 where he engaged in farm labor until he obtained land near Ritzville. He was joined there by his brother, Jacob, in 1901 and in the following year by their father, John Adam, and other brothers, Christian and Henry. All but Adam (he joined them later) filed on quarters in the same section of land near Quincy in the spring of 1902 and began irrigating from a single well put in the middle of their property.[43] It was difficult to begin farming the dry, sandy loam and Conrad later remarked that he thought of leaving the area more than once "but we were too poor to get away, though we had plenty to eat and feed for our stock, as well as a roof over our heads."[44]

Jacob Weber did relocate in 1909 to the famous orcharding district of the Wenatchee Valley near Dryden where Bessarabian Germans had settled as early as 1884. Other Russian Germans later settled at Peshastin, Cashmere, and Wenatchee. The number of first generation Russian Germans in Grant County swelled to approximately 377 in 1920 while Chelan County registered 68.[45] In 1916, Conrad Lautenschlager filed a homestead claim on land which had just been opened on the Colville Indian Reservation near the mouth of the Okanogan River. Lautenschlager, a native of Yagodnaya Polyana, Russia, immigrated with his family in 1900 to Wisconsin and eventually to Endicott, Washington. He "broke out" the reservation land for wheat and pasture in 1916 while the family remained in Endicott until the following spring when they joined him and established a Volga German presence in that scenic region of north central Washington near Brewster.[46]

In the late 1890s demand grew in the world market for soft winter wheat. This brought a new prosperity to the Inland Northwest since the region was well adapted to the growing of this crop and was rapidly being settled. These factors, combined with the negative effects of the Ukase of 1892 on the Russian Germans and recurrent crop failures, prompted more to leave their homeland. During this decade an interesting corollary to great northwest Volga German settlement occurred. The movement to Alberta, Canada, began with the arrival in the Palouse Colony in the spring of 1891 of the Peter Poffenroths, the Henry B. and Adam Scheuermans, and Adam Schmick. This group had all departed their native colony of Yagodnaya Polyana in the spring of 1888 and endured together with other "Yagaders" the Atlantic voyage in May on the SS *Hungaria* from Hamburg to New York.[47]

After spending three years in the vicinity of Florence and Newton, Kansas, some of them decided to join friends in Washington. Arriving in Endicott in March 1891, the Poffenroths, Scheuermans, and Adam Schmick boarded in a three-room dwelling in the Palouse Colony until they found farms of their own.[48] Emigrants arriving from Yagodnaya Polyana the following year included several other Poffenroths, all brothers who settled at Moscow, Idaho: Christian, Henry, George, and Peter.[49] The summer of 1892 was particularly hot and dry, severely damaging the crops and Adam Scheuerman, who was renting a farm, resolved to personally investigate settlement possibilities in Canada where it was rumored good land was still open for sale at reasonable terms.

Although the Canadian Pacific Railroad had been completed in 1886, Scheuerman found it cheaper to join four other men, not Volga Germans, in a long trek north led by a prospector en route to the Kootenai goldfields. Scheuerman's son, John, also accompanied the party as they loaded his father's breaking plow into a wagon and set off with seven horses to points northward in what was intended to be a three-week journey. Had they foreseen the struggles ahead, they would probably have chosen an alternate route. The road they took led them north of Spokane into the Rocky Mountains but soon deteriorated into a rocky trail impassable for the wagon. Not to be defeated, they constructed a large raft to hold two of the men and the wagon while the Scheuermans continued on horseback over the rugged terrain. John nearly drowned several times while testing the depths of the swollen rivers with a rope tied to his horse and anchored to shore.

After weeks of arduous travel and near drownings, they finally emerged from the mountain wilderness at Banff, both horses and men facing starvation. They managed to meet the two men with the wagon and continued north to Wetaskiwin, Alberta, arriving six weeks after leaving Endicott. Scheuerman filed for a homestead on unsurveyed land thirty miles southeast of the town near the present site of Bashaw.[50] He went to work on the construction of the railroad between Edmonton and Calgary at fifty cents a day and, not wanting the rest of his family to endure the same trip, procured free passes for them on the railroad. They lived in a cave-like enclosure on the farm the first winter subsisting largely on wild rabbits for meat.[51]

The Henry Scheuermans also arrived in Canada in 1892, homesteading a quarter section southwest of Red Deer Lake next to Adam's property. More adequate buildings were constructed the next year and a large influx of foreign immigration to the area began in 1894; many came from the province of Volhynia in Russia, though later settlers were also from the Volga.[52] The newcomers organized a congregation, St. Peter's Church, in 1897 under the auspices of the newly formed German Evangelical Lutheran Synod of Manitoba and erected a beautiful country church in 1903.

Volga German immigration to Calgary was also hastened in 1894 as the four Poffenroth brothers—Christian, Henry, George, and Peter—together with John Geier and others, moved there after emigrating from Yagodnaya Polyana to Endicott. Land was more readily available in Alberta where, under Canada's 1872 land law, individuals could secure title to 160 acres for a mere ten dollar registration fee and three years' residence. This factor, together with the availability of Canadian Pacific Railroad land, induced many to settle in the Pine Creek district near DeWinton. Plantings were confined to the spring due to the harsh winters and many found employment in the city. In 1902 the Volga Germans organized Emmanuel Lutheran Church in the Riverside area of Calgary which became known as "Little Yagada" (after the mother colony Yagodnaya Polyana) and by 1913 it was estimated that nearly one thousand Germans were living in Calgary, most in the Riverside district.[53] Many came direct from Russia through such Canadian ports of entry in the East as Halifax, Nova Scotia.

• • •

About the turn of the century Volga Germans from Kolb began settling in Tacoma where they found employment in sawmills and factories. Among the first to go there was George Miller who had immigrated earlier to Hastings, Nebraska, where he heard of the opportunities for work in the Pacific Northwest. He journeyed west about 1899 to Tacoma and was soon joined by other Volga Germans from Kolb, many of whom had worked in the Ritzville area until the harvest season was over. Other early emigrants to Tacoma included Peter and John Jacob Koch, Peter Miller, and a Yukert family.

Later Volga German arrivals there were families named Achziger, Adler, Bauer, Meininger, Muench, Rehn, Reiber, Ruth, Thaut, Thorn, and Wilhelm. Although they were predominantly from Kolb, others also came from Frank, Hussenbach, Walter, and Dönhof.[54] This group established a beautiful neighborhood of white houses dotted with their churches, known as "Little Russia," between South 19th and 23rd Streets along Ainsworth, Cushman, and Sheridan Avenues.[55] After the turn of the century a considerable Volga German nucleus formed in Bellingham with most of the men employed in lumber mills. George Schmidt, a native of Frank, was among the first to arrive there from Russia, coming in 1885. However, he later relocated to Walla Walla.

• • •

In eastern Washington the population in the Big Bend country continued to rise during the first decade of the new century; the totals are taken from the 1910 census: Ritzville, 1,859; Lind, 831; Odessa, 885; Sprague, 1,100; Harrington, 661; Davenport, 1,229; Wilbur, 757; Ephrata, 323; Quincy, 264; and Wilson Creek, 405. The influx of Black Sea Germans between 1900 and 1905 was particularly heavy to the districts of Odessa, Ritzville, Krupp, Ruff, Wheeler, Warden, Ralston, Packard, and Lind,[56] and Russian German settlement in the next decade continued to Cashmere, Peshastin, and Dryden in the Wenatchee Valley.[57]

The Palouse country witnessed a similar growth during the same period involving many Volga Germans, although a number of Black

Sea Germans who had immigrated earlier to Parkston, South Dakota, relocated about 1905 in the vicinity between Colfax and Lacrosse near Dusty. In 1910 Colfax, the county seat, contained 2,783 inhabitants, Endicott had 474, and Volga Germans continued to settle between there and St. John to the north which had 421 residents in 1910.[58]

Walla Walla grew to nearly 20,000 inhabitants by 1910 as Volga German immigration to that city continued through the first two decades of the new century and by 1920 approximately 715 first generation Russian Germans lived in the county.[59] Most were still coming from Walter, Walter-Khutor, and Hussenbach, although emigration to Walla Walla from Kautz had begun around the turn of the century. Some of the families from Kautz later joined relatives in Laurel, Montana, where many had found employment following the construction of a large beet sugar refinery at nearby Billings in 1906.[60] Volga German immigration to these and other points in the Pacific Northwest continued unabated until 1914 when war broke out in Europe, and decreased to an insignificant number after the 1917 Bolshevik Revolution, when Russia became embroiled in a Civil War and the victorious Bolshevik later restricted travel over the borders.

In the spring of 1917, the U & I Sugar Company recruited Russian German laborers from the Ritzville and Odessa areas to work in the

Henry Bauer combine near Ritzville, 1919. *Courtesy Harland Eastwood*

beet fields of the Yakima Valley near Toppenish, Wapato, and Union Gap. A number of Volga German families were grateful for the opportunity to find work there including those of William Eichler, George and Henry Wuertenberger, George Wortt, and George Kissler. Most of these families originally came from the villages of Frank and Neu-Dönhof.[61] By 1920 there were about five hundred first generation Russian Germans living in Yakima County.

Russian Germans living in the three Pacific Northwest states by 1920 numbered approximately 21,480, contributing to an impressive national total of over 303,000. About one-third of this number (118,493) had come from the Volga,[62] and in several Washington counties Volga Germans amounted to over 30 percent of the total foreign-born population.[63] Clearly, the Volga Germans had made a major impact in the region during the dynamic era of pioneer settlement, playing an integral role in the development of business and agriculture in the Pacific Northwest.

6

Pioneering Mission Work

Glaube der Väter, heil'ge Glut
Zum Liebesdienst im Kampfe hier
Dich fünden wir dem Freund und Feind
Durch sanftes Wort un Tugendzier.

Faith of our fathers, we will love
Both friend and foe in all our strife:
And preach thee, too, as love knows how,
By kindly words and virtuous life.

—*"Glaube der Väter,"* verse 3, Traditional

The Volga Germans continued to be devout people in America. As their numbers grew in the Midwest, they perpetuated their faith through associations with several denominations, and as immigration streamed to the Pacific Northwest during the 1880s, they established churches there as well. Approximately 85 percent of the Volga Germans who settled in Oregon, Washington, and Idaho were Protestant and the remainder were Catholic.[1] Of the Protestants, the majority continued to be Lutheran although the German Congregational Church also developed into an important denomination among the Volga Germans. Other Russian Germans joined the Methodist, Episcopal, Reformed, and Seventh Day Adventist Churches. It was German Congregationalism, however, that gained the earliest religious prominence among Volga Germans in the Pacific Northwest, as its missionaries were most readily available to the German immigrant population. Furthermore, its doctrinal position was well adapted to alleviate disputes that the German Pietists had known in Russia.[2]

The German Department of the Congregational Churches had its inception in 1846 among German immigrants who had settled on the

Iowa frontier. It was primarily occupied with missionary efforts to the scattered areas of settlement in the Midwest, but with the surge of immigration in the 1850s and 1860s, it soon became a leading force among German Protestants in America. The German Congregational Church held to traditional evangelical church doctrine while encouraging the free use of the German language in religious work. Of equal importance to the Volga German Pietists, it held to the principle of the autonomous local church.[3] Elements of their religious fervor had long been thwarted by the Lutheran consistory in Russia, and it was thought by many that association with the Congregationalists would provide the opportunity for a fuller realization of the Christian faith.

It was Emmanuel Jose, a German Pietist from the Odessa District in Russia, who made the initial contact between the German Russian Pietists and the Congregationalists in America. Immigrating to America in 1874, he was raised in the atmosphere of the brotherhood in Russia and continued to espouse its theology through his preaching in Nebraska and the Dakota Territory. He worked there with others supported by the American Home Missionary Society. Through the efforts of Jose and his associates a number of churches were organized among German immigrants in the Midwest; congregations composed entirely of Volga Germans were formed in 1880 in Sutton and Culbertson, Nebraska. In a report to the American Home Missionary Society in 1881, Rev. H. Hetzler described Jose's mission in Culbertson:

> I found quite a settlement of Russian-Germans...Most of these are homesteaders, on the vast prairies now Culbertson...Isolated, these people live in their sod-houses, scattered all over the prairie. Here they pray and sing praises to the Lord. Brother Jose, who resided in Sutton, served these people about once in three months. They are as sheep, having no fold and no shepherd. Not a church of any kind did I see in that whole region of country.[4]

As more churches were organized and received into the Congregational fellowship, the needs for more effective organization and qualified pastors became apparent. Crete Seminary in Nebraska was opened in 1878, followed four years later by the formation of the German Department of the Chicago Theological Seminary. In 1883 a General Conference was organized known as *Die Allgemeine Evangelische Kirchenversammlung der Deutschen Kongregationalisten*, altered to the General Conference of the German Congregational Churches in 1888.[5]

With the arrival of the Volga German Nebraska colony in Washington in 1882, German Congregationalism was carried to the Far West as well. The Volga Germans who settled near Ritzville in 1883 had encountered a pastor, Reverend F. Frucht. He ministered to their spiritual needs while they wintered in Walla Walla and gathered them into a church in 1882 that is considered the first German Congregational Church in the Pacific Northwest. It was permanently established near Ritzville. This church, however, existed as an independent organization until 1888 when it was officially received into the Congregational Church, adopting the name *Erste Deutsche Kongregational Kirche*.[6]

Through Pastor Frucht's missionary efforts several other congregations were organized in the area among Volga Germans. In 1883 a church was formed in Walla Walla, apparently by those Volga Germans who remained in the city, and in the same year Frucht organized a church in Endicott.[7] Volga German settlement at this latter location had begun in 1882 by members of the Kansas colony who were ministered to for a time by an English Congregationalist, Reverend Thomas W. Walters, resident pastor of Plymouth Church in Colfax.[8] By 1887 the membership of the German Congregational Church in Ritzville

Rosenoff Congregational Church near Ritzville. *Courtesy Harland Eastwood*

had grown to forty-three and in Endicott to twenty-two. However, in the same year Rev. Frucht withdrew from the district without a replacement proficient in German. The lamentable situation was evident in the Association's 1887 Minutes: "Pastor Frucht, who has served them (the Volga Germans) for some time, now leaves them, and they know not where to look for another pastor to lead them in their church work."[9] For them it was an act of providence when a Volga German Pietist entered the field of Northwest Congregationalism the following spring.

A dynamic evangelist who had recently come from Russia, Johannes Koch arrived in Ritzville and accepted a pastoral call extended to him by the Volga Germans gathered there. He soon became acquainted with two prominent leaders of the Congregational Association of Washington Territory, Reverend Thomas W. Walters of Colfax and Reverend George H. Atkinson, who served as General Missionary and Superintendent of Home Missions.

Since the English Congregationalists were not proficient in German but realized that large numbers of Russian Germans were settling in the region, they met with Koch in 1888 at Endicott and ordained him into the ministry of their church.[10]

This meeting marked the inception of German Congregationalism on the West Coast as Koch's churches in both Ritzville and Endicott were accepted into that fellowship at the time. As "Missionary of Pacific Coast," Koch became the leading force behind German Congregationalism in the American West and through his efforts hundreds of Germans from Russia became members of the Congregational Church. He served as pastor to churches in Ritzville (1888–91, 1893–95), Endicott (1888–93), Portland (1895–99), Ralston (1899–1904), and Sanger, California (1909–1912).[11]

Reflective of the revivalistic spirit engendered by Koch and others is this description written by Koch on February 6, 1893, of a series of meetings being held in Portland:

> We have not had a single evening without a meeting since Christmas. Last week our Brethren felt that the evenings would no longer suffice. We therefore had meetings hither and thither, beginning at nine o'clock every morning and closing at nine o'clock at night. People who were considered to be beyond the reach of grace have been carried along by the power of revival. Old perverse sinners, drunkards and hardened men; down to the age of fifteen, have been reached and humbly sought

forgiving grace. Last Sunday we had reception of members. The church was packed full. Forty-eight converts gathered about the altar. All freely confessed Christ as their only Savior, after a very searching address. Then they were strongly exhorted to steadfastness in the Christian life and the Apostolic Confession of Faith was read to them, to which they all responded with a loud "yes". Then while the church sang the hymn:
"To each other we give covenant
The faithful, fraternal hand"
I gave to each the right hand of fellowship. Then all went down on their knees, sometimes a half hour at a time. Every man wanted to thank the Lord that he had sought him and found him and given him his hand of fellowship...Thus the work goes on. God be praised![12]

In 1897 several Swiss and German congregations in the Northwest united with the Congregational Church, and this addition prompted the formation that year of the Pacific Conference. Embracing both Oregon and Washington, the first conference met on March 5 in Portland at the Ebenezer Church with fourteen delegates representing seven churches.

The following thirteen churches were received with their pastors into the newly formed conference: Alkali Flats (near Lacrosse, Washington), Ballard, Beaver Creek, Beaverton, Endicott, New Era (Oregon), Portland, Ritzville First, Ritzville Emmanuel, Ritzville Zion, Seattle, Stafford, and Walla Walla. Later in 1897 Rev. Gottfried Graedel organized a congregation northwest of Ritzville at Packard. In 1899 churches were organized in Quincy (Salem) and Ralston. Rev. J. C. Schwabenland pioneered missionary work in the Odessa area to which large scale German immigration from Russia began about 1900. In that year he organized the congregations of Odessa Pilgrim and Batum Hoffnungsberg. With the aid of Rev. Graedel, new churches were formed in 1902 including Marlin Zion and Odessa Friedensfeld. These two men ministered in this extensive field for many years and churches later established in the area included Odessa Emmaus (1904), Odessa Zoar (1904), Odessa Tabor (1907), and Odessa St. Matthews (1916).[13]

German Congregational membership continued to rise after the turn of the century and by 1910 it reached 1,249 in Oregon and Washington. In 1915 California was detached from the Pacific Conference to form its own division and by 1937 the Pacific Conference had grown to twenty-seven congregations with a total membership of 1,631.[14]

As was the case elsewhere in the nation though, most Volga Germans who settled in the Pacific Northwest remained Lutheran and became associated with several leading synods. Two of the largest German Lutheran bodies in the United States during the nineteenth century were the Joint Synod of Ohio and Other States and the German Evangelical Synod of Missouri, Ohio and Other States.[15] The Joint Synod, formed in 1818, was the second oldest Lutheran synod in America and was composed of both English and German speaking members.[16] (It later merged with the Buffalo and Iowa Synods to form the American Lutheran Church in August 1930). The German Evangelical Synod of Missouri, Ohio and Other States (changed to Lutheran Church–Missouri Synod in 1947) was organized in 1847 and was also instrumental in forming the transition to American Lutheranism of many Russian German Lutherans. The efforts of both synods were directed primarily in the Midwest and East while their interest in expansion to the Pacific Northwest waned until the influx of Germans there in the late nineteenth century attracted their attention.

Both synods entered the field of Northwest missionary activity at the same time, and through the years their work was often typified by intense rivalry. Peculiar circumstances linked both groups with the inception of organized Lutheranism in the Northwest. Associated with the Joint Synod, Reverend Anders Fridrichsen arrived in Portland in 1871 and immediately began to gather Scandinavian Lutherans into a fellowship which resulted in the formation of the first Lutheran Church there that same year. Fridrichsen was of Norwegian background, but he did not limit this missionary work to Scandinavians. Indeed, he actively sought Germans and others as well. His repeated appeals to the synods in the East for more pastors had little effect. Finally, in 1876 Reverend August Kentner responded by resigning his Minnesota Synod pastorate and traveling to Oregon. He organized St. Paul's Lutheran Church in Sherwood under the auspices of the Missouri Synod. In 1878 this synod boasted the establishment of its first church in the Pacific Northwest.[17]

Reverend Edward Doering, who served a Missouri Synod congregation in the Chicago area, accepted a call to Oregon issued at the Western District Convention of 1880. He arrived in Portland in September 1881 where he became increasingly interested in ministering to the Germans of the Portland area. Through his labors, Zion Lutheran Church was founded in the city of Portland. Doering soon became the prime mover in Northwest missionary work for the synod, traveling extensively throughout the region and serving at a multitude of scattered points of German settlement. One of Doering's fellow pioneer pastors described him as:

> a very modest, unassuming man, of simple habits. He was not graced with great oratorical gifts, but rather somewhat hampered in his enunciation by brogue, nevertheless by preaching the Gospel in its simple beauty, to the best of his ability, his efforts crowned with success. As he was of sound bodily health, and an indefatigable worker, he could quite regularly cover his large field.[18]

The Missouri Synod's position was further bolstered in 1882 when Fridrichsen's Portland Church was transferred to Missouri control in accordance with Fridrichsen's will. This situation arose out of the fact that the church building site was apparently owned by the pastor himself who, believing that the Joint Synod would not consider work in this distant field at that time, decided to will the church to the Missouri Synod, which had already placed men in Oregon. This was accomplished shortly after his death in 1882 despite the opposition of some members in the congregation.[19]

The entrance of the Ohio Synod into Northwest religious affairs began in 1881 because of a doctrinal dispute with the Missouri Synod over its adoption of Lutheran theologian C.F.W. Walther's interpretation of predestination. This event caused a division among many clergy in the synod, resulting in the withdrawal of Dr. H. A. Allwardt, D. H. Ernst, C. H. Rohe, J. H. Doermann, and other prominent church officials. These men then became affiliated with the Joint Synod, which in 1882 established the Northwestern District with limits defined as "everything west of Chicago!" Allwardt was elected president; Ernst, vice-president; Doermann, secretary; and J. L. Gruber, treasurer. Through the influence of these men, Luther Seminary was founded in Afton, Minnesota, in 1885 (later moving to St. Paul and then merging with Wartburg Seminary at Dubuque, Iowa). Under the tutelage of Professors H. Ernst and W. Schmidt at Luther Seminary, a number of pioneer Lutheran missionary pastors were supplied to the Pacific Northwest while others came from Capital University in Columbus, Ohio.[20]

By 1887 a synod publication indicated that the "boundless" Northwest District of the Joint Synod had taken on some definition, although this scarcely restricted its immensity. Appearing under "Miscellaneous,"

Lutheran Ohio Synod Regional Conference, Endicott, c. 1920. *Richard Scheuerman collection*

an article that year in the *Lutheran Standard* specified the Northwest District as "reaching from Duluth, Minn., to New Orleans, La., and from Michigan City, Ind., to New Tacoma, Washington Territory."[21] The outpost in Tacoma was the home of Frederick N. Wolf, a man later known to many as the "father of the German and English Lutheran Churches of Washington."[22] Pastor Wolf was called to this fertile mission field through Capital University by Empire German Lutheran families who emigrated from Ohio to Tacoma in the early 1880s. He accepted the call to this area of the Far West, void of any Lutheran clergy, and organized the first Lutheran church there, the Evangelical Trinity Congregation on March 22, 1884. A building was soon erected and dedicated on July 18, 1885.[23] (The second Joint Synod congregation in Tacoma was not organized until 1900 when Peace Lutheran Church was established among Volga Germans from Kolb, Russia, under Pastor George Koehler.)[24] Inasmuch as Pastor Wolf was totally occupied with missionary activity in the Puget Sound area until his semi-retirement six years after his arrival, many enlarged their vision to the Inland Northwest where, as one pioneer Lutheran observer noted, three new towns were being platted every day.[25]

At the Northwest District's sixth annual meeting in the spring of 1887 at Michigan City, Indiana, a traveling missionary was recommended to the General Mission Board to be sent to Spokane Falls in Washington Territory. An interested supporter immediately pledged a year's salary of three hundred dollars to support the position.[26] The missionary, Pastor Karl Anton Horn, responded to what was considered a

Macedonian call issued through Mr. Henry Knostman, who resided several miles north of Spokane Falls. This community in eastern Washington was growing rapidly, and Knostman with other Lutherans had considered forming a church. However, they felt that the need for a pastor was essential. A petition was therefore forwarded to the Ohio Synod and Pastor Horn embarked on his journey in May of 1887.[27] Thus, he opened another field to Lutheranism in the Pacific Northwest.

Pastor Horn was originally from Saxony, Germany, born in 1855 in the village of Oberbobritzsdez near Freiberg. After attending the missionary seminary in Breklum, Schleswig-Holstein, he accepted the call to the United States where he assisted Reverend Henry Rieke in his Wisconsin mission field.[28] Pastor Rieke, also a native of Germany, had arrived in America in 1884. He had been born in Döhren, Hannover, and immigrated following the completion of his formal education at the missionary seminary in Hermannsburg. Rieke was accepted into the Joint Synod and established Cicero, Wisconsin, as the center of his missionary endeavors. He was joined there by Pastor Horn who was ordained in the synod in 1887. These two men later played leading roles in pioneer missionary work among the German-speaking populace of the Northwest.[29]

Upon arriving at Spokane Falls in May 1887 Pastor Horn immediately set out to minister to the needs of German immigrants throughout the region. In the manner of a traditional circuit rider, he preached at numerous towns including Spokane, Fairfield, Genesee, Colfax, Endicott, Walla Walla, Ritzville, and in the Marcellus district of Adams County. Pastor Rieke joined his former associate in the fall of 1887. For two years they ministered together as the only Joint Synod missionaries in the Inland Northwest, performing baptisms at the Palouse River Colony of Volga Germans near Endicott, administering the Sacraments to others who had homesteaded near Ritzville, and organizing new groups in Farmington and elsewhere. Reflective of the work undertaken by these and other early Lutheran missionaries is the following synopsis of "Fifteen Days in the Mission Field" of eastern Washington beginning with Palm Sunday:

> In fifteen days we preached thirteen times, gave catechetical instructions three times, one evening, one-half day, one full day; delivered four addresses; examined and confirmed a class of twelve catechumens; administered the Lord's Supper twice; baptized two children; visited sick four times; made two other calls; and to do this we had to travel 185 miles by team, 100 miles by train, and six to eight miles on foot.[30]

Later a member of the Idaho legislature, Reverend George Finke was also active in the early work of the Joint Synod in the Northwest. He described the joint ministry of the pathfinders Horn and Rieke in the following terms:

> A burning love for the savior filled their hearts, as well as the desire to bring lost souls to the Savior's feet. Pastor Horn, the Saxon, acted up to the royal command and would not pass a person on the road, or a house where people lived, without offering them salvation with Christ or damnation for their sins without Christ. His horse knew his master so well that he would not pass a gate without entering it. There is no doubt that many a person will confess on that day: "I have found my Savior through the instrumentality of Horn."
>
> Pastor Rieke, with his North-German organization talent was more for organizing congregations where the Gospel would find a home and souls could be drawn to the light of Christ. When he heard of any settlement of Lutherans, he went there with his message. No distance was too great, no road too bad (and we had bad roads here in the Northwest), no weather too stormy or cold or rainy, no snow too deep. Pastor Rieke did his duty, as our Lord expects us to do.[31]

Rev. Henry Rieke.
Concordia Center for Volga German Studies, Portland

The year 1887 marked the extension of mission work by the Missouri Synod into eastern Oregon and Washington. Their pastors on the Pacific coast realized the need to form their own synodical district since the vast Western District was headquartered in St. Louis. Accordingly, a new district was organized at the Delegate Synod of 1887 held in Fort Wayne, Indiana, and this Pacific District was further subdivided into Southern and Northern Conferences, the latter comprising Oregon and Washington. Frederick Selle, a candidate with the synod, was called into service as their first resident missionary east of the Cascades in the Northern Conference, establishing his residence in Pendleton, Oregon.[32] Selle ministered to groups throughout the region, visiting Volga Germans in eastern Washington until his work was interrupted by health problems. His health worsened and he died in 1888 on his way East seeking treatment.[33]

Pastor J .H. Theiss reported to the Synod Mission Board following a trip to the Inland Northwest in 1888 about the need for a replacement to continue the work. Later in the year, Candidate J. Ehlen was dispatched there although reasons of health also compelled him to suspend missionary activities within two years.[34] In the spring of 1890 Ehlen stopped in Tacoma en route to California for recuperation but encountered a number of Lutherans there who were without a pastor. They prevailed upon him to preach several sermons and through him Zion Lutheran Church was founded there in June 1890.[35] Rev. H. Haserodt became their first resident pastor later in the year as Ehlen continued on his trip to California where he died in Fresno shortly after his arrival. Again the Missouri Synod's work in eastern Washington was interrupted at a time when additional men from the Joint Synod were entering service in the region.

With more and more of their time spent ministering to the widely dispersed groups in the area, Pastors Horn and Rieke of the Joint Synod welcomed the arrival to Spokane in August 1889 of Rev. Paul F. Hein.[36] Pastor Rieke had resided in Spokane since 1888 but then moved to Genesee, Idaho. Pastor Horn had journeyed to The Dalles, Oregon, and thus divided the vast field of eastern Washington between himself and Rieke.[37] Reverend Hein also conducted missionary trips in the area while establishing his base in Spokane which underwent its catastrophic fire the very month he arrived. He immediately set out in what one observer called the "city of tents" to gather a few Germans together

and preach to them in a small house. Though it was a humble beginning, fraught with financial difficulty (typical of most early Northwest
missionary activity), a congregation was soon organized with the first
installation of officers on September 1, 1889. The construction of a
building was completed the following year and Emmanuel Church was
dedicated on Easter Day, 1890.

Reverend Hein resigned his duties at Emmanuel in March 1893 to
devote his full energies to work among the English-speaking populace
of the community. These labors reached fruition with the formation of
the First English Evangelical Lutheran Church in Spokane on March
1, 1893.[38] About the time the financial panic of 1893–94 struck the
Pacific Northwest, and in the decade the region took to fully recover,
the district's pastors endeavored to enlarge their parishes. They did this
despite the fact that their salaries were lowered, some receiving as little
as fifteen dollars per month.[39]

During the late 1880s the need for additional men to work among
the Germans in the Puget Sound area was growing and was answered
by 1890. At this time pastors entering service with the synod in Puget
Sound included C. Lembke at Lake Bay, A. Krause in Tacoma's "New
Addition," and L. H. Schuh who replaced Reverend Wolf at Trinity in
Tacoma. Significantly, the contrast between the great potential of the
entire Northwest District for the church and the acute lack of clergy
did not fail to gain attention at the 1889 Diaspora Conference in Germany. The Reverend Dr. Borchard, who had visited the work in the
Pacific Northwest, reported in an address to that body that:

> It is beyond all doubt, that the states along the Pacific Coast are of
> the greatest importance for the future of the United States and of the
> German Evangelical (Lutheran) Church. I therefore commend to
> your activity the mission work of the German Evangelical Church and
> school on the Pacific Ocean, especially the fruitful Washington Territo-
> ry, West Oregon and California.[40]

Echoing Horace Greeley's adage, "Go West, young man," Pastor
Schuh in Tacoma wrote, "Young preacher, go West" in a May 1890 field
report to the synod filled with hope and detailing the present needs of
the district.[41] The response by several missionaries who journeyed West
about this time is significant in that it contributed to the organization
of an effective Joint Synod pastoral network among the Germans in the

Northwest. This occurred at a time when many in the synod were advocating a policy of retrenchment and consolidation in the more firmly established districts of the Midwest and East.[42] Reverend Schuh's article announced the recent arrival of Pastor C. Pitzler, who would soon be assigned to Fairfield, Washington, and told of plans to place a man in Walla Walla.[43] It was Pastor C. F. Vollmer who responded to the call there in 1890 at Emmanuel Church, but was compelled to resign the following year due to tuberculosis and returned to the Midwest. The work in Walla Walla was carried on by Pastor A. F. Gillman from 1892 to 1895 who was in turn succeeded by Pastor A. Eberle from 1895 to 1899.[44]

The Schuh article also reported on the continuing activities of Pastor C. Lembke at Lake Bay and Reverend A. Krause, who was ministering to a mission of forty communicants in Tacoma. Within a year Pastors C. Haase and J. Willers arrived to serve congregations in Leber and Tacoma respectively. While citing Spokane, The Dalles, and Tacoma as the centers of the three principal fields of missionary activity, the area of roughly 3,000 square mile served by Pastor Rieke in southeastern Washington and northern Idaho did not escape Schuh's attention as he mentioned the district's intentions to place two additional men in openings there. Certainly the arduous tasks involved in serving such a field never escaped Reverend Rieke's thoughts but financial considerations had precluded the assignment of additional support there. Nevertheless, writing from Colfax on May 5, 1890, Pastor Rieke issued a call to Paul Groschupf who, like Rieke, had emigrated from Germany to the United States after studying at the mission institute in Hermannsburg:

> Mr. Paul Groschupf of Afton, Minnesota as my assistant pastor in my congregation at Genesee and in my mission territory. I expect of you, dear Brother, that in assisting me in the discharge of our difficult but also precious vocation, you will faithfully stand at my side, so that, in every way, the honor of our God and our salvation and the souls entrusted to us, may be promoted…God give you grace to accept this call and follow it real soon![45]

In an accompanying letter Pastor Rieke promised Groschupf free lodging in his home, a horse, an annual salary of $250, and offered other arrangements if he chose to reside elsewhere.[46] The call was readily accepted; Groschupf moved to Cameron, Idaho, and was ordained to begin a prominent career as a missionary in Idaho and Washington.

Later, he began his lengthy tenure as president of the district. One historian wrote the following graphic account of Groschupf's work:

> All the missionary's work had to be done on horseback for two reasons: the roads were very poor and the missionary's pocketbook was too slender for a buggy. (His horse was named Flora.) Groschupf was a wild rider. Instead of opening gates, he with Flora jumped over them. He rode her through deep overflowing creeks, crossed the Clearwater River with her on a ferry, went down steep mountains and climbed them. The deep canyons were full of rattlesnakes. In order to escape their deadly bites, the rider had to lay his feet on the horse's neck and his back on the gown and books, which were tied in the saddle.[47]

Groschupf was called to Emmanuel Church in Spokane in 1895 and served faithfully there until his death in 1924.

It soon became clear to the Joint Synod that activities in the vast Northwest District were becoming too complicated to be dealt with as a single home mission field. For this reason the district was divided in 1890 into the Minnesota, Wisconsin, Kansas-Nebraska, Texas, and Pacific Districts.[48] This latter district convened for the first time April 23–29, 1891, at Pastor Schuh's Trinity Lutheran Church in Tacoma.[49]

One of the first orders of business was to legitimize the district's official name which, while it presumably would be called the Pacific District, was named the Washington District largely due to the difficulty for the German tongue in pronouncing the former term. Basing his text on I Corinthians 15:28, the newly formed district's senior pastor, Rev. F. N. Wolf, sounded the theme of the assembly in his address with the words: "The Lord hath done great things for us; whereof we are glad."

A large portion of the conference was dedicated to the delivery and discussion of the report by Pastor P. F. Hein entitled "*Das Missionwerk im fernen Nordwesten.*" It detailed the current status of the work and outlined methods for future endeavors among Russian Germans and other immigrant groups in the region. The report also dealt with the three-fold problem that would reoccur throughout the pioneer period: the need for more self-sacrificing men, the lack of financial support, and the dangerous proselyting of the fraternal lodges and sects.[50] The entire district was composed of thirty-two congregations and mission points numbering 780 souls. The district was divided into an Eastern (Spokane) and Western (Tacoma) Conference with the 120th Longitude being the dividing line, roughly corresponding to the crest of the Cascade Mountains.

Pastor A. Horn was assigned the chairmanship of the Spokane Conference which met for the first time in Cameron, Idaho, November 17–19 in 1891. The train only went as far as Kendrick, Idaho, at that time and the pastors were compelled to ride on horseback over a snowy mountain to Cameron, nearly getting lost in the process. Nevertheless they succeeded in assembling for the conference where they elected the resident pastor, P. Groschupf, secretary, and P. F. Hein the conference president.[51]

The second annual conference meeting was held in Spokane October 25–27, 1892. Following the election of officers, the assembly adopted a resolution requesting the Home Mission Board to "send three men, respectively to La Grande and Palouse City...and if possibly the third one to the 'Big Bend County,' Washington. Thus the field is enlarging and the great missionary work advancing."[52]

The 1890s were also marked by slowly expanding missionary efforts in the Pacific Northwest by the Missouri Synod. At the beginning of the decade, seven synod pastors functioned in the region, most west of the Cascades, and in December 1890 Trinity Lutheran Church in Albina, Oregon, was organized by Pastor J. H. Theiss in an area inhabited by many Volga Germans.[53] With the addition of only one man in 1891, Pastor C. J. Heuer, missionary efforts by the synod were renewed east of the Cascades as Heuer located that year in Pendleton to serve the area. Moreover, his efforts took him to Endicott, Washington, where he organized the Zion Evangelical Lutheran Church in 1891 among German and Volga German immigrants who had settled between Endicott and St. John.

Candidate F. Schoknecht replaced Heuer the following year with the latter relocating to Sherwood, Oregon, while Schoknecht shifted the center of his mission work northward to Endicott. His goal was to serve the Volga German immigrants and others who were moving to eastern Washington.[54] The Endicott congregation continued to grow and Schoknecht opened a parochial school there while establishing additional preaching points in the area until he moved to Minnesota in May 1893.[55] Pastor F. Verwiebe began work in Spokane in 1893, but his responsibilities there prevented normal service to the Zion congregation and others in rural areas. As a result, many families in these areas transferred their memberships to established Joint Synod churches in eastern Washington and northern Idaho which numbered eleven by 1893.

Noting the change in Ohio's strategy, it soon became clear to Missouri Synod pastors in the Northern (Pacific) Conference that if effective organization and growth was to be achieved, a separate synodical district was needed solely for the Pacific Northwest. Such a proposal was submitted and adopted in April 1899 at the St. Louis Delegate Convention. This led to the formation in August of the same year of the Oregon and Washington District. The district met that month for the first time with six lay delegates, nine pastors, and one teacher assembling at Zion in Portland. They elected as President Reverend H.A.C. Paul of St. Peter's Lutheran Church in Blooming, Oregon, who in his sermon for the occasion challenged the district to "be ever conscious of its tremendous mission duties, and try to do justice to the obligations which this vast territory of these three states—Oregon, Washington and Idaho—places upon it."[56]

Mission work soon expanded to northern Idaho as Candidate William Koss began ministering in 1900 to groups in the Camas Prairie at Grangeville, Denver, and Lowie.[57] By the time the 1901 district convention met, five new men had been added and services were being conducted on a regular basis in Odessa, Menno, and Yakima.[58] St. John's Lutheran Church had been founded in Spokane in 1900 after years of labor there by Pastor Verwiebe and the work among Volga Germans of Endicott was revived the same year as Pastor Heuer accepted a call there, replaced in 1902 by Pastor Schmelzer, who was then followed by Pastor H.A.C. Paul (1902–1906).[59]

Pastor Edward Doering continued to be one of the prime motivators of mission work for the Missouri Synod throughout his forty-year career in the Pacific Northwest. A meticulous chronicler, the following selection from a 1902 journal and letter indicates the extent of their work among the Russian Germans and others in the Big Bend country as well as the rivalry with the Joint Synod:

> February 8—Saturday. Trip to Odessa, city of the Russians. Here almost everything is German. Our people live twelve miles south of here; they have founded a congregation; six members have joined, three have announced their intention of joining, still others want to come from the East. As soon as the Ohioans heard that a school was to be built, they began to hold their services nearby in a school house. Ohio is always right on the spot, they have their "pioneers" stationed everywhere. The Mission Board is certainly not familiar with the importance of this

field. Therefore I shall describe it a bit. The so-called "Big Bend" is a district unequaled. The prairie extends about 150 miles long, 150 miles wide, and is covered partly with bunchgrass, partly with sage brush. Since people have discovered that the soil is exceptionally good for the raising of wheat the farmers are moving here from cold Minnesota and Dakota; yes, they are coming by the hundreds to establish homes here. Therefore, it is absolutely necessary that help be given to the congregation at Odessa to obtain a pastor who can gather and serve our people.[60]

Russian German settlement expanded westward along the recently completed route of the Great Northern Railroad and Doering decided to inspect this area as well. It is clear that the Missouri Synod had not been aware of the dynamic changes taking place there since the construction of the Crab Creek line in 1892. Doering was astonished to see how rapidly the small communities were progressing.

> February 10—Monday. I rode westward to Wilson Creek. As I arrived there, I found half the town under water. The creek had overflowed; I rode out into the country on a boat, for which the brave boatman demanded his "nickel." I was told that a year ago only one hut stood here, now over fifty houses have been built, three hotels, stores, a bank, even a newspaper office, two schools, and the like. The roads are practically impassable, the snow is beginning to become soft, the "coulees" (ravines) are running full of snow water. On Tuesday I found an opportunity to ride in the direction of a German settlement. I rode along, but still had to walk two miles and then found the Germans. They moved here last fall from Minnesota, but are Evangelical and are being served every two weeks...
>
> Since there is now a vacancy at Endicott and the confirmation instruction which had already been begun should be concluded, I shall go there and finish it.
>
> Most respectfully,
> Your humble servant of the Word,
> (signed) Ed Doering[61]

Congregations of both Lutheran synods generally increased in size through the first decade of the twentieth century although problems resulting from lack of pastors continued to plague them and put tremendous strain on those who functioned in the Pacific Northwest. In the Washington District of the Joint Synod alone some forty pastors withdrew to other areas between 1891 and 1914.[62] The Joint Synod, however, was the largest of the six main Lutheran bodies in the Pacific

Northwest by 1916, with its Washington District composed of sixty congregations, twenty-three missions[63] and had an adult membership in the state of 4,461.[64] At the same time membership in the Synodical Conference in Washington, of which the Missouri Synod held the vast majority in 1916, numbered 2,740.[65]

It has been said that the pioneer period of Lutheranism in the Pacific Northwest drew to a close with the outbreak of the World War I, which suspended European immigration to the region.[66] The Bolshevik Revolution in 1917 further curtailed emigration from Russia of Volga Germans and ushered in a period of tragedy for those who remained. Conditions there would have worsened considerably had it not been for Northwest Russian Germans who undertook a massive famine relief campaign through their churches. It was a remarkable demonstration of the cooperative spirit which continued among Volga German groups throughout the United States and Canada.

In 1920 and 1921 catastrophic droughts struck southwestern Russia where the people refused to harvest their crops in protest of requisitions by the Communist authorities. The 1921 harvest was only 37 percent of normal for the region and led to the great Russian famine of 1921–23.[67] News of the disaster soon reached Volga Germans living in the Pacific Northwest who united with others nationally in what Herbert Hoover, chairman of the American Relief Administration, termed "efficiency and devotion" to deliver hundreds of thousands from starvation.[68]

Between 1914 and 1921 the population in the German colonies on the Volga dramatically fell from 600,000 to 359,000.[69] This was due to many factors including the Russian Civil War, starvation, executions, and some resettlement. Letters streamed to Volga Germans in the Northwest from their families in Russia begging for help. The following letter from the Peter Morasch family in Yagodnaya Polyana, Russia, sent during the 1920s to relatives in Endicott, Washington, was typical of the confused state of affairs.

> I will let you know that we are without parents. Where they are is unknown to us. Mother all this time was in Yakutsk (Siberia). But where they are now is known only to God…It (their assumed arrest) was a very bitter pain for us the children…
>
> Will you not take mercy on us because we are lost and without money? It is dear uncles, everything so high priced that rye flour costs 70 rubles per pood [36 pounds] and the potatoes, a sack is 40 rubles, so

we cannot buy them. Will you not take pity on us because if not we will not be long on this earth. We have to put everything in the hands of God, what God does that is well done.[70]

Such correspondence evoked great sympathy and willingness to help on the part of Russian Germans in North America and when the Volga Relief Society was formed an effective network was established to channel funds to the areas of greatest need. News of the disastrous famine received widespread coverage in the Western press during the summer of 1921. At that time Mr. and Mrs. George Repp of Portland had been considering methods to aid the suffering Volga populace. Like hundreds of Volga Germans in Portland, the Repps were natives of the Volga colony of Norka. Discussing the various alternatives with John W. Miller, Mrs. Repp's brother, it was decided to organize a relief society and before a meeting was formally arranged, Miller cabled the following letter to American Relief Administration (ARA) on August 8, 1921:

> There are approximately fifteen hundred people in Portland that came from German colonies located in Russia near city of Saratov along Volga River. These people are anxious to help get food into that stricken district of Russia. They have received letters from relatives appealing for help. Will you be good enough to wire us how to proceed…There will be a mass meeting Thursday evening among our people and a regular relief committee organized for German speaking colonies in Russia… Have hopes extending work of this committee to other places where our people are located in California, Washington, Idaho, Montana, Colorado, Dakotas, Nebraska, Iowa, and Kansas. We figure that there are in the United States approximately a hundred thousand people interested in these German speaking colonies along the Volga River and that good work can be done with proper help from reliable source like yourselves. Would it be possible for us to send an American citizen of our people be endorsed by you or even sent by you as one of your workers so that he would have proper protection.
> John W. Miller[71]

The following day Miller received a telegram from Edgar Rickhard of the ARA expressing their willingness to channel contributions for relief work, although it would be confined to feeding children. Funds could not be designated for assistance in any particular locality in Russia until later. Encouraged by this response, the Repps and Miller held a public meeting attended by about one hundred people at Zion Congregational Church in Portland on August 11, 1921 and organized the Volga Relief Society.[72]

On August 18 a second meeting was held as interest spread and $6,075 was taken in pledges for relief to twenty different Volga German colonies. Plans were discussed to form a national organization, and this was effectuated through the sending of a circular letter to German Congregational churches throughout the United States and Canada. Other denominations soon became involved in the program, principally Lutheran and Evangelical churches that had large Volga German memberships. The organizational meetings of the society in Portland particularly benefited from the advice of Congregational Pastors H. Hagelganz II, George Zocher, and John H. Hopp, Reverend Peter Yost of the Brethren Church, and an Evangelical Church minister, Reverend Jacob Hergert.[73]

On August 21 permission was given to the society to send a delegate to Russia who would work with the ARA staff in their distribution program. George Repp was selected to go on what would become a great humanitarian venture. At the same meeting a strategy was planned to actively involve other Volga German communities. Reverend Zocher was sent to California and Reverend Hagelganz was assigned to Nebraska, Colorado, and Montana. A separate group was being formed in the Midwest, organized in Lincoln during September as the Central States Volga Relief Society which cooperated with the Portland group, and a third organization was established later in Denver, the Rocky Mountain States Volga Relief Society.

In September Pastor Hopp began traveling throughout eastern Washington in order to organize several branch societies of the Portland group. He met an enthusiastic response in Odessa where the work was spearheaded by Rev. J. H. Eckhardt. Both Volga and Black Sea Germans joined efforts through the next year in contributing the remarkable sum of $4,184.84, a total exceeded only by the cities of Portland, Fresno, and Denver. Additional meetings were held by Rev. Hopp in Ritzville, where the work was directed by Rev. Jacob Morach and William Thiel and in Dryden where Pastor John Reister of the Congregational Church was assisting in fundraising.

Branch societies were also organized in Endicott under the guidance of Rev. C. J. Wagner and in Walla Walla under the leadership of Pastor Paul Krumbein. Within three weeks of their receipt of Miller's original circular letter, $3,236.81 was received from these two groups. Additional support was given through the National Lutheran Council and the American Red Cross.[74] Local Ladies Aid auxiliaries in Lutheran churches in the Northwest and other denominations in the region initiated a massive campaign in the fall to send clothing to Volga German families in need. In October the Soviet authorities agreed to a program of Food Drafts suggested by Mr. Miller and others through which aid could be designated to specific families.

George Repp's arrival in the Volga German villages was heralded by great excitement, and he became referred to as the "father of our children" by the people. Despite the inevitable transportation delays caused by the Russian winter, the aid society nevertheless succeeded in regularly feeding 40,000 children by February 1922.[75] The pastor in Messer, Rev. Edward Eichhorn, reported on the situation in his village on New Year's Day:

> The 1200 children who are now being fed in the American kitchens send their utmost sincere thanks for the food which they receive. Their parents, however, look into the year 1922 with fearful hearts, and can only pray that their lives will be spared. In the past year 800 people in Messer died of starvation and an additional 400 left for other sections where they hoped to find bread. Messer now contains 3,600 inhabitants as compared with its former population of 5,000. Our people live on mere scraps of food; their clothing has been sold, and they lift their arms in despair to an unmerciful heaven.

Eichhorn's letter also noted how inflation had caused soaring food prices in Russia.

> Prices are exorbitantly high; one pound of black bread costs 14,000 rubles; one pound of meat, 13,000 rubles; one pound of fresh butter 50,000 rubles; one cow, 3,000,000 rubles; one pair of oxen, 28,000,000 rubles, etc. These figures may give you some idea of our present struggles for existence.[76]

Food Drafts remained the only way through which adults could receive food and this system, introduced in October 1921, was not always reliable at first. Some were drawn out in January in Norka by several inhabitants who responded with thanksgiving in the following note:

> Although conditions in Norka get worse every day, we were greatly encouraged last Thursday when ten sleighs of provisions were brought to our village. Each of us received nine poods from our relatives in

America. Many families who were on the verge of despair, have now been given new hope of being able to survive until the next harvest. We wish to thank everyone who helped in sending this food to us, and pray that God's richest blessings will reward them for what they have done.[77]

During 1921 and 1922, the Volga Relief Societies contributed approximately $550,000 worth of food, clothing, and other materials. Combined with the services rendered by the National Lutheran Council and through various charitable organizations for relief work to the Volga Germans, the total figure amounted to over one million dollars.[78] An equal sum was used in ARA relief work to aid Germans living in the Black Sea region, Volynia, and elsewhere in Russia.[79] Praising the role of the Portland society, an official in the ARA New York office wrote: "You may rest assured that not only have no other communities of Germans equalled the efforts of the Volga Relief Society due practically entirely to the activities of your Portland organization, but no other organization outside, of course, of the various members of the European Relief Council, of any race or religion has equalled yours."[80]

With good crops assured for the 1922 harvest in July, George Repp departed Russia for America. The following November the Portland, Lincoln, and Denver societies united to form the American Volga Relief Society, which continued for several years, rendering service when needed until the Soviet government prevented further assistance. The society also served of great value to Volga Germans in the Pacific Northwest and throughout the nation as it facilitated communication and fellowship while perpetuating elements of their distinct culture.

Epilogue

The late nineteenth century was characterized by the greatest westward migration of people in the history of the United States. Many individuals who had been affected by the Civil War were eager to move into the great expanse of the Trans-Mississippi West at the conclusion of the conflict. Others who moved onto the "Great American Desert" came from abroad, from the many countries of the Old World. Some of these new immigrants were influenced by factors pushing them from their European homelands while others were lured by conditions in America, the land of promise. Millions of immigrants flooded to the United States, and they greatly influenced the course of American history. This was true of the many groups and successive waves of immigrants who traveled to this country to begin life anew. This certainly was the case for the Volga Germans.

Much of what had occurred in their past prepared the Volga Germans for their migration to and settlement in the United States. Their earlier move from Germany to Russia had prepared them well for their immigration to the American West. The Volga Germans had experienced the trauma of leaving their homeland, their families, and their identity with Germany. Despite the rigors of the move to the Volga region, they maintained as much as possible their cultural identity as Germans. This contributed to the cohesiveness of the people, but it did not endear them to the Russians, who were suspicious if not envious of the Germans. The Volga Germans had established colonies in Russia, and this pattern of settlement was used to good purpose by the people when they made the journey to America.

Four major factors resulted in the migration of the Volga Germans to the United States. While some traveled to the United States to seek adventure and be a part of the exaggerated glamor of the Western American experience, these individuals were very few in number. The majority of Volga Germans moved to the United States for more practical reasons. Most immediate was the fear of being drafted into the Russian army, a fate so dreaded they were willing to flee their homes and families to seek sanctuary in the United States. Economics was another reason for migration. It was difficult, often impossible, for the Germans

129

in the Volga region to purchase more land. As the years passed, the lands owned by the Germans had been divided time and again among the men. After successive generations, the parcels were too small to make a good living. There was little hope that this trend would change in the later part of the nineteenth century. In fact, conditions for those Germans who remained in Russia would become worse, much worse.

Discrimination against the Germans in Russia grew in the nineteenth century, and contributed significantly to the migration of the people from Europe to the United States. There were two forms of discrimination, one that affected all of the Germans in the Volga region and one that affected a large portion of those who left Russia for religious reasons. The form of discrimination that influenced all Russian Germans originated from a force external to the German colonies. It emerged from the native Russians and their government. The official Russian policy in dealing with the Germans evolved from paternal care to passive neglect and finally to one of aggressive Russification. In the mid-nineteenth century the Russian government decided to force their German colonists to acculturate and assimilate into Russian society. This change in governmental policy was most pronounced in the demand that the Germans educate their children in the Russian style which, of course, required the use of the Russian language, not German.

In addition to discrimination from the government, there were conditions within the German colonies that resulted in the discrimination of a portion of their own group. The internal conflict was religious in nature and emerged within the Lutheran Church. The Brotherhood, a Lutheran splinter group, was formed as a result of doctrinal disagreements. Many of the first Volga Germans who moved to the Midwest were members of the Brotherhood and, in response to the discrimination they faced from the dominant church, they formed a separate denomination once they arrived in the United States—German Congregationalism.

Another factor contributing to the migration of the Volga Germans, indeed many Europeans, were the huge and effective advertising campaigns that were launched to attract settlers to the United States. Steamship and railroad companies worked diligently to encourage large-scale European migration. The immigrants were extremely important to the transportation businesses of the United States. The Europeans purchased fares for the ocean crossing, tickets for their journey by rail once they had arrived, and necessities of life while they were in transit. Moreover, the immigrants purchased land owned by the railroad companies.

The transportation companies realized that once the immigrants had settled, they would use their systems as a means to transport their products to foreign and domestic outlets. The railroads had much to gain in the short and long term, so they established bureaus of immigration and land departments. They bombarded Europe with advertisements, all of which made the American West appear to be as attractive as Heaven itself. The Volga Germans and other Europeans conjured up an image of the West from viewing the many picturesque posters and reading the mass of colorful prose printed in the promotional brochures produced by the transportation companies. By the time the Germans began their journey to America, they were convinced that the American West was a Garden of Eden, a virtual "land of milk and honey."

While the Volga Germans shared many experiences with other immigrants of the era, they were unique in some ways. For one, many moved to America and onto the Great Plains as colonial groups. Most immigrants, whether they were Irish, Italian, Polish, etc., traveled to the United States as individuals, not as colonies. The Volga Germans differed greatly then in this respect. Not only did they travel as a unified body, a colony, but they came to America with a plan of how they would immigrate, settle, and make a living. The Volga Germans were of rural origin, not urban, and therefore they planned even before departing to settle on farms in the Trans-Mississippi West. This was important not only to their immediate well-being, but to their image as recent immigrants to America, and set them apart from immigrant groups who became associated with the urban problems of the United States. The Volga Germans never planned to remain in the industrial cities of the East and thus were spared the nativist fervor directed at many recent arrivals. In addition, they did not suffer religious persecution known to Catholics and Jews who remained in the cities.

The international phenomenon of immigration to the United States brought the Volga Germans to the shores of their chosen country. Once they arrived, they began their journey overland by railroad to farmlands on the Great Plains. As colonies they moved to Kansas and Nebraska, which years before their arrival had been part of the large Indian Territory. There were Indians residing in Kansas and Nebraska after the

Civil War, but the Volga Germans had little contact with them. The newcomers spent the bulk of their time trying to eke out a living on the prairies of American's heartland. There were many problems for the new settlers to overcome, yet most of them remained in spite of the prolonged droughts, harsh winters, and destructive grasshoppers. A few returned to Russia. Other Volga German groups decided to pick up their roots once again and move west because of the promise of new opportunity in that region. Their experiences, lessons they learned when things did not turn out the way they had expected, helped them immensely when they resettled in the Pacific Northwest.

Like so many other immigrants, the Volga Germans were lured to new lands farther west as a result of advertising. They moved to the Pacific Northwest, in large measure, because of the efforts of the Northern Pacific Railroad and its subsidiary organizations. The Northern Pacific Railroad encouraged immigration to the Northwest by paying the fares of members of immigrant groups undertaking exploratory expeditions to the region. This technique worked very well for the transportation companies, and once the representatives of the Volga Germans saw the Columbia Plain, they were convinced that they could in fact transform the region into a "land of milk and honey." With favorable reports of the area in hand, the Volga Germans began their move to the isolated regions of the "New Northwest," migrating overland by wagon roads and steel rails. They would make their homes in this unique region of the United States, and they would offer much to the overall economic development of the Pacific Northwest.

The settlement of Volga Germans on the great Columbia Plain was more than a story of one "farmer's frontier." The Volga Germans were part of a much larger settlement pattern in the United States and the American West. They peopled an area that had once been the sole domain of Indians who had hunted and gathered on the lands that were to be cultivated by those who had only recently arrived in the "New World." By the time the Volga Germans had arrived in the Northwest, the government had forced the first Americans onto reservations and had liquidated their title to the vast hills and prairies. The Indians had lived in harmony with the land, and they had not, for the most part, farmed. For hundreds of years the land had remained virtually untouched by the hands of man. The Volga Germans, however, and other white immigrants in the region, had come to till the soil, to work the land, and to produce a livelihood from farming.

• • •

Volga German settlement of the Pacific Northwest significantly changed the region. The face of the land itself changed dramatically as the farmers turned the soil, planted their crops, and harvested their produce. Economics therefore changed in a land that had once been dominated by the Indian trade, fishing, and livestock grazing. The presence of Volga Germans in the Northwest changed the social fabric of the region. They and other immigrants created a patchwork of newcomers in the Northwest. Although the Volga Germans were quick to understand the social structure and cultural elements of the larger society, they held steadfastly to some of their customs, teachings, and general techniques of their past lifeway. Some of them held onto the cultural heritage of their Volga German ancestors, a heritage that was centuries old and had emerged through both the German and Russian experiences. This was particularly apparent in their religion. Some of the doctrine had changed, but the role of the church in society had not. Religion and the church were the center of life in the Volga German community. Political, social, and cultural matters were discussed and handled in and through the church. Thus, the church was an institution within Volga German society that remained significant once the immigrants had moved to the United States.

Nowhere is the lasting importance of the Volga Germans seen better than in the realm of economics. Farming in the region has been a

Lautenschlager, Poffenroth, Scheuerman threshing outfit near Endicott, 1911. *Richard Scheuerman collection*

continuous crucial economic factor in the Pacific Northwest, indeed the world. Volga Germans contributed much to the growth and development of agriculture in a region that otherwise would have suffered more severely from soil depletion. They introduced new methods of soil fertilization and crop rotation. They turned the dry prairies of the Columbia Basin into productive fields by irrigating their crops, and thus helped drive the economic development of the Northwest.

The Volga Germans were part of a national movement to fill up the land and make it productive. In so doing, they played an important role in the nation's destiny. Along with the business communities of the East, the farmers of the West were the engine behind the emergence of United States as a world power in the early twentieth century. The Volga Germans were a part of dramatic expansion, and their significance to American history and the American West, too long unappreciated, was indeed great.

PART II

Volga German Stories from the Pacific Northwest

Collected and retold by Richard D. Scheuerman
Illustrated by Jim Gerlitz

The Empress nodded to Fidgen in a gesture of familiarity.

Introduction

Clifford E. Trafzer

Stories exist in all cultures and provide us truths about people and communities, even when the stories are presented as fiction. They tell us of cultural values, beliefs, successes, and failures. They tell us of joy and sorrow. Stories tell us who we are at certain times in our history, and how we have changed—or not—over time. Stories can contain deep meaning and purpose, guiding us in our understanding of peoples of the past. They give us ways of knowing and sharing knowledge crucial to our understanding of people and places, past and present.

In former times, people shared most personal accounts in the oral tradition, passing down stories so that younger generations could know about their ancestors. The stories are like traveling to far-off foreign countries. They do things differently there, just as our ancestors did things differently, often out of necessity. Over time, people wrote down their stories so that future generations would have the old tales and never forget what went before. The stories offered by Richard Scheuerman are presented here for the first time in written form. He learned these stories through the oral tradition of his people, Germans from the Volga region of Russia. In an age of mass communications, cell phones, email, twitter, and texting, stories shared in the oral tradition might seem passé and backward. Written stories take far more time to develop than a five-line tweet. And they make far more sense as they contain content, development, thought, and feeling. Readers might consider taking their time reading the following short stories, and to contemplate and consider each story and its larger meaning. The stories may have multiple meanings for the storytellers, authors, and readers. They are participatory with those presenting and those receiving—who, hopefully, will pass them along to others.

Many storytellers from the past—relatives and non-relatives—took time to share their knowledge of the old days with Scheuerman. All of the stories presented here are historical and hold truths about Volga German immigrants to eastern Washington. These hardy people

138 Hardship to Homeland

migrated to make new and better lives for themselves, their people, and their children. This is an ancient refrain shared by many cultures.

During the nineteenth century, German immigrants moved into the Volga and Black Sea regions of Russia to make new lives for themselves and their families, and prospered through hard work and perseverance. Within Scheuerman's family, a story has survived many generations that tied his family to Tsarina Catherine the Great. Some might say that the story of "Fidgen and the Orange Tree" is mere myth, but consider this: family elders have always believed the story to be true and have treated the tale as fact. Thus, the story is a truth for the family and community. The coin given to Fidgen in the story remains in the family as an heirloom, a treasure. Like the coin, the family story remains a treasure, but one they wish to share with others. In this way, the stories are a gift of history and culture of one immigrant group.

While still living in Russia not far from the great Volga River, families spent most of the winter months hunkered down against the elements. In his story, "The Gift," Scheuerman describes a dramatic winter encounter, and an unusual gift that saved the lives of Anna Marie, Martin, and Fedda (uncle) Honna. The gift, a blue enamel teapot, remains in the family to this day. It is a symbol of another place, another time. The teapot is a mnemonic device that reminds members of the family and the Volga German communities of the United States of the threat the wolves posed to travelers in Russia.

In "The Homeland Garden" Scheuerman provides a moving account of a Russian German family making their way from the Volga River region to Washington Territory in the 1880s. After years of toil farming the Volga hills, discrimination provided a push factor that encouraged many Volga German families to relocate to the American West. The opportunity to buy parcels of land, own their own farms, and till the soil in America appealed to families who saw immigration as a way of making a new start in a new land.

Through these engaging stories, Scheuerman captures the excitement and joys, the anxieties and fears, of pioneer immigrants settling the American West. "Aurora's Ghosts" invites readers into the new settlements of Russian German people of eastern Washington. Working communally at Palouse Colony, the new immigrants witnessed the spectacular Northern Lights, which some worried were a sign of impending doom. But their religious faith and leadership sustained them and lessened their fears about surviving in the new country. The elders passed along their faith and belief to younger generations, which nurtured the families and helped to make them strong. These hardy settlers built their first homes into the vast Palouse Hills, and with time and equipment they cut lumber to build new homes, barns, churches, and schools. They respected the Indian families living nearby, including the extended family of legendary Chief Kamiakin.

The Palouse Country is known for its changing weather and the potential for violent storms. Immigrant families had long known the importance of weather, but they learned by experience about the changing weather of eastern Washington. During the winter months, wind, snow, ice, and blizzards blanketed the hilly plateau above as well as the inland valleys along the river systems. Palouse Colony children attended school on the plateau above the canyon, traveling up and down the steep canyon walls every day to attend school. With keen perception and moving prose, Scheuerman tells of a dangerous blizzard and the Old World power of an elder that saved the school children from a tragic fate.

Stories found in this volume offer more than tall tales. Scheuerman provides colorful accounts of the early settlement of one community of European immigrants in the American West. Similar colonies of immigrants banded together to settle lands throughout the West. Before their arrival, Native Americans had been the sole inhabitants of the lands settlers claimed, purchased, and farmed. The Russian German settlers maintained friendly relationships with the Snake River-Palouse Indians who lived in the region and with whom they traded. Immigrant farmers focused on developing their own farms, communities, and collectively helping each other succeed and survive.

As a descendent of some of the first immigrants to the Palouse Colony, Richard Scheuerman uses stories to retell accounts he heard growing up near Endicott and walking the trails of the Palouse River Valley. The elders shared their gifts of knowledge through stories, which Scheuerman has never forgotten and has chosen to share with us here through his gift of storytelling.

A southering flock of great gray and black birds.

Fidgen and the Orange Tree

By the first of October brisk east winds blowing across the Baltic Sea can chill to the bone. Twelve-year-old Sophie Keller and her older brother, Andreas, had endured cramped quarters for nearly three weeks with their parents and four dozen other families in the lowest hold of the creaky, three-masted *Dipperman*. The vessel had been sailing north-easterly since early September 1766 from the German port of Lue-beck for Oranienbaum near the Russian capital of St. Petersburg. The Kellers and others had begun a great trek eastward from their native Hesse where peasant families had labored through generations for area landowners in the hilly Vogelsberg area near Frankfurt am Main.

Sophie could still recall the moment earlier that summer when her kindly father assembled the family around a table in their tiny home to tell them of the move. "The Kaisarina Katharina of Russia has invited poor families like ours to her empire to receive rich farmland along the river Volga. It's all for the taking and our travel costs will all be covered by the crown," Phillip Keller explained. He then leaned toward Andreas and said, "And no army service either to fight these endless wars for the nobility. We will be safe there."

"But Russia," her mother, Anna, whispered apprehensively, "it sounds like the end of the earth."

Sophie realized the importance of the announcement, and in spite of her mother's misgivings she had rarely seen her father so excited. But his tone had also turned somber that evening. "We must make preparations soon," Papa told them in the mellow candlelight, for the last transports would sail in September. The tearful good-byes to her grandparents, the careful packing of their meager possessions, and the wagon ride to Luebeck all seemed a dream now. The foul smells from the hold and brown-green oozings along the sloped walls near her bunk bed made Sophie wonder if the journey would be worth all the discom-fort. Maybe Russia was at the end of the earth.

"Papa," she pleaded, "may I join Anna and the others going on deck for some fresh air?"

"Stay by the door, Fidgen, and don't linger," her father replied. "They will be serving supper soon."

Sophie pulled her gray woolen shawl from a muslin sack on her bed in the gloomy surroundings and wrapped its soft folds around her brown hair. She put on her coat and carefully ascended the narrow wooden stairs toward the soft afternoon sunlight. Sophie soon emerged on deck and fully breathed in the fresh salt air. She leaned against the shingles of an elevated vent and squinted to see wooded tongues of land appearing to the southeast through the deepening grayness. Great stands of birch and linden lined the shore in clumps of green and yellow. Overhead a southering flock of great gray and black birds bellowed as they flew against the ship's direction. *Dipperman*'s three enormous canvas sails filled fully with the brisk breeze and cut a wake in the dark waters.

"I count fourteen!" said Veronica as she looked up toward the birds. "How many ducks can you see, Anna?"

"Yes, maybe that many," answered another girl Sophie's age standing nearby. "I can't imagine how they stay in the air hardly moving their wings."

The sound of the birds, the feel of the waves, and changing colors of distant bluffs lanced by sunbeams were altogether marvelous to Sophie. She closed her eyes to breathe in the memory.

"You probably couldn't see the birds if your eyes were open," interrupted Veronica loudly.

"Well, I know the difference between a goose and a duck," Sophie answered.

"Too bad you can't tell a number from a letter," Veronica replied as she led the rest of the girls back below deck.

Sophie enjoyed stories from the few books she had read at the village church school attended by the children during the winter months back home. She had memorized the catechism and Bible verses assigned by Pastor Schneider but had been slower to answer his questions than some others. Sophie was sometimes teased about being a daydreamer, but her faraway look was usually a vain attempt to see in the distance what seemed clear to most everyone else.

A few moments later she joined her family downstairs where they gathered with others on benches around several short tables for a meal of thin cabbage soup with crusts of brown rye bread. She used her wooden spoon to rescue the last gristly morsel and carefully reached down to place it on the floor next to the yellow-orange cat that had become her best friend on the voyage. At the same moment, one of the deck hands entered the cramped room. The unshaven fellow, perpetually dressed in a red woolen stocking hat and brown long-coat, had taught the children a few Russian expressions. He called for everyone to listen.

"Captain Rohn says that we will be arriving late tomorrow morning at the Russian port of Kronstadt for transfer to Oranienbaum," he announced in a peculiar brogue of German flavored with a Finnish accent. "You must be ready down here with all your gear packed by morning's second bell," he continued, "but don't bring your things up top before you're told to do so." He feigned a salute to a toddler standing on a nearby bench, turned to leave, and then swung around to add, "And heads of households, be sure your documents are available for inspection. You're about to become subjects of the Russian Empire."

The thought of swearing allegiance to another sovereign was somehow unsettling to Sophie's father. For decades Kellers had tilled the fields of Vogelsberg landlords. They had paid taxes from their meager earnings and served in the army when ordered to do so by local princes. Would he simply be exchanging the bonds of servitude in a small principality for that of an empress who ruled the largest domain on earth? Perhaps all the promises had been a ruse to raise a new vanguard of soldier-serfs to battle frontier conditions and wild tribes half a world away. Venturing into the unknown for the sake of a stable future might be worth personal risk. But what fate awaited his wife and two children? Phillip fretted at not knowing the answer.

A few feet away Sophie struggled to sleep next to her mother as the boat gently rocked and groaned. She heard purring beneath her and reached down. "I wish you could come with me," she whispered as she petted the cat's head, "but I don't suppose you have the proper documents." Sophie had heard so many stories of life in Russia from the other children and her parents that she wasn't sure what to expect. Andreas heard that the country's only season was winter, but their mother said the wheat and rye they were to raise only grew in places with warm summers. Veronica said their new neighbors would be fearsome Persians and Chinese who spoke languages no civilized person could ever understand.

Sophie had asked her father about the "Tsarina Katherina" he and others often mentioned.

"She is one of us, Fidgen," he once explained as Sophie listened earnestly. "A poor princess from Pommerania who speaks our tongue;

somehow married to Tsar Peter the Great's grandson, who recently died leaving her to rule the land."

Thoughts of winter and Persians and tsarinas danced through Sophie's mind the whole night through, but she awoke to the gray gloom of morning and found the cat sleeping comfortably next to her. Her parents were visiting quietly on the side of the bed and she greeted them with a yawned "good morning." Moments later she joined them and Andreas at a table for a breakfast of hot tea and barley loaf.

Soon a bell sounded and the Keller family slowly climbed on deck where they huddled with others against a cold wind that spit snow against their faces. Heaped clouds as plump as galleons blew across the fortress island of Kronstadt toward the mainland in the distance. Farther to the east they spied the golden spires of the Cathedral of Saints Peter and Paul in the harbor of St. Petersburg, the city Sophie knew had been named for the apostle who walked with Christ.

Kronstadt's harbor seethed with activity as *Dipperman* pulled alongside a mammoth wooden dock where stevedores lashed ropes from the ship to enormous iron capstans along the pier. Crewmen soon guided the expectant families down a gangplank and along a wide walkway onshore toward an immense stone building where they assembled in lines before clerks who stood behind high wooden lecterns. Heads of households were asked in German to name all accompanying persons and these were compared to passengers listed on *Dipperman's* manifest.

As Sophie waited in line with Andreas behind their parents, she wondered if there would be some kind of examination that might prevent them from entering the country. Perhaps the Kaisarina's officials would find them unfit for life in Russia. Sophie couldn't imagine returning to Luebeck in the ship's dank hold. Finally, she heard her father say, "Sophie, my daughter, age twelve," a phrase repeated by the bearded clerk who scribbled names in ink before them.

Shortly afterward the Kellers and other colonist families were led to a dock on the southwestern side of the small island where several substantial rowboats ferried them across the choppy waters of the gulf to the nearby city of Oranienbaum. Veronica sat shivering with her parents and four brothers and sisters in the same boat. Sophie could see that she seemed distressed from either sickness or their bewildering morning, and Sophie smiled at her. Veronica raised her eyebrows and managed a reassuring grin in return.

"Finally, we'll be able to walk on land," Sophie said.

"And finally," replied her mother, "maybe we'll be able to take a bath."

• • •

The families were met at the Oranienbaum docks by a burly Russian commander with bushy sideburns and red cheeks. He stood near a dappled gray stallion and spoke brief words of welcome in broken German with a deep, granular voice informing the immigrants that they would be taken to lodgings nearby. He directed the families onto horse-drawn wagons driven by soldiers and with a hearty laugh occasionally shouted *"Bistro, bistro!* (quickly!)" which Sophie and the others took as encouragement to quickly load.

The early afternoon sky began to brighten and as the column got underway Sophie felt the warmth of the sun on her face for the first time in many days. They passed through a loosely tumbled terrain on the outskirts of town and noticed the imposing onion-shaped domes of an immense cathedral in the distance. White and black birch trees lined both sides of the rutted road and the cool breeze blew leaves from their darkened strings like swarms of orange and yellow butterflies. They passed along a street of ramshackle buildings where shopkeepers stared blankly at the foreign passers-by. After a brief foray of bumpy transit, the Russian commander turned his horse next to three long barracks and called for the wagons to stop.

"Here is your first Russian home!" he shouted to the colonists, and ordered the soldiers to assist in directing the people inside.

Sophie and her family were in the last wagon and entered the lodgings closest to them. The white-washed wooden building was divided along a corridor into a dozen small rooms that each held two bunkbeds. A large kitchen was located at the entry and Sophie was delighted at the aroma of roasted meat with potatoes, carrots, onions, and black bread. A gray-haired woman clad in a loose white blouse and long black dress labored over an enormous kettle on a wood stove and smiled to greet her guests. She struggled to say something but the sounds were incomprehensible to Sophie and the others.

A boy's voice appeared from nowhere and translated into familiar German, "She says 'I hope you like potatoes; we have them for every meal here!'"

Their nods and laughter needed no interpretation. The boy stepped farther into the kitchen from a closet where wood was stored and placed a pile of kindling into a metal box behind the stove. He then walked toward the door and passed by Sophie.

"*Spaseba*," she thanked him in the best Russian she could summon from her brief shipboard lessons.

"*Pazaulsta*," the boy replied, and hurried out the door.

In the days that followed, Sophie learned from her father that even though the fall weather had turned pleasant, officials who oversaw settlement of the colonists advised against traveling to the lower Volga until spring. The families would remain in Oranienbaum for the winter, apply their trades to local needs, and learn something of the language and culture of their new homeland. Although some complained of these arrangements, Sophie thought their surrounding a wonderful place. Her father and Andreas soon found work in the stables nearby caring for the soldiers' horses. Veronica had learned a new version of hide-and-seek called Cossacks that she taught to the other children, though Sophie was not usually invited to play.

Each morning the boy who had first welcomed them delivered a load of wood for the kitchen where Sophie helped the women by cleaning and peeling vegetables. She understood their Russian cook to say that the boy's name was Daniel. He seemed to be about Andreas's age.

"So can you teach me some Russian?" she asked Daniel as she followed him outside after his delivery the next day.

"I am not a teacher," he said shyly.

"But you know both German and Russian," Sophie continued. "How is it that someone your age is so smart?"

"It's not intelligence, but experience," Daniel explained. "My father came to Russia from Holstein, and met my mother who is Russian. I grew up hearing both languages. But you've probably had more school than me and know numbers and things."

"What little schooling I've had hasn't taught me what you know," said Sophie. "So is your father a farmer like us?"

"In a way, yes," explained Daniel who began to talk more freely as he split kindling behind the barracks with a bruised iron hatchet. "He is a gardener for the tsarina's new estate yonder, the *Kitáyskiy Dvorets*— The Chinese Palace. It's on the top of that hill." Daniel motioned to a southeastern forested slope with a piece of wood he had been holding.

"You mean your father works for the Kaisarina Katarina?!" Sophie asked in wonder.

"First off, we call her the tsarina; sounds like 'kaisarina' and means the same thing, but she is a Russian empress now, not German. But no," he chuckled, "my father does not work for Her Majesty. He helps one of the gardeners tend the greenhouse. I don't think either of them has ever seen the empress or so much as a princess. They live in their palaces in St. Petersburg most of the time, and when the tsarina does come to Oranienbaum to Peterhof or some other place, nobody the likes of us could ever get close enough to see her. And be glad it's so, or it might be 'off to Siberia' for you to be never heard from again."

Sophie couldn't tell if Daniel was serious or joking. The conversation, however, raised a thousand other questions.

"But you said," she continued, "that your father works at her 'Kitai, Kitai…,'" Sophie struggled with the strange sound she had heard Daniel effortlessly pronounce.

"*Kitáyskiy Dvorets.* They've been working on it for several years now; who knows how long until it's done. Not anytime soon even though it's small as palaces go. Mother says ten women worked every day for three years sewing glass beads for tapestries to line the walls of just one room. My mother knew one of the sewers who said the beads were so tiny each one could sew just a couple hundred a day."

Sophie quickly considered the numbers in her head. It was not a difficult problem: so many sewers, so much work, so many days. "In that case," she reported moments later, "the room has about two million beads."

"There is no such a number!" Daniel shouted.

"Oh yes," Sophie said flatly, "two million is just twice one million. Of course I can't imagine that many colored beads hanging inside a room."

"Well they're not colored," Daniel added restoring some dignity. "They're supposed to all be clear to shimmer under the White Nights."

"I think you're making fun of me," scolded Sophie.

"And I think you're making fun of me with such numbers," answered Daniel. "We are so far north that the summer nights stay bright and in winter we have snow and the Northern Lights that shimmer in the sky with greens and reds. The beaded panels are being installed this winter and I suppose the salon will be a wonder at nighttime."

"Do your parents tell you about all these things, Daniel?" asked Sophie.

"Sometimes I hear them talk about what is happening hereabouts, but I can also see for myself," Daniel replied. "I help my father water the oranges and limes up there twice a week."

"Oranges in snowy Russia?" exclaimed Sophie.

"Don't you know where we are?" asked Daniel incredulously.

"Yes, this is Oranienbaum," answered Sophie, who then paused to repeat the name slowly. "Oranien-Baum. Does it mean what I think it does?"

"Yes, '*Oranien*' is old German for 'orange', and you know *Baum* means "tree". My father told me that oranges have been grown here in greenhouses for the royals since the days of Peter the Great. That's how this place got its name."

"So have you ever had one?" Sophie asked mischievously.

Daniel looked around and whispered as if divulging a secret. "It's forbidden for any of us to take the fruit. But sometimes if it is blemished or won't properly ripen at Christmastime, father is permitted to give one to us."

"Ah yes," Sophie recalled wistfully, "I've seen bowls of dried oranges and nuts in shop windows at *Weinachten* back home."

"Well, this fruit is fresh," Daniel said proudly, "and grows here even when it's cold outside. Of course when winter comes we line them up inside the entry hall of the palace so they don't freeze. Father says we'll need to be doing that soon."

"So may I help you for something to do while my family waits here, and you could teach me some Russian words?" asked Sophie.

"Perhaps," Daniel considered with a smile, "if you could help me learn numbers."

• • •

For several days each week that fall, Daniel and Sophie met in the late afternoon to study numbers and the Cyrillic alphabet. If the weather permitted they sat on the barracks steps, and when the days drew colder they studied at one of the tables in the kitchen.

"At least our numbers are the same in both languages," Sophie said one day in frustration. "But these letters don't make any sense at all. The 'P' is an 'R', and the 'C' is an 'S'. I still can't spell my own name without looking!"

Daniel's father and mother, Andrei and Anna, occasionally came by
to visit the Kellers and in late October the parents agreed that Sophie
could help with Daniel's greenhouse chores. On her first trip up the
twisting footpath to the Chinese Palace, Sophie turned to marvel at
the scene around them. To the north they could see whitecaps on the
Gulf of Finland and the stone fortress on Kronstadt where she had first
landed. Daniel pointed east to the grand city of St. Petersburg where
silhouettes of palaces and cathedrals glittered in the distance.

Finally they emerged from the trees onto a broad grassy plain where
a small army of workers noisily toiled amidst an array of magnificent
plantings and fountain sculptures surrounding a tiny lake. A group of
masons and brawny youths used a wooden derrick to unload a massive
red granite slab from a wagon onto a framed walkway. Others carried
tools and wooden beams around the beautiful fairyland palace of pink
stucco walls with curving white cornices that rose in the distance amidst
sweeping tissues of fog.

The voice of Daniel's
father called out to them as
she admired the spectacle.
"Fidgen," Andrei said while
approaching, "welcome to
Kitáyskiy Dvorets!"

"I might as well be in
China!" she replied, "It's like
another world up here."

"In that case I shall tell
Monsieur Rinaldi that he has
succeeded," Andrei laughed.
"The architect wishes us to
fashion what he calls 'an
enchanted place of escape' for
the burdens of Her Majesty.
But there's plenty of burdens
in this world for you two," he
continued. "Harvest is long
since passed and we are about
to prune the cherry and apple

Sophie's first glimpse of the Chinese Palace.

trees. You can start today by picking up all the windfall apples and leave them by the wagons. Then be sure the trees in the greenhouse get watered, Daniel."

Sophie and Daniel set about gathering the decomposing fruit into baskets. The smell was at once corrupt and exotic. They set the baskets near a wagon that Daniel said would carry the fruit down to the village where some might be salvaged for baking. The rotten ones would be taken to the soldiers' quarters where Andreas and the stable boys could feed them to the animals.

They then walked across the broad lawn to a long greenhouse situated in an open southern exposure near the tree line on the far side of the estate. Daniel opened a wooden door and they stepped inside where Sophie immediately felt the warm air and saw two rows of potted dark green plants along the length of the glass enclosure.

"It feels nice in here after being outside," Sophie said, "but after a while it must be stifling."

"We open windows when it gets too warm," Daniel explained, and as he walked along the greenery a black and red butterfly fluttered past Sophie's face. She jumped back and giggled. Daniel turned and watched two more alight from a nearby branch.

"They love bright colors so maybe they're attracted to your rosy cheeks," Daniel said. "Here, Fidgen, look at this." Daniel pushed away a branch to reveal an enormous orange.

"It's beautiful," marveled Sophie. "I've only seen small dried ones. I never knew they grew so big."

"Well, they taste better than they look," Daniel said with a wry smile. "But of course I'm not supposed to know that."

Over the next two weeks Sophie visited the grounds of the Kitáyskiy Dvorets with Daniel several times to water the orange and lime trees and make preparations to move them into the heated corridor of the palace. As they were gathering dead leaves from the pots one chilly afternoon, Andrei entered the greenhouse and asked for Daniel to join him.

"Monsieur Rinaldi is expected sometime soon and the masons want to finish setting two stone caps along the walkway," Andrei said. "They're short-handed and could use some help to steady the horses."

"Just finish watering the pots, Fidgen," Daniel called as he left with his father. "We'll try to send somebody with another bucket."

Sophie continued her chores until she noticed a cocoon suspended near a ripening lime that seemed to move. She watched mesmerized as the glistening creature struggling to break free, and did not notice someone enter the greenhouse until the woman moved her hand toward one of the orange trees.

"Oh, thanks, but I don't think we'll need any more water," Sophie said. "Besides, we'll be moving these in the morning and it's probably better not to add much more weight." The woman drew back a garnet velvet bonnet but said nothing. Sophie realized she had spoken in German to someone who probably only spoke Russian. It was time she put her lessons into practice.

"*Ah, nee nuzhen pomosch* (Ah, I do not need help)." Still nothing. "*Mnye zovoot Fidgen, ee ya* (My name is Fidgen, and I…)."

"'Fidgen' you say?" interrupted the gardener in perfect High German, and as she turned Sophie noticed the woman wore a long grey robe trimmed in thin black fur. "I haven't heard that name in years," she said wistfully and gazed through the window somewhere far beyond

the waning sunlight. She touched a ripened orange and said, "What do you do here, child?"

"I help my friend tend Tsarina Catherine's fruit trees," Sophie explained, "while my family waits to travel to the Volga next spring."

"So you are one of the *kolonisty*," she said more than asked. "Have you tried the fruit?"

"No," Sophie replied earnestly, "and anyway we can only take the spoiled ones. I've have no idea what an orange tastes like. Papa says some people have oranges and nuts at Christmas because they represent the light of God's Son and new life."

Sophie meets a stranger in a long grey robe.

"And Russians believe," said the woman, "that long ago St. Nicholas the Wonderworker secretly gave gold to a father who otherwise would have lost his three daughters. He is the patron saint of children, and oranges represent St. Nicholas's special gift. So be sure to take one of these nice ones with you when you leave."

With that, the woman turned and walked out the door where she was greeted by two rambunctious greyhounds. Sophie finished watering a pot and then walked toward the door but saw a ripe orange at the base of the tree where the woman had been standing. She picked it up and touched it to her nose to smell the sweet fragrance. How delightful to give it to Andreas for Christmas, or to her mother to make marmalade, or to peel and eat it now! After the fashionable woman's kind offer, she decided it was worth the risk of dreaded Siberian exile and put it in her pocket to share with the others.

• • •

The next day was Sunday and Sophie joined her family and those of Veronica, Anna, and others at Oranienbaum's beautiful blue and white Lutheran Church where they had faithfully gathered each week with other colonist families since arriving in Russia. Her parents enjoyed hearing the liturgy and hymns sung in their native tongue and on this day Daniel's family also joined them at worship. Although they usually attended the Orthodox Church, Sophie and Daniel had agreed their religious beliefs were more alike than different. Daniel sat next to Sophie and in the middle of the pastor's sermon, he reached into his side coat pocket and pulled out a ripe orange. "It fell from the tree and now it's yours," he whispered. "You can have it for dessert this afternoon."

On this day the service would be followed by the oath of allegiance to the Russian crown that was often administered in a brief ceremony by the black-robed Lutheran cleric. He rose at the end of the service to lead the congregation in singing a postlude to the pipe organ's stirring music. As they stood to sing, a smartly dressed Russian officer walked down a side aisle and briefly spoke to the pastor who smiled broadly. When the music ended, he raised his hand to make an announcement.

"My dear friends," the pastor said in a loud voice, "as is sometimes the case on such special occasions here in our church, we are to be favored by the appearance of a most special guest, Her Imperial Highness the Tsarina Catherine, who has been in residence nearby at Peter-hof these past several days."

As the congregation gasped the main doors swung open, eight uniformed officers took up positions down the aisle and stood at attention. Sophie strained to see what was happening through the rows of people until Phillip lifted her up onto the wooden pew next to the aisle. She peered through the open doors to see handsomely attired horses and an ornate gold coach outside flanked by a crowd of soldiers, several exquisitely attired women, and gathering townspeople.

Then, rising from the stairway into the church at the head of the procession was the elegantly dressed Tsarina Catherine the Great, whom Sophie instantly recognized as her greenhouse helper! She wore a gleaming sable cloak and hood that hung over her shoulders and a jeweled dress of ruby silk with gold lace that rustled as she stepped forward. Her full hair was gathered into a long braid that swirled tightly around her head to form an auburn crown in which was placed the iridescent feather of a Chinese pheasant.

Four soldiers in brown leather vests followed to close the church doors and remained there in a row. As if on cue, the commander nodded to the pastor who then led the colonists in an oath of allegiance to their new homeland and to "Catherine the Second, Empress of all Russia, Tsarina of the Volga and Siberia, Lady of the Entire North Region, and Sovereign of Many Others." Sophie couldn't imagine one person having so many grand titles. The Empress then took several steps forward and Sophie saw her sparkling diamond broach and matching earrings set with fiery topaz gems.

"I bid you welcome to Russia," she said firmly in German, and offered brief words of appreciation for the "noble work" pledged by the new arrivals to prosper their lives and her empire. The empress's tone was reassuring to the families who remained standing in awed silence. As the tsarina turned to leave, she saw Sophie standing at the edge of the pew holding the orange. She nodded in a gesture of familiarity noticed by many, and Sophie coyly raised her fingers from the fruit and smiled. The tsarina then walked back to descend the church steps. She paused momentarily to speak to the commander before entering the imperial carriage which departed with a clattering detachment of mounted grenadiers.

The tall officer reentered the church and walked up to Sophie who had just stepped into the aisle with her orange to be surrounded by all the children. He leaned over and asked in Russian, "Are you Fidgen?"

"Yes, I am," Sophie answered warily in the same language.

He reached into his pocket and said, "Then Her Majesty wishes you to have this newly minted *pyatak* bearing her initials as a memory of your friendship, and for your service to the imperial household."

With that he placed an enormous copper coin into Sophie's other hand, stood to nod respectfully toward her parents, and departed.

"Come!" shouted Daniel gleefully. "Let's see if an orange weighs as much as five kopeks."

"I think I know which one tastes better," joked Andreas.

"Indeed, princess," said Phillip with a festive smile as he put his hand on Fidgen's shoulder. "And I think you have some explaining to do."

⌐ Afterword ⌐

Our families have many memories of community elders telling about Catherine the Great and her famous 1763 Manifesto of the Empress inviting European settlers to colonize the fertile lands along the lower Volga River. Some 27,000 people responded, mostly peasants of German background. Grandpa related the story as if "*die Kaisarina Katarina*" had personal contact with the colonists, and in later years I learned that she was known to occasionally greet the newcomers in their native tongue soon after their arrival at Oranienbaum. The Russian city near St. Petersburg had been named for the oranges mentioned in this story, where Catherine maintained a summer residence.

Catherine the Great (1729–96) was born Princess Sophie Augusta Fredericka of the small German principality Anhalt-Zerbst in Stettin, Pommerania. Her nickname "Fidgen" comes from *Sophiechen*, a diminutive of Sophie. She was engaged to the Russian Grand Duke Peter III, grandson of Peter the Great, in 1744 and given the name Ekaterina Alekseyevna (Romanov). She assumed the throne upon Peter's death in 1762 and ruled for thirty-four years. One of her first official acts was the organization of the Guardianship Chancery for the settlement of foreign colonists in Russia.

Although Catherine usually resided in the Winter Palace and adjacent Hermitage in St. Petersburg, several royal residences were located

Catherine the Great's Chinese Palace at Oranienbaum. *John Clement*

in the vicinity of Oranienbaum. These included Peter the Great's spectacular Peterhof, the Grand (Menshikov) Palace, and Catherine's splendid personal retreat, *Kitáyskiy Dvorets*—the Chinese Palace, constructed from 1762 to 1768. This stunning structure is Italian designer Antonio Rinaldi's preeminent original example of Russian Rococo architecture and is the only imperial residence of the style that escaped damage during World War II. Many of the state rooms are adorned in nineteenth-century chinoiserie, Chinese décor featuring hand painted silk wallpaper, porcelain pictures, and exquisite inlaid wall panels and parquet floors of ivory and such exotic woods as amaranth, palisander, lime, and maple.

Catherine conceived of the Chinese Palace as an extraordinary artistic place where the "Eastern Dream" of balance between art and reason could be experienced. One of the building's masterpieces is the allegorical painting *The Union of Europe and Asia* by the artist-brothers Guiseppi and Serafino Barozzi that graces the ceiling of the Great Chinese Cabinet. The palace's famed Glass Beaded Salon still displays the twelve tapestries made of Lomonosov milky glass beads, correctly calculated by Sophie to number some two million, sewn in patterns of exotic birds and plants that shimmer in blues and mauves beneath the Baltic's White Nights. Catherine delighted in her periodic

Fidgen receives a token from the Tsarina.

visits to Oranienbaum away from the court intrigues and bustle of St. Petersburg, and stayed at her summer dacha some fifty times.

I visited the Chinese Palace in 1993 with the eldest living relative of my grandfather's family, his 86-year-old niece, Eva Litzenberger Baldaree, who said that the names Sophie and Catherine had been passed down for several generations in our family. When Eva passed away in 2009 at the age of 104, her nephews examined the contents of a small strongbox brought by her German grandparents from Russia's Volga region to America in 1876. Inside were yellowed family documents, faded photographs mounted on cardboard, a packet of flower seeds, and a five kopeck copper coin minted in 1765 bearing the initials "IE II" for "Impress Ekaterina II"—Catherine the Great.

The Gift

"And when they were come into the house, they saw the young child with Mary his mother, and fell down, and worshipped him: and when they had opened their treasures, they presented unto him gifts; gold, and frankincense, and myrrh."—Gospel According to Matthew

Anna Marie almost knew the story by heart. Each year in the December Advent season, her father, the village schoolteacher Martin Fischer, gathered the family before bedtime near the rounded earth oven in the center of their home and read from Luther's Book of Sermons. Twelve-year-old Anna Marie and her younger brother, Phillip, listened attentively as their father recounted the story of Mary and Joseph, guiding star and stable, and Nazareth and Bethlehem. The children's mother, Katya, rocked quietly nearby where lately she had been putting the finish touches on a thickly knitted brown woolen shawl.

"Herod and Judea were not much farther away from our Volgaland," Father informed the children, "as, say, the tsar and St. Petersburg."

"Then might we see the bright star?" eagerly asked Phillip.

"No, no," replied Father with a kindly smile, "the heavens above are bright with starlight these cold nights, but there's nothing like the one God provided to lead the Wise Men."

Anna Marie and Phillip listened attentively.

"And Jesus isn't in Bethlehem anymore," Anna Marie informed Phillip and then turned back to her father, "but can I go feed Rudy and the colt with you tonight and see outside anyway? The windows are too frosted to see the stars."

"Yes, you can be a shepherd tending our stable scene, Anna," Father replied before Katya could protest, "but you'll need to bundle up after we finish the story."

Martin then continued reading. "Though the Wise Men saw but a tumbled-down shack and a poor young mother with a little babe, not like a king at all…they did not shrink. In great, strong faith they cast out all misgivings of common sense, and, following simply the word of the prophet and the witness of the star, accepted him for a king, fell on their knees, worshipped him, and presented their treasures…. If we Christians would join the Wise Men, we must close our eyes to all that glitters before the world and look rather on the despised and foolish things, help the poor, comfort the despised, and aid the neighbor in need."

Martin looked up and asked his children, "So do you understand now what sacrifice means?"

"Like helping others," Anna Marie said matter-of-factly.

"Like when we fill Grandpa's root cellar with potatoes and carrots from our garden," added Phillip as he fidgeted on the floor.

"Yes, all that and more," said Martin. "Only Jesus came to entirely give himself."

"Stop poking my feet, Phillip," Anna Marie complained before Katya leaned down to touch his shoulder.

Martin carefully closed the black leather book and reached for his pair of felt boot liners that Katya had lined up with three other sets near the oven. Nearby sat a large tin can half full of dark caramelized sugar syrup.

"Put your *Feldshtievel* on, too," Katya told Anna, "if you're intent on going or a few minutes out there will chill your feet to the bone. And Phillipya—it's off to bed for you."

Martin then put on his black wool coat and gloves and took the warm can. Moments later Anna followed her father out the side door to the adjacent barn that sheltered the family's milk cow, four sheep, and two horses—a powerful roan gelding named Rudy and the unnamed colt Martin had recently purchased from his brother-in-law, Johann, Anna Marie's Fedda (uncle) Honna. She stepped on ground hard as stone and heard the movement of animals against the far wall of the enclosure. There tall Rudy's head appeared amidst the shadows as he gave a snort of anticipation. Martin took a three-pronged wooden fork from its familiar place near the hay pile and began to toss the green roughage over the stalls.

"Sprinkle the oats on top of the sheep's hay," he told Anna Marie, and after she did so Martin poured on the dark steaming concoction.

"The old ewe has been moving slowly of late," he said. "This should help give her some strength." The animals eagerly munched the fodder while Anna Marie walked to a door in front of the barn and lifted the wooden catch to peer outside. The sky was alive with glistening jewels. As she marveled at the sight, Anna Marie felt her father's gentle touch on her head.

"Even with a new moon it seems the starlight is bright enough to cast shadows," he whispered.

Anna Marie looked up to catch a twinkle in his eye and ventured the question she had pondered all day.

"So what did Momma say? May I go?" she asked expectantly.

"Yes, *Schodsche*, Mother says you may go to Saratov in the morning with me and Fedda Honna, but before..."

Anna Marie turned her head and interrupted her father with a great hug and sigh.

"But before we go," he continued, "you must be prepared for colder weather than this. Winds on the steppe and even in the forest can be as unforgiving as the wolves, and we'll need to be ready to go by daybreak. The city is full sixty *verst* away and we can't risk a late start.

"I'll be ready!" Anna Marie said excitedly, "I can even make breakfast!"

"No need for that," said Martin. "Just get a good night's sleep and don't worry your mother."

"Can I let the colt lick what's left of the syrup?" Anna Marie asked her father.

"Ah, such a treat for that spirited one. Why not?" Martin replied as he handed Anna Marie the warm can. "After all, he'll need his strength, too, since he's coming with us tomorrow."

"Oh, that's wonderful!" Anna Marie exclaimed, but then paused with concern.

"You're not thinking of selling him, are you?" she asked.

"No, no Anya," Martin reassured her, "but everything has a purpose and besides, he's dying to stretch out those long legs."

With that Anna Marie stepped over to the attentive colt and held out the can to its muzzle. He licked the sweetness and whinnied in delight.

Anna Marie tried her best to follow her father's advice to get to sleep. But her mind simply couldn't rest at the prospect of visiting the grandest settlement—the only real city in the entire region. Anna Lise, Marikia, and most of her other friends had already been to Saratov and told her of the wonders it held. But not even they had traveled so far in the dead of winter. Imagine seeing the majestic Volga, Mother of Rivers, now so frozen that horse-drawn sleighs were said to travel beyond sight far to Pokrovsk and Samara on the eastern shore.

Samara. It now occurred to Anna Marie that it sounded like "Samaria" from the Bible. Maybe the places her father had been reading about were closer than she thought. At school Marikia had told of an Orthodox church in Saratov with a two-story entry of multicolored jeweled glass as if something from a fairy tale. And Anna Lise described a brick Lutheran church with bells that were truly deafening. No wonder she didn't hear very well. Anna would be careful to keep her distance.

• • •

The next morning Anna Marie awoke to the familiar sounds of her parents' hushed voices in the kitchen. She also recognized the laugh of Fedda Honna and dashed from under her thick covers to the warmth of the kitchen to give him a hug.

"Adyea, good lady," he said, and gathered her up in his arms where she felt his soft black beard. Fedda Honna twirled her around in a circle while singing a familiar melody.

Anna Marie, Anna Marie,
Ich habe ein schöner Traum
Ein Baum wuchs in die Höh,
Ein wunder, ein schöner Baum.

Anna Marie, Anna Marie
I had a wondrous dream:
A tree grew up into the sky,
A wondrous, beautiful tree.

Anna Marie giggled while Katya shushed her brother to keep his antics from waking little Phillip.

"Anya," her mother smiled, "hurry to dress and eat while the men get the horses harnessed. You mustn't be on the road at night and it's a long ride to Saratov."

As the men went outside to tend the animals, Anna returned to the room she shared with Phillip who was still sleeping beneath the patchwork quilt and put on her warmest underclothes. She rushed to the table and drank a glass of milk her mother had set out next to a warm bowl of *Hirsche* (porridge) and piece of rye bread.

Fedda Honna twirled her around in a circle.

"Momma," she asked, "what shall we bring you from the city?"

"Yourself in good health," Katya replied. "It's a long way and you'll only have time for your Papa and Fedda Honna to pick up supplies for Fedda's shop. After that outbreak of influenza last month he's running very low on medicine, and with all the New Year's weddings he wants to be sure there's enough ribbon and candles."

Katya then reached across the table to a pile of soft brown wool. "Here, this is for you, Anna. I finished it last night so you could stay warm during the trip."

"Oh, Mamma, thank you!" Anna Marie gushed, "It's beautiful and soft as down."

She used her bread crust to wipe the bowl clean of sodden oats while Katya closed the metal fastener on a leather valise and put it next to the door just as Fedda Honna entered it wearing his golden brown Beltz sheepskin coat thick with curls. Tiny icicles hung to his beard beneath his nose.

"Get going all you," scolded Katya playfully, "or Phillip will wake up and think the *Belznickle* has come for him!"

"Well if he keeps pulling my niece's braids that's exactly what will happen to him!" Fedda Honna laughed. He took the bag and walked back outside with Anna Marie as Martin stepped inside to kiss his wife.

"There's half a loaf of rye bread and cheese wrapped inside," Katya said; "and I packed a good-sized link of sausage in that pail of lard. You also find two pairs of socks in case any of yours get wet. Do be safe."

"Don't worry;" he reassured Katya, "we'll be back by supper time."

He then turned to join Honna and Anna Marie in the wagon the men had converted to a sleigh by replacing its wheels with long iron runners attached to the box with a sturdy wood frame. Rudy and Fedda Honna's dappled gray mare, Dotchka, were harnessed in front and Anna Marie noticed the colt's bridle was tied by a long rope to the side of the wagon.

"So does this mean we have a troika like the Russian people do?" joked Anna Marie.

"We wouldn't go without the colt," Martin said as his eyes met those of Fedda Honna, "but we're mostly just a *dvoika* [twosome]."

There was enough room on the high front seat for two persons but Martin sat behind with Anna Marie on a bench in a make-shift enclosure of thin boards. Behind them rose a small pile of hay covered by a sheet of dark canvas. Anna Marie was bundled in a heavy coat and clutched her treasured new shawl around her arms and over her head. Martin had a placed a heavy folded quilt beneath their feet and Anna Marie felt something hard inside it. She gave a kick and looked down to see the end of her father's single-barreled shotgun sticking out.

"Are you afraid of the Belznickle too, Father?" she asked nervously.

"I don't think we'll be seeing him on this trip, Anya" he replied; "but you never know when a hare might scamper across our trail and offer a meal."

Fedda Honna gave the reins a jolt and the wagon suddenly lurched forward toward down the lane to the main road that led south through the village. In minutes they were beyond Anna Marie's beautiful home and she turned to see tiny clouds of smoke arising in the hazy distance from the chimneys. Soon the village disappeared among the gentle curves of the road that led through Aspenwald. She leaned against her father and settled into the lulling tempo of Rudy and Dotchka's gait and fell asleep to another of Fedda Honna's melodies:

Hei dei dolga!
Fahren m'r iwer die Wolga,
Fahren m'r iwer die Nei-Kolonie,
Mit mei Schodsche, Anna Marie.

Hei dei dolga!
We're going across the Volga,
To the village of New-Colony,
With my sweetheart, Anna Marie.

The wagon sped over the gently rolling hills and light snow fell as Anna Marie and her father and uncle continued farther and farther south. She awoke at the sound of Fedda Honna's shout to the horses to slow down. She looked up just as another sleigh met them carrying a load of logs.

"Where are we, Father?" she asked and then felt the cold sting of fresh air against her face.

"Almost to the city, Anya," Martin said.

"You've been sleeping all morning like a bear in winter," Fedda Honna turned to say. "Did you get any sleep at all last night?"

"A little I think," Anya replied, "but I mostly thought about the city."

"Well look up, little one," Fedda Honna said, "those buildings in the distance are the outskirts of Saratov. See there the golden domes of *Starii Zabor* (Old Cathedral)."

In another half-hour Anna Marie found herself riding along the city's main boulevard amidst more sleighs and pedestrians than she had ever seen in one place her entire life. Snow was piled high on both sides of the way and in the middle. The horses trotted on for several more blocks and Anna Marie marveled at the opulent green, turquoise, and mustard-colored building facades rising four stories and crowned with ornate white cornices. Finally Fedda Honna reined the horses left through a small snow pile and stopped in front of a store with enormous windows. Above the door a sign read "Schmidt Brothers" in both German and Cyrillic script to identify the familiar name of a leading Saratov merchant firm.

"I'm sorry we're not here on a pleasure trip, angel," Martin said to Anna Marie as he jumped down from the wagon and turned to lift her. "You'll have time to look around the store and we'll eat here, but then we must head back."

Fedda Honna tied the two lead horses to a wooden post and brought the colt up next to them. He tossed some fresh hay beneath the animals, and then stepped up to the boardwalk alongside Anna Marie who was peering in a display window. Fedda Honna reached into both his pockets and pulled out two fists.

"Candy kopecks for one niece, none for the other," he said, "better make your choice."

Anna Marie had played against her brother in this game before, and knew there would be little risk.

"That one!" she shouted, pointing to her uncle's left hand.

"*Ach, du liebe.*" Fedda Honna mumbled, pretending defeat as they walked inside. "Your daughter beat me again, Martin."

A beautiful teapot for Mama.

As the men walked up to visit with a clerk standing behind a wide counter counting colorful banknotes, Anna Marie looked around in wonder at the vast storehouse of goods neatly arranged on the two floors she could see from the entryway. Kitchen tinware, colored bolts of cloth, brass samovars, birch baskets, dried fruit and nuts, and jars of ribboned hard candy and other *Konfekt* were on display near an enormous wooden abacus. But before she made her way to the sweets, Anna Marie stepped closer to the window display she had seen when they arrived. A beautiful teapot of bright blue enamel decorated with painted flowers in yellow, pink, and white was surrounded by six matching teacups. Then she felt her father standing near.

"So you saw it, too?" he asked.

"Yes, Papa, wouldn't Mama just love it?" Anna Marie cried. "And I have two rubles I saved and the money from Uncle to contribute. Please let me help."

"I had my eye on it for her myself," Martin said. "You buy some candy for yourself and Phillip with the kopecks," Martin told her. "And if you wish to help with the rest then it will be from both of us."

The thought of seeing her devoted mother open such a present was delightful, and Anna Marie watched as a clerk came to fetch the vessel from the display and carefully box it up. Fedda Honna's transactions took longer than expected, which gave Anna Marie time to consider the many flavors of hard candy. She eventually settled on two berry flavored sticks and a pair that tasted of horehound. As the men carefully loaded the supplies into the wagon, Martin noticed that a bolt was missing from one of the metal brackets holding the right runner to the wagon frame.

"That won't do with the distance we've yet to travel," he observed, and led all three back inside to find a properly sized replacement. A clerk led them into a back room lined with small wooden boxes on all four walls that contained nuts, bolts, and fasteners of every size imaginable. Soon the proper one was found and put into place while Anna Marie ate the lunch her mother had prepared. After the repair was finished, Martin thanked the storekeeper and checked his pocket watch while Fedda Honna helped Anna Marie back into the wagon.

"Time to bundle up again, Anya," he told her as he glanced at the leaden skies to the north.

He then turned to his brother-in-law. "Hannas, looks like we'll need to make up some time on the way back home. Now it's my turn."

Martin then sat at the front of the wagon and Fedda Honna settled in next to Anna Marie. She turned to look in every direction so not to miss a single detail of Saratov's wonders and smiled when she heard the clanging afternoon church bells as they drove through the outskirts of city. Soon they were riding through the creamy white countryside again and she looked back to see to see the colt keeping pace with the wagon. A flock of rooks swooped low along a field to the left where fuzzy rows of stubble were barely visible rising from the snow. The air felt colder to Anna Marie and she noticed that Rudy and Dotchka's breaths exploded in geyser-like blasts to the tempo of their gait. She wondered what her mother would say when she opened their special gift, and soon Anna Marie drifted again into dreamland.

Anna Marie couldn't tell how much time had passed when awakened. She had been leaning against Fedda Honna, felt him move, and opened her eyes. She didn't recognize the vicinity and sensed it was late afternoon. The road was shrouded in dense stands of birch and linden with occasional patches of evergreens. She noticed Fedda Honna, who was munching on the sausage, held the shotgun in his right hand and was scanning the right side of the trail.

"Did you see a hare, Uncle?" Anna Marie inquired.

"No rabbits hereabouts," replied Fedda Honna, "but best stay awake now and hold tight to my coat and the seat."

Anna Marie became attentive at Fedda's cautious tone. She looked up to her father who snapped the reins to advance the horses' pace.

"We can't be sure, Anna," her uncle explained, "but Rudy's seems a bit spooked. May be some sign of wolf."

The very word "wolf" sent a shiver down Anna Marie's spine. She had heard tales of their presence on the steppes but few her age claimed to have actually seen one. An instant later her father nodded to the right toward shadowy phantoms only momentarily visible.

"Off there, Johann!" he shouted and Fedda Honna raised the gun.

"Get under the bench, Anna," he ordered sternly, "and cover your ears."

The lead horses seemed to pull in jerks and Fedda

She glimpsed the fearsome dark form of a wolf.

Honna looked back and forth the icy road. He suddenly swung the weapon to the left as Anna Marie curled up under the seat while the horses struggled. But she didn't cover her ears. A moment later she heard the loudest explosion she thought possible and was instantly seized with terror. She plunged her head into the quilt as Fedda Honna clicked open the barrel to reload. The blast immediately thundered again and Anna Marie heard her uncle shout something about the trees. She risked looking ahead in the winter gloom and felt pieces of snow thrown by hooves hitting her face. She then glimpsed the fearsome dark form of a speeding wolf lunge at Rudy's underside. A third shot thundered and the creature disappeared amidst the noisome melee of panicked horses, careening wagon, and shouting men.

"It's a pack!" yelled Fedda Honna.

Her father hollered back, "Cut it now!"

Anna Marie was paralyzed with fear but opened her eyes to see Fedda Honna drop the open gun on the floorboard next to her. She winced at the acrid smell of gun smoke and watched her uncle grasp his lower right leg with both hands. With a single motion he pulled a hunting knife from its sheath in his boot and drew it to the taut rope beside him.

"Not the colt!" shrieked Anna Marie as she pulled down on Fedda Honna's arm.

As he pushed Anna Marie down, Fedda Honna glimpsed the pail of lard and jerked it up. He dropped the knife, tore off the lid, and just as he struggled to take off his coat Anna Marie tore off her precious shawl and offered it to him. Fedda Honna smeared some of the creamy gray mass on the fabric and then threw it behind with all his might. Anna Marie heard a fiendish howl, closed her eyes tighter than ever before, and felt her heart thumping. She then felt her uncle's hand on her head and heard him say, "Now you know why we bring a colt on these winter trips."

The wagon soon resumed a steady motion as Rudy and Dotchka settled down. The horses and colt kept a brisk pace in the growing darkness and Anna Marie heard nothing more from her father and uncle. Her fright abated but she remained motionless under the seat until they reached home shortly afterward. The horses pulled up to the barn and she heard the men step down from the wagon. Anna Marie felt exhausted and lay still until her father called her name. Martin leaned over the sideboard and lifted Anna Marie into his arms.

"We've all learned something about sacrifice this day," he whispered, and the two hugged each other very tightly.

✎ Afterword ◠

This story is based on experiences related to me by Amalie "Mollie" Hergert Bafus of Endicott, Washington, in 1980. She emigrated from Schöntal, Russia, on the lower Volga's eastern *Wiesenseite* bank as a young girl and had vivid memories of life in the German colonies. I often visited Mollie in her tiny home "across the tracks" until her passing in 1994. Whenever returning from a visit to Russia, I would stop by to see her with an update on my travels. She and her fun-loving husband, John—whom she survived by many years—were great friends of our grandparents, who lived a short distance across town. They had grown up in another world and loved entertaining us younger ones with stories of the Old Country.

Reference to the terrifying *Belznickle* comes in part from the dark and dank basement of our youth on our family farm near Endicott. A large black bear coat hung from a post there and I once asked my father about it. He told me it was our Uncle Yost's "Belz" that likely came with the family from Russia in 1888. Years later I heard the story of the Belznickle, a monstrous ogre of the steppes clad in a bear coat or sheepskin who terrorized naughty children in the villages at Christmastime. Fortunately such threats were tamed by the *Christkind*, an angelic maiden dressed and veiled in white and gold who followed to give a gift of nuts, dried fruit, and candy.

The Homeland Garden

Farewell. I feel the west-wind blow;
The Asian dream is o'er;
And Europe's in the sunset glow,
That gilds thy sandy shore.
I go where other streams will shine,
But none so lone, so grand as thine.
—Edna Dean Proctor, "Farewell to the Volga" (1878)

Martin could not remember ever going all night without sleeping. He was warmly wrapped in the dark blue quilt Grandmother Bauer had given him several years before when he had turned ten. Now his lanky body hardly fit beneath its heaviness without bending his knees. In the dimness of early morn, he heard his parents talking quietly as they moved about in the adjacent kitchen. But Martin's imagination still kept him from slumber. The Wagner family—Peter and Maria, their thirteen-year-old son Martin, and his nine-year-old sister, Leah, would be leaving in the morning. The thought of setting out on their adventure to America was thrilling to Martin, if also a bit fearsome.

Several years earlier a half-dozen young men from his native Oberfeld and neighboring Volga villages had ventured across the Atlantic to explore prospects of life in that fabled land. Tsar Alexander's worrisome manifesto of 1871 decreed that Russia's German colonist farmers must now pay state taxes, and also serve in the Russian army. But on the other side of the world opportunity seemed to abound. "Maybe not the land of milk and honey," reported *Galotya Heinrich* (Shortcoat Henry), "because we didn't see many trees or bee hives on the great prairies, but plenty of cattle, and for farming, grasslands without end!"

Since the scouts' return, word had reached Martin's parents of fertile valleys and prairies newly opened to colonists in America's Pacific Northwest. His mother's oldest brother and Martin's namesake—Uncle Martin Bauer—was now living with several other relatives along the Columbia River in jurisdictions with odd-sounding names—Oregon and Washington. Herr Schneider, Oberfeld's longtime schoolmaster, told Martin that the Columbia was a mighty river though not as grand as the Volga, and a place where Indians roamed much like the pastoral Kirghiz and Kalymk tribes who still ranged across their eastern Volga *Wiesenseite*.

"I can't say whether they are peaceful or not," Herr Schneider had told Martin. "One hears strange things from America. But your Fedda Martin is a wise man and would not bid you to come if it were not safe."

Young Martin had few memories of his American uncle, who four years before had first taken up residence in Kansas. Now Uncle Martin's letters told of the beautiful forests and available farmland in faraway Oregon. No locust plagues and wind storms there like their people had known on Galotya's Midwestern grasslands. The thought of joining his uncle in America appealed to the boy's adventuresome spirit, but he knew the idea was not popular with everyone in the family—especially his elderly grandparents. But Peter and Maria Wagner had other considerations.

Taxes imposed by the tsar in distant St. Petersburg were one thing for thrifty country folk. But military conscription brought the unsettling likelihood of years of contentious dealings with Russian-speaking soldiers for young males not much older than their son. Even after they had lived for more than a century on the Volga, some Russian officers as well as conscripts considered the prosperous Germans to be foreign interlopers who had too long remained aloof from their Slavic neighbors. Several young men from the village were serving in remote border areas of the Caucasus Mountains, while the oldest brother of his friend Anna had been sent far to the east of the Urals. Not only were the Volga Germans derided for their incomprehensible amalgam of archaic Hessian sprinkled with misspoken Russian, the Catholic and Protestant Germans were also considered forsakers of the ancient Orthodox way. Martin himself had lived in Russia his entire life, but had no Russian friends, and only knew a few practical words like "food" and "help" for use when visiting the great city of Samara with his father. Of course area inhabitants of all backgrounds knew the Russian expression for the fabled Volga waterway of song and story—*Mat'h Reká*, Mother of Rivers.

Martin eventually dozed off, only to be awakened soon afterward by the sound of his mother stirring nearby. He smiled at the thought of no longer having to fetch wood in the chilly morning air for the enormous corner stove. It had kept at least four generations of Wagners warm against the piercing Volga winters. Last time as well to tend the horses and cattle in the stalls of their home's adjacent thatched-roof barn. Of course there might be chores in America, but at least there, according to Schoolmaster Schneider, everyone was treated as equals. Moreover, he said it was forbidden to make fun of foreigners and raise your voice except to animals. But might this also be the last time to see his lifelong playmate and neighbor, Anna Roth, and other friends with whom he had spent so many afternoons exploring the flowered banks and eddies of the nearby Yeruslan River? Martin felt instantly sad at the thought of not seeing them for who knows how long. Perhaps never? He could hardly bear that melancholy prospect.

The children's parents had told them to spend more time than usual the previous week with kindly Grandfather and Grandmother Bauer, Maria's parents, and Peter's widowed mother, Grandma Wagner. She could be severe in dealings with other older women in the village, but Martin and Leah saw their grandmother's tender side whenever they needed refuge from parental correction. She could always cheer them up with a story from her Oberfeld youth of long ago, related over a

cup of hot tea flavored with licorice root and a warm slice of buttered rye bread. They had spoken little of the family's long journey that week, but only yesterday Grandma Wagner presented the children with pairs of newly made woolen mittens for him and his sister. Martin held her fast in a tearful embrace when they parted.

The boy quickly dressed in his dark trousers and blue shirt and tied the laces of the soft black leather boots he had polished the night before. No sooner had his mother given him a warm hug and bowl of steaming *Hirsche* than they heard a knock at the door. Someone

Martin held his grandmother in a tearful embrace.

must not have said a final good-bye after yesterday's worship service in the stately white church that rose in the heart of the village. As Leah slowly emerged from the bedroom still clad in her nightshirt, Martin looked toward the door that his father opened to admit the unexpected visitor from the frosty dawn air.

"Dear Frederich!" Peter said as both men clasped hands. "Thanks so much for coming to see us off," Martin's father said with conviction.

"I had to conduct services for Pastor Walter over in Heimatsdorf yesterday," Herr Schneider explained, "and was not able to return until evening. You know how much I shall miss you all." He nodded toward Maria and smiled to the children.

Martin watched their guest take his parents into his broad arms for a final, silent embrace. As much as anyone, Martin knew he would greatly miss the man who had taught him to read and cipher at the village school for the past several years. Some of the children thought Herr Schneider to be a stern taskmaster, but not Martin and Anna. He seemed to appreciate the inquisitiveness both children had showed from earliest youth.

While other boys could talk only of soldiering and playing jokes on each other or some decrepit village elder, Martin was fascinated by their teacher's Bible stories and lessons about the mysteries of nature and life in distant places. He often stayed after class to visit about what they had studied in class. Somehow Martin's teacher seemed to have knowledge about most everything, and when he didn't, he would learn from one of the many books from his considerable personal library. But Herr Schneider could not tell him much more about life in America than what was described on the pages of the delightful *Poems of Places* book they sometimes read together after school. As Herr Schneider stepped away from his parents that last morning, Martin recognized the small green volume that his teacher held out toward him.

"Martin Pyotrvich!" he shouted using the patronymic usually reserved for formalities, "You have been my faithful student of English these past months as we've explored worlds in this wonderful book. I wish you for to have it for your journey and new life in America."

Martin did not know just what to say in response to such a special gift, and was nearly overcome at the sudden realization that he might never see his beloved mentor again. As when leaving Grandmother Bauer, tears welled up in the boy's eyes. He stepped forward with downcast eyes to accept the book, then looked up to give his teacher a warm hug. As Herr Schneider departed, Martin rushed to the door and shouted, "Fredrich Adamovich! I shall never forget you!" as Herr Schneider disappeared into the morning mist.

The front room table was laden with several parcels Martin's parents had carefully packed for their departure. They contained blankets and nightshirts, brown woolen shawls, a dark green enameled coffee pot, small broadaxe, and other necessities. His mother also packed a separate wooden box with rye bread, smoked pork sausage, and cheese. They had sufficient money for trip expenses and a new start in America after selling their house on favorable terms to the eldest son of the village miller. Peter would carry their cash, passports, and tickets in a fabric satchel fashioned by Martin's mother to be tied securely around his chest.

Along the wall near the entry rested the *Feldstievel* boot inserts that would keep their feet warm during the long journey by wagon, train, and ship. On the floor next to the shoes were two medium-sized chests that held his father's black *Beltz* bearskin coat and smaller coats for him and Leah made of coarse gray *Wadmal* (wool), wooden bowls and spoons, a brown glass bottle of hearty *Brannvin* for medicinal needs, and the family's few precious books—black leather-bound Bible, catechism, and *Volgagesangbuch* (Volga hymn book).

"How would they carry it all?" Martin wondered. But he knew his parents had made careful preparation for several days. Just then Martin heard his Fedda Yost arrive outside with a wagon and team of snorting horses for the brisk morning ride some fifty miles westward to the bustling Volga city of Samara. They would then cross the Mother Volga by ferry to the railhead in the provincial capital, Saratov.

"Don't forget this!" Martin's spirited uncle said as he stepped inside the house carrying a small, brightly painted blue wooden chest by its handle.

"Thanks again, Yost, for helping us dig them yesterday," said Maria to her heavily bearded brother. "I can't imagine life somewhere else without our beloved iris."

"Yes, Marikia, may the purple ever remind us of our Lord's message of love wherever home may be, and the yellow for sunshine in your life. Now if the bulbs will just keep until they find some good black earth. I also wrapped some rhubarb root, cucumber seeds, and *Schwartzbeeren* (blackberries) so you can plant your own *Heimat Garten* (homeland garden)," Yost added with an affectionate smile, and Maria leaned over to closely hug him.

Martin decided to keep the book of poems in the small knapsack that he would keep close at hand throughout the trip. Herr Schneider had suggested that he take a small tablet, pen, and ink in order to keep a journal of his travels and write short letters to family and friends back home as time and post permitted. Reading the book of poems would benefit his limited knowledge of English. He lifted the cover to see words written in Herr Schneider's familiar flowing hand:

To my young seeker and friend, Martin Wagner—
May the Lord ever guide, protect, and bless.
Herr Frederich Schneider
Oberfeld, Russia—March 19, 1882

Beneath the inscription, Martin recognized lines from a favorite poem in the book that he had already memorized during his study of the new language:

To east and west I reach my hand;
My heart I give my native land;
*　I seek her good,—her glory;*
I honor every nation's name,
Respect their fortunes and their fame,
*　But I love the land that bore me.*

After carefully placing the precious volume into his leather bag, Martin joined his father and uncle in lifting their trunks, boxes, and sacks to Yost's substantial wagon. Peter made room for his wife and children to sit as comfortably as possible for the three-hour drive and ferry ride to Saratov. After the last of their goods were finally loaded in the wagon, Martin looked wistfully down the familiar lane that led to his grandparents' home. Through the dim morning mist he could see two hunched figures like a pair of mute statues just outside the front door, silent and frozen in time in a pose that would be forever engraved on his mind. The wagon jolted as Yost jerked the lines, and the Wagner family disappeared into the overcast distance followed by a wagon carrying the family of Martin's Fedda Conrad and Vess Marillis Wagner, who were traveling with them. They would all meet up in Saratov with Henry and Anna Mueller who were leaving with their infant daughter, Katya. The Muellers, natives of nearby Schoendorf, were longtime friends of Martin's parents who had farmed near the Wagner's fields for many years in the *Khutor* (countryside) several miles away from their home villages.

As a flurry of snow brought a sudden chill to the travelers, Martin pulled up the collar of his coat and closed his eyes hoping the rhythm of the ride might bring more sleep. But the strange mix of feelings from a peculiar sense of loss to exhilaration at the prospect of unfolding adventure prevented any rest. He looked up and saw Leah leaning her head on their mother's shoulder as they slightly bounced in unison, while Maria looked ahead silently as if in a trance. The brightening morning revealed a countryside of scattered trees and grain fields Martin had rarely traversed, and by early afternoon the families reached Samara and took a slow-moving ferry across the river. After procuring tickets at the Saratov train station where they met the Muellers, the families transferred their belongings to an assigned passenger train car. The group then settled in for the long ride to the Polish border, across the old German homeland to Bremerhaven on the North Sea, and transfer by ship to the great port of Liverpool, England.

April 24, 1882

Dear Anna,

I hope this letter finds you and your family all in good health. We are by the grace of God safe in our travels now to Liverpool in England where we will sail in three days to America. Our way was long across Russia and Europe. In ten days we went by railroad all the way from Saratov to Edykuken at the border with Poland and through Germany to Bremerhaven on the ocean. It was a marvel to hear our language spoken in so many places, but many folks think our Schveza ("talk," dialect) is like sound from the long forgotten past.

Please tell Herr Schneider how thankful I am for the book of poems he gave me. Papa says he will need me to serve as our translator in Amerika. How I wish I spent more time on my lessons with our teacher. The poems seems to me like a window on so many places of the world I had only heard or read about before, but now am seeing. This one now I have almost memorized during travel through the German *Heimatland*—

Before all tongues, in east or west,
I love my native tongue the best;
    Though not so smoothly spoken,
Nor woven with Italian art,
Yet when it speaks from heart to heart,
    The word is never broken.*

*George Phillip Schmidt, "My Native Land," *Poems of Places—Germany,* 1878

We enjoy the bread and sausage Mama packed for our journey, and we can buy food like fruit and drinks. We are lodged here at Liverpool near the place where the ships depart, and our passage to New York will be on the *Linden* which we can see being prepared for our sailing. Leah plays the Mill game that you gave her so I thank you for that. We use buttons for the pieces and she often wins even when I try not to let her! She is smart like you and also misses our friends there.

Papa and Fedda Conrad bought the tickets for our families and we will travel with the Muellers from Schoendorf who came with their three children. Mr. Mueller says all in America are equals, and that boys cannot approach a girl without asking her permission. It is like a law.

As soon as we get to our new home I will write again.

Sent with a kiss of love,

Martin

• • •

A cold, piercing Atlantic wind blowing across the Liverpool harbor caused the Bauer, Walter, and Mueller families to cluster with a horde of other immigrant families who gathered the second week of May to board the *Linden* for the long Atlantic voyage to America. After a tiring pre-dawn wait to board the vessel and inspection of passports and tickets, all seventy-eight emigrants filed across the railed wooden passageway onto the place that would be their home for as long as a month depending on conditions at sea. The adults were mostly silent in apprehension at the prospect of so long a voyage in such limited space, while Martin and other youngsters gazed in wonder as the brightening day brought a soft breeze filling the broad sails of the three masts that pierced the awakening sky.

The families were directed across the wooden deck toward the entrance to the hold by one of *Linden*'s two mates, who joined a bosun, three able-bodied seamen, three deckhands, and a cook for a crew of eleven that included fifty-year-old Captain Edward Mitchell. The voyagers felt the alien sensation of unsure footing as the floor beneath them slightly heaved as they stepped on board. Farmers who had only known the soil and stone solidity of unmovable steppes fumbled about to a wooden stairway that led to the darkened levels below. Maria glanced to her right and saw a man she assumed was the captain standing in the distance along the outer rail. He filled a clay pipe with tobacco and seemed indifferent to the new inhabitants of his domain, and then sauntered away. Maria and the families were directed by a deckhand to the hold as the morning mist abated and the day's breeze grew stronger.

The passengers struggled to adjust to the darkness below where one of the mates motioned families to one of the two ends of the cavernous interior. Long sheets of gray canvas divided the area into spaces where small families would reside with double bunks that held mattresses of loose straw. A second mate led a group of single men and older sons down into the bottom deck where all would reside with less privacy and sleep on similar beds fastened to the bulkheads along the side of the vessel. Martin placed the blue chest containing the precious iris bulbs and plant starts with other belongings at the foot of their bunks as others did in their fabric cubicles. Three crude, narrow tables stretched along the center of the hold where the immigrants would take their meals in shifts or eat while standing.

The burly crewman who had first guided them onto the ship then motioned everyone to gather around as he loudly proclaimed the rules of the sail in a pantomimed mixture of English and German.

"Good thing you paid attention to Herr Schneider's English lessons," Peter said to Martin. "Leave it to one of us to get lost on the ship without you to help us understand," he smiled.

"I'll do my best, Papa," Martin replied with no little worry about his ability to comprehend the strange tongue.

Grabbing one of two brooms that rested against a nearby bulkhead, the mate explained that everyone's area was to be swept clean each morning with sawdust thrown upon vomit and wetness and gathered for disposal, and that mattresses were to be turned and checked for bedbugs. He had scarcely begun the narration when little Katya Mueller began to cry and Anna walked away to rock the child in her arms, though the child's crying did not subside. The speaker shook his head and continued with instructions about mealtimes, while Maria winced at the revolting thought of sea sickness. She had already glimpsed the telltale tiny red spots made by the repulsive little creatures on the necks of some of the passengers. How could a respectable German mother abide their presence?

The mate motioned toward two wooden barrels and several tubs secured beneath the stairway and said they held a week's supply of that level's ration of flour, dried peas, herring, sauerkraut, salt pork, and cheese. Families were to share the small galley space toward the bow of the ship and appoint someone to throw all refuse and sweepings overboard, and not allow any unaccompanied children on deck. One half-gallon of fresh water would be supplied daily per person, except in case of wild weather when the hold might be locked, so all were urged to conserve for drinking and washing. As another baby joined the incessant cry of Katya the whole group shifted slightly portside as the *Linden* lurched away from her moorings and began to slowly head along the docks toward the open sea.

The combination of motion with thoughts of sickness, storms, and uncertainty about their ultimate destination brought a lump to Maria's throat. What if they were lost at sea, or if the Columbia River were nothing like the Volga? What if the good land had already been claimed and only desolate waste and natives who disliked foreigners await? Peter sensed his wife's unease, tightened his arm around her, and mustered a smile of assurance. He pulled back Leah's black headscarf and ran his fingers through the little girl's hair. She looked up silently and leaned against him. As the mate finished his oration and disappeared above deck, Martin asked his father if he could follow to explore the ship.

"You should have understood the instructions better than any of us," Peter said. "There are to be no youngsters up there without a parent. You may not be a child anymore, but you're not a man yet either, Martin. We'll not be starting out this trip by getting crosswise with the captain and crew."

Martin thought his father's tone to be oddly severe, and he sat down on one of the bunks assigned them and drew out Herr Schneider's book of poems from the satchel he had carried on board. He scanned several pages for something that might relate to their journey, and found reference to America and the ocean in lines by William Cullen Bryant:

The Prairies. I beheld them for the first,
And my heart swells, while the dilated sight
Takes in the encircling vastness. Lo! they stretch
In airy undulations, far away,
As if the ocean, in his gentlest swell,
Stood still, with all his rounded billows fixed...

Martin only knew a handful of the words, but understood enough about ocean vastness to spark both fear and excitement. Since he had been up most of the night in anticipation of their departure, the boy had not noticed his fatigue until straining to comprehend some of the poem's words. Now denied opportunity to go above and surrounded by the gloom of the rocking ship's hold, the boy drifted to sleep.

• • •

During the first week at sea, the Wagner and Mueller families joined with the others in a daily routine that began with the morning meal served soon after sunrise. The Germans slept uneasily amidst the groans and rolls of *Linden's* nighttime sailing, and were early risers. The women carefully divided the dried sausages, bread, and cheese they had packed to supplement the ship's bland offerings, and young mothers breastfed their infants. Most of the men spent time on deck visiting and playing cards while boys and girls enjoyed games of checkers and mill, scanning the great ocean waves for signs of life, and imagining creatures in the shapes of passing clouds. On a crisp, sunny day during the second week of the voyage, a deck hand beckoned onlookers to the peculiar sight toward the rear of the ship where a formation of some half-dozen lithe creatures swiftly rose and fell in together as if their glistening gray bodies formed a ship's escort. Several children shrieked in amazement and Martin hurried below to excitedly report the sighting to his parents. He found his father sitting on his mother's bunk holding a cup of water and then saw Uncle Conrad bring a brown bottle of *brannvin* and pour some of the golden liquid into the drink.

"Your mother is feeling a bit low today, Martin," Peter said, "so it will be up to us to prepare our food and keep Leah busy."

"It's nothing that a few minutes of fresh air topside and some of Grandma Bauer's *Ruschimilch* can't cure," Maria suggested. "I'll be just fine if I can rest comfortably for a while."

"Well, we can certainly take you upstairs for a walk," Conrad replied, "but the *Ruschimilch* will have to wait till we find an American cow and hot stove."

"Someone heard the captain say we'll likely pass the half-way point in the next day or two," offered Martin reassuringly; "so it won't be long before we have milk and eggs again, Mama."

Maria smiled at her son and thought happily of prospects for her children's new life in a land where they needn't fear the tsar's armies or persecution of their faith. Yes, against all the tumult of uprooting the familiar ways of village life back home, Peter had been right in his decision to join his brother and the vanguard of *usu Leut* (our people) in the faraway Pacific Northwest. So what if they hadn't seen the Columbia Land? Did not the Scripture say, "The just shall live by faith, not by sight"? There would be plenty to see in the weeks and months ahead, and it would be good. Now she just needed to rest.

As Peter returned from visiting with a young German emigrant to his wife's side, Conrad led Martin back toward the stairs. He told his nephew to keep an eye on Leah who had joined Anna Mueller and the baby on deck. Martin described the remarkable sea creatures they had appeared along the ship's stern.

"Martin!" Conrad scolded, "You mustn't speak of such things to your mother. Haven't you heard that such beings of the waters who breathe the air of mankind seek the spirits of the living? Pray they may depart us, young man! Carry something with you to throw and persuade them to leave us alone."

Martin had wanted to sneak some pickled herring to feed the mysterious creatures, and now realized the danger that might have invited.

"I had no idea what they were, Uncle," Martin explained.

"Let this be a lesson, Martin, that as we encounter strange places," Conrad warned. "We must be on guard against the wiles of the Wicked One. It is written that he wanders about as a roaring lion on land, but who knows what form he can take here on the high seas. God be praised that He has spared us ill weather, and let us pray that good fortune continues as we near our new home."

Fair winds continued to guide *Linden* into the third week of the long voyage and stalwart Captain Mitchell's periodic updates to the passengers expressed hope that this sailing might be one of the calmest in his twenty-six years at sea. Martin was pleased that he could get the gist of conversations among the crew that he overheard, and he started to teach Leah how to pronounce certain words he thought might be helpful in America—yes, no, help, food. After several more days their mother's condition had not improved, however, and she had begun to run a slight fever. But other adults and children were also unwell and Aunt Marillis reported with some unease that ill health on such a journey could be expected. Maria's sister-in-law prepared a daily serving of hot broth nourished with barley and sour cabbage which seemed to give her strength. Sometimes music could be heard from the men's deck further below where an Irishman broke out a fiddle tune and others of all nationality laughed and danced arm in arm.

One day after some hours of unusually calm air, the winds shifted to the southwest and white-capped swells rose and fell that sent waves washing across the deck, which necessitated closing the hatch. Peter's old friend, Henry Mueller, was a great storyteller and at such times or just before bedtime would gather the children around for a tale about the tribulations of life in the Old Country they had forever escaped, and how they should always be grateful. Way back when, Pugachev the notorious bandit claimed to be Empress Catherine's resurrected husband, the murdered Tsar Peter III, and he ravaged the peaceful Volga villages of their ancestors with fires and hangings. The children's parents preferred Henry's stories of the wonders awaiting them in enchanted America, the land of milk and honey such as God had promised the Children of Israel. Only in America there were no Amalakites and Canaanites, but friendly Indians who some claimed spoke the language of the ancient Jews and welcomed all strangers.

Scarcely without any indication of illness save occasional fussiness, the infant of a Swedish couple ran a high fever one night in the third week of the voyage and died the following morning. The bosun was summoned for the sorrowful task of sewing the tiny corpse inside a canvas shroud. Peter kept close to his family in their fabric compartment as the sobbing couple and comforting friends filed above deck. Captain Mitchell performed a brief ceremony that concluded by lowering the wrapped body into the passing depths. Martin heard soon afterward that as the solemn service ended a member of the crew noticed coastal seaweed in the water. The next morning shouting on deck summoned many of the weary passengers upstairs to see a large gull circling above the foremast, and by noon at least two dozen were flying around the ship and alighting in the rigging. A warm, contrary gust arose from distant shores and Martin heard one of the able-bodied seamen say the "America Wind" was beckoning. *Linden* would be entering New York Harbor by morning.

Martin relayed the good news below deck and his words reached through Maria's delirium as if an angel's revelation. Sister-in-law Marillis, who with Peter had taken turns at Maria's side for the past week, thought her fever lessened during the night though she continued to fall in and out of consciousness. The next morning found all the German families joined to sing their familiar anthem *Gott ist Die Liebe* (*God is Love*), and with newfound spirit Maria whispered the familiar refrain: *"Drum sag Ich nach einmal, Gott ist die Liebe, Gott ist die Liebe, Er liebt auch Mich."* She saw Martin and Leah standing in the distance with broad smiles and wondered if she was back at church in Oberfeld or in some other place. Days of dank and gloom soon gave way to sunshine so brilliant that she struggled to shield her face just as someone thankfully placed a white kerchief over her eyes. The invigorating bite of fresh air swept through her body as the stretcher on which she had been placed emerged from the ship's dark interior. Maria thought of familiar lines from Psalm 65—the "Psalm of God's Abundant Favor":

> *By awesome deeds Thou dost answer*
> *   us in righteousness, O God of our salvation,*
> *Thou who art the trust of all the ends*
> *   of the earth and of the farthest sea....*

Maria realized that she was being carried off the boat to finally arrive in the Promised Land of America. She grasped Peter's wrist and smiled at the thought of stilled seas now behind them and the rejoicing hills of flowers and grain.

The immigrant families looked somewhat disheveled and disoriented as they walked down *Linden*'s gangplank in the fresh May morning's air to Castle Garden's massive wooden pier on the southern tip of Manhattan Island. Peter and Conrad knew that Maria's condition would complicate the family's entry since a doctor's approval following the medical examination in the holding area would be required. The Wagners and Muellers prayed that Maria could summon the strength to manage the inspection. Like most others, Martin and Leah felt dizzy while taking their first steps on America's solid ground. Maria rallied sufficiently after being carried to the wide walkway of tan stone and masonry to ask Peter to help her stand. To everyone's amazement she rose and smiled before resting her head on Peter's shoulder as he placed his arm around her waist to help her slowly bring up the end of the immigrant herd. Captain Mitchell, who had been visiting quietly to the side with a custom's official, approached the slow-moving couple. Peter feared for the worst, as he had heard stories about those unfortunate souls who had reached the doorstep of America only to be turned back after a diagnosis of typhoid, cholera, or some other malady.

"I told the doctor," the captain explained to Peter in his best German, "that your wife's condition seemed to us to be more of a prolonged sea-sickness than contagious disease. These things happen and they maintain a small infirmary where people in such condition can spend a couple of days to recover. If that's not the case then perhaps something more will have to be done."

Peter was relieved to hear that special care for Maria would be provided, and decided not to ask at the moment about what the "something more" might mean. His wife seemed to be improving, and surely one or two days of decent food and accommodations in a warm, secure place would restore her health. As he pondered the matter, Conrad continued to speak with the captain and doctor using Martin for periodic translation for certain words like "permit" and "rule." Uniformed officials who had guided everyone into the cavernous main hall then led the Wagners and Muellers into its doors and Conrad explained to his brother that the children would not be allowed to remain in the medical facility with Peter and Maria. They could stay in a hostel beyond the processing area for the cost of board and room, or join their accompanying relatives on to the group's intended final destination.

Both choices seemed unsettling and Peter dared not discuss them with his ailing wife who sat with Marillis and the children on a massive wooden bench nearby. "So Marillis and I will stay here in the city with the children for a couple days, Peter," Conrad interrupted. "This is not such a big problem; the main thing is for you to stay with Maria and we can all continue on in no time at all."

"Without question we should do all we can to remain together, brother," Peter replied. "But the cost—we know how limited our funds are, and with so much travel across the country still ahead of us...." Peter's stared ahead as his words fell off in sober silence.

"Leave this to me," said Conrad firmly as both men felt the eyes of the inspectors encouraging them to proceed. "Let the Muellers proceed if they wish, but Marillis and I could use some time to recover from our long trip as well, and Martin can help me send messages between us. You tend to Maria and we'll all be fine. *In Gottes sagen ist Alles gelegen* (Everything depends of the grace of God)."

With the commotion ahead of them beginning to subside, the two men turned toward those in uniform and explained their decision. Konrad beckoned Marillis to his side and Peter walked over to his family and knelt on one knee to embrace his daughter and son.

"As you may have heard, Mama and I will stay here for a short time," he explained. "We will then join you in the city so we can continue our journey together."

Maria, who had been sitting peacefully between her children, placed her hand to her lips and touched each of them on the forehead. "Go with God, my precious one," she said softly to Leah, and then turned to her son to recite a familiar village proverb: *"Wie der Vater, so die Buben; wie der Acker, so die Rüben* (As is the father, so will be the sons; as the land is tilled, so the harvest comes). You always make us so proud, Martin. Be sure to keep our flowers and seeds safe."

With another group of immigrants entering the pavilion, one of the officials led Peter and Maria to the infirmary while Conrad gathered the children and walked with Marillis toward an open stall ahead where a gruff agent asked for their passports. Martin took a fabric bag that Leah struggled to lift, and also retrieved the small blue chest. The children kept their eyes on their mother and father until they disappeared into the noisy crowd across the hall. By noon all four had cleared immigration and clumsily carried their belongings several blocks north in the bustling city where street vendors barked names and prices of apples, plums, and cherries displayed next to crates of potatoes, carrots, beets, and other strange vegetables, and eggs piled in baskets. Further on they encountered a row of meat sellers with large cuts of pork, sides of bacon, and ribs as well as wide wooden tables with twisted *gehinks* of smoked sausages, freshly butchered chickens, ducks, and rabbits, and smelly fish covered with flies. Fedda Conrad paused at a tub of red pork sausage that looked almost identical to the familiar *wurst* he and his brother made every winter, while Marillis looked longingly at a pile of bread loaves and other baked goods in the open window of an adjacent storefront.

"It would take all day just to decide what to eat!" Conrad shouted. "Our lodging is only a block or two more so let's first get settled and then we can tend to mealtime."

The weary sojourners continued on to the address provided at customs and found an imposing four-story brick building teeming with men, women, and children wearing all manner of dress and talking and yelling in incomprehensible sounds.

"Perhaps we've arrived at the Tower of Babel instead of New York," Conrad joked as he led them inside to register and trudge up a dark stairway to the small room where they would spend their first days in America.

July 18, 1882

Dear Anna,

I greet you in the name of our Lord but write with a heavy heart. We have been staying here in New York America where Mama died soon after we arrived. It is very sad for Papa and all of us. She was not well since the long voy-

Arriving in the bustling city of New York.

age. We came on July 8 to the Castle Garden harbor and she waited there with Papa for three days so she could improve enough to join us. We then traveled together to this place not from New York called Pine Island where there are other people like us. But Mama's fever returned and Papa has decided that we should stay here for now. Fedda Conrad and Vess Marillis have gone ahead by the railroad to Washington by the Pacific Ocean to join our relatives there.

Papa and Leah and I live in a house with two other families from Oberfeld. Papa earns some money by working in the onion fields. He leaves on Sunday after we meet a house for services and we do not see him again for several days. There is no pastor here but one from the English church came when we buried Mama, and Papa has been heart-broken ever since.

We must have hope in this new land which has so many strange things. I miss our beautiful rolling hills, but the soil here is dark and wet and the people are friendly. I am so glad Herr Schneider taught me some English and the older people rely on me to help them understand

things. Here is a poem from Herr Schneider's book that tells about the
far west of America where I still hope that we live—
> *Dark hollows seem to glide along and chase*
> *The sunny ridges. Breezes of the West!*
> *Who toss the golden and the flame-like flowers,*
> *And pass the prairie-hawk that, poised on high,*
> *Flaps his broad wings, yet moves not,—ye have played*
> *Among the vines and limpid brooks*
> *That from the fountains of Sonora glide*
> *Into the calm Pacific.**

Anna, we live so far apart now but I always think of our walks along
the stream and in my dreams I hear the water flowing. Perhaps we will
meet again here someday. Please write and tell me what is happening
with our friends. We heard that the family of *Moslanga Yerich* (Sunflower George) may be coming to America here soon. If that is true and he
is still there, Papa asks that you tell him to bring a screwdriver and sickle
for him if there is room since tools here are expensive.

Sent with a kiss of love,

Martin

• • •

The widower Peter Wagner remained with his children in Pine Island,
New York, for three years. Weather-permitting he worked each week
in the vegetable fields surrounding the tiny community in southeastern
New York State that supplied onions, potatoes, carrots, and other vegetables to the produce markets and restaurants of the city. Martin and
Leah attended the local school where both acquired fluency in English
more quickly than their clannish Volga German elders. Martin especially wanted to continue westward to the family's original destination
in the Pacific Northwest where Fedda Conrad and Vess Marillis had
gone on to join Uncle Martin in the rolling hills of land they called the
Palouse. Martin sensed that his father also did not feel at home helping
raise vegetables for others in the flat wet soils, but the unspoken presence of his mother seemed to tie Peter to the place.

"It's a lovely land here and the people are good," Peter once told
Martin, "but too wet for my liking or for growing rye and wheat."

By the third year of their residence there, Martin had grown as tall
as his father, and the once reserved Leah had blossomed into a beautiful
girl of ten who seemed to have more friends at school than anyone else.

*William Cullen Bryant, "The Prairies," *Poems of Places—America* (1879)

The two often joined their father on his weekly pilgrimage after church on Sunday to Pine Island's little cemetery on the edge of town where copses of oak and hackberry signaled the entrance to his wife's final resting place. Although they could not afford a proper stone memorial, a small wooden cross surrounded by blue and orange iris marked her grave's location. They spoke little on the way back to the small house where they rented two basement rooms. Peter was a respected worker who earned enough to afford better lodging, but continued to save his money for reasons even he could not fully articulate except for the desire to have land of his own someday.

The threesome's simple living arrangements were made more pleasant by the fellowship of an elderly couple upstairs, Henry and Anna Wiegand, and their spirited daughter Katrillsie. She laughed easily, sang, and played the pump organ for church. Peter and the children appreciated her uplifting presence, and she often invited the Wagners to join them upstairs for delicious meals of pork and sauerkraut, and the watermelon and flavorful *Klees* dumplings that reminded them of family fare back home in Russia. Peter was especially fond of Katrillsie's thin *Suesspleena* egg-batter pancakes filled with berries and sour cream, and soon Leah had learned the art of frying them to golden perfection.

On many evenings the entire household would listen to the familiar hymns Katrillsie would softly sing in German as she played on an upright piano. The music wafted downstairs through an open heat register with bass notes that sometimes vibrated the exposed ceiling rafters. Martin especially enjoyed hearing tunes like *Vor dreihunerttausend Jahr* (Three Hundred Thousand Years Ago) that wove their faith with mystical happenings shrouded in the distant past:

Vor dreihunderttaausend Jahr,
Wie de Welt es noch im alten war,
Ei, da stand eine Kaisrin auf,
Wollte suchen das Kruz Christi auf,
Wo es liegt in der Erd.

Three hundred thousand years ago,
When the world was still old so,
And empress did exist,
Who wanted to find the true cross of Christ,
Where it lay buried in the earth.

On Martin's thirteenth birthday in late August 1885, the Wagners and Wiegands assembled around the family's broad oak table in the upstairs kitchen to enjoy a layered *Suesspleena* cake of the plate-sized delicacies slathered inside with honey and jam made from the finest Pine Island strawberries. Mrs. Wiegand poured steaming tea for everyone from the stately brass samovar they had brought from Russia. Martin grinned and began to heartily thank his hosts for the celebratory presentation of such a festive dessert—"too beautiful to cut!"—but was interrupted by Katrillsie who said that Leah had done most of the work. Peter then stood up with a small glass of cherry schnapps in his hand.

"Martin," he began happily, "how you have made us all so proud by your hard work in the fields and studies at school. You may still be too young to drink the glass I raise—though you may take a taste!" Everyone laughed and then Peter grew wistful. "I give you a special gift, my splendid son, as I know you have longed that we join our family in faraway Columbia Land." Peter then looked across the table toward the Wiegands. "I have spoken to Henry and Anna about the matter, and to their daughter. Katrillsie and I are soon to be married, so you and Leah shall soon again have a mother, and then the four of us shall move on to the land of rivers and hills of grain."

Martin was so startled by his father's announcement that he could hardly speak. Of course the news was welcomed, but signaled so much change that he could scarcely take it all in.

"Papa, I think it's wonderful!" exclaimed Leah to break the awkward silence.

"Yes, it is wonderful," Martin firmly followed, and stepped to hug his father and the bride-to-be who had joined him. "And now," the young man continued, "I think I will have that taste!"

The group eventually retired to the front room and Katrillsie took her place at the piano as the others stood behind her.

"Surely you will recognize this song," she said loudly while playing an introduction from *O Susanna!* "I know the Americans have their own version, but I like ours better," she laughed, and together they all began to loudly sing:

O Susanna! Wunderschöne Anna!
Ist das Leben noch so schön.
O Susanna! Wunderschöne Anna!
Is das Leben noch so schön.

O Susanna! Beautiful Anna!
Life is still so wonderful.
O Susanna! Beautiful Anna!
Life is still so wonderful.

Martin and Leah eagerly joined in preparations for their coming travel adventure to the Far West. Both felt some disappointment that they would not begin the school term with the many friends they had made in Pine Island. But their father's rediscovered happiness brought new life into a household that had long been melancholy. In early September Peter and Katrillsie became the first couple to be married in the white church recently build by the community's Volga Germans. With preparations under way in the Wiegand household for the Wagners' imminent departure, the children stayed for several days with Pastor Rehn and his wife in the parsonage adjacent to the church where Martin had been confirmed the year following their arrival. Pastor Rehn read them an article that appeared in a summer issue of the denominational journal about the Northwest's Columbia District circuit-riding ministry. It favorably mentioned places like Walla Walla and Plainville that Fedda Martin Bauer had mentioned in his letters from Washington Territory, and told of available land for prospective settlers and abundant harvests of grains and fruits.

On their last Sunday in Pine Island, the Wagners and Wiegands attended church and dined at the parsonage with Pastor Rehn and his wife. After the sumptuous meal, Peter left with Martin and Leah for a last visit to their mother's grave. The Volga iris were no longer in blooms, but the children were pleased when their father said he would remove some of the bulbs to transplant at their new home. The next day, Peter made one more trip to the onion fields to bid farewell to several area landowners who had given him work since coming to the area, and to earn some additional cash by finishing some promised projects. He told his family that all was in order for their Thursday departure from the main train station in New York, and trudged off with a shovel over his shoulder to return the following evening.

By midweek the Weigand's porch was piled with several of the same trunks both families had brought across the ocean. Their mother's precious blue chest was securely locked, and Peter nailed shut a wooden box he had especially built to hold the well-wrapped samovar that the Wiegands had given to couple as a wedding present.

"How can we ever thank you?" Peter said to his elderly in-laws as he and Martin finished loading the wagon that would take them to New York's Grand Central Station. "Your precious daughter, the samovar, and such care that has sustained us."

"Was mei und dei is, is aach unser (Whatever is mine and yours is also ours)," Henry said struggling to smile. The families embraced each other one last time, and the Wagners boarded the wagon for the drive northward in the late summer's morning warmth.

"Don't get so good with your English, Martin, that you can't write to us in German!" Anna Wiegand cried out as they left. The young man turned with a teary nod, and waved.

The family reached the train station by noon in plenty of time for their late afternoon departure. The chaos reminded Martin of their arrival in the city three years earlier, but this time he did not feel the unease surrounding those events. He had never given up hope of reaching their original destination beyond the grand Rocky Mountains, and now the long awaited dream was coming true. In dress and language and outlook he was now an American, and now joined his father in hopes of finding land where he could work hard to make a home of his own.

Martin and his sweetheart Anna back in Oberfeld had continued writing, and in her last letter she mentioned some possibility that her family would also come to the United States. Martin's heart soared at the prospect and in the ten days of train travel that followed across the grand American countryside, he alternated rereading from her letters and the precious green book of poems he had safeguarded since the day the two had parted. Katrillsie had prepared them well for the journey. They ate well from their food bundles and occasionally bought fresh fruit and bread at station stops along the way to St. Paul, Minnesota, where they transferred to the Northern Pacific line that would take them all the way to Palouse Junction in eastern Washington Territory and the last leg to tiny Plainville.

The wagons especially jerked and rocked while crossing the Rocky Mountains through Montana, and for the first time all four wore the heavy coats they had been using as cushions on the hard board seats. Though some other passengers seemed affected by changes in altitude and temperature, the Wagners stayed healthy. Martin's tall frame did not conform well to the benches so he frequently strolled up and down the center aisle to remove the stiffness in his joints and visit with the few other youngsters his age.

As they descended the forested western slopes a fertile landscape of greens and golds appeared with broad fields along rivers and streams. Cattle grazed in grassy meadows and men with horse-drawn binders were still harvesting bountiful crops of wheat, barley, and oats. Some waved to the passing train that periodically sounded a piercing wail and left a smoke-filled trail in the still September air.

"Are we now in Columbia Land?" Martin asked the courteous conductor as they approached the bustling city of Spokane.

"I guess you could put it that way, young man," he replied; "since all the streams hereabouts flow into that great river. We'll cross it just below Palouse Junction about where you'll be transferring as I recall."

Martin thanked him for the geography lesson and then turned to the family.

"I've been waiting a long time to read something to you," he said. "One of the poems in the book Herr Schneider gave me so long ago now I've read over and over again because it's titled 'The River Columbia.' Now that we're finally here I thought you might like to hear some lines from it."

"Of course we want to hear it," Katrillsie replied, and so Martin recited verse by William Gibson from memory:

Look; use that one sense only; not to listen
Have you in the sweet calm. Superbly flowing
By pines and banks of basaltic forms,
Lo! the smoke-purple river like amethyst;
While the sun rises a discoloring mist in
With luster like full-grown iris in colorful bloom.

"Martin," Katrillsie smiled, "you are such a blessing to us."

• • •

September 24, 1885

Dear Anna

I write to you by God's grace from our new home near a place called Plainville in Washington Territory, America. It is a beautiful land of hills and streams and reminds us all very much of our Volga homeland.

We live north of town along a river that is lined with reeds called cat-tails for their fuzzy heads. This time of year they blow wonderful puffs like cotton throughout the air—you should see Leah chase them!

Papa has married Katrillsie Wiegand as her Heinrich died last year. So we have a new mother now and she has been very good to us. We all wish for a better life in this faraway Northwest and hope it will be our real home. The long journey took us still farther away from you, but maybe now that we are here in such a good place your family will think to come.

Here we have about 70 hectares (160 acres) of fine land both flat and hilly along a great canyon. Most all is in heavy grass as high as a horse's belly but Papa and I have already been clearing a wide area with sickle and scythe. He will soon begin to plow with equipment from our neighbor who is Gigal (Rooster) Adam. We also have one horse and two cows. Papa says there is still time to seed some of the winter wheat, and in the spring we will plant our homeland garten of tomatoes, rhu-barb, and blackberries with what we have saved all this time.

At home in Columbia Land.

You must not be fright-ened, Anna, when I tell you that our home for now is in the earth! Yes, it is true and like the *zemlyankii* (earth homes) the old ones told about when they first lived in Russia. We have two rooms dug into the hill and Papa has lined the walls and ceil-ing with boards for now but all will be better in the spring when we will build a prop-er wooden house. We have a stove in the middle where Katrillsie cooks our meals and also keeps us warm. Leah is afraid of the big spi-ders that sometimes visit but Papa says they just know a good thing.

There is a German pastor named Becker who visits the families all around. Because there are many of our people living here, he would like to lead services by our home so the men are also now building a small place where we can gather. I think you would like it here, Anna, so if your family decides to come to America it would be wonderful if you could join our colony. There is work for the railroad and good place to farm. Papa says that if all goes well that he will soon help me get my own place. Perhaps we could have a life together in this new land.

Sent with a kiss of love,

Martin

ᴄᴏ Afterword ᴗᴗ

Among the first Russian-German families who immigrated to the Pacific Northwest were Phillip and Anna (Rothe) Green, natives of Rosenfeld, Russia, who journeyed to Oregon in 1881 before relocating to Washington Territory in the fall of 1882. A century later, a cache of fourteen letters from the 1870s and '80s that were written to them from family members in Russia and the Midwest was found in the bottom of an oak file cabinet that had belonged the Greens' youngest daughter. The distinctive style of the letters and information they contained guided creation of this story's selections. The letters offer rare insight into daily life and conditions of travel and settlement experienced by the immigrant pioneers prior to completion of the Northern Pacific Railroad in the 1880s.

In those years a vanguard of Russian-German pioneers had established settlements in the frontier towns of Portland and Walla Walla, and in the rural Endicott-Colfax, Ritzville-Odessa, and Bickleton districts where they planted their grains, raised cattle and horses, and gathered fruit and berries. Here the immigrant parents would remind their children that they had indeed been led to "a land of milk of honey," a story related to me by Conrad "C. G." Schmick of Colfax who lived for some weeks at the Palouse Colony near Endicott after arriving in the region. Like Martin and Leah of this story, my paternal grandmother, Mary (Litzenberger) Scheuerman, arrived from Russia as a child with her parents in New York but lost her mother shortly after setting foot in the new land. Grandma grieved for the rest of her life because the kindly young woman was apparently placed in an anonymous Pine Island grave. Jim Repp of Colfax shared additional details about Volga German immigrant experiences to the Northwest—where his father had immigrated by himself as a boy after becoming separated from his family.

I learned about the pioneers' earth homes from the Greens' granddaughter, my Aunt Una Mae Scheuerman, and from Connie Lust Taylor and Kathey Benner Birdsell at a festive gathering in 2017 to commemorate the 250th anniversary of Catherine the Great's historic Manifesto of the Empress inviting colonists to settle in Russia. In many places in the Northwest, the immigrant families lived temporarily in earth-homes dug into the hillsides and reminiscent of the fabled *zemlyanki* their ancestors first inhabited when they arrived in Russia in the eighteenth century. These primitive abodes, like the one fashioned by Martin's family in this story, were often substantial, wood-framed two-room dwellings. Some were eventually reinforced with concrete to serve as expansive cellars and storage rooms usually connected to the main house by a covered porch. Remnants of these historic structures can still be seen at homestead sites throughout the Columbia Plateau.

The locked blue chest that Martin's father safeguarded did come west with one of these pathfinder families and in later years was kept in a closet of the family's country home. His strict instructions were that it never be opened and that it be buried with him. When he died many years later, the chest was found to contain the carefully wrapped bones of his beloved first wife who had died soon after reaching the United States. In accordance with his wishes, the couple was interred together and their remains rest today among lilacs and irises in a rural Palouse Country cemetery.

Aurora's Ghosts

Swing out into the night
Beneath the glowing Northern Light.
Swing low stars above
And touch the eyes of my baby love
That he may see as he wanders far
Into the land of amber stars,
Mountains of ice and valleys of snow
Where beautiful flowers and grasses grow.
Swing out over the snow, spirit of my baby…Joe.
—Thomas B. Holmes, "Northern Lights Lullaby"
  Pullman (WA) Herald, January 17, 1891

Joseph had seen the magnificent creature several times that fall brows-
ing among the scattered stands of pine and hawthorn that grew along
the meandering river. The buck grandly displayed no less than four
points on both sides of its rack, but getting close enough to tell for
sure had eluded the boy all year. The shot he had just fired as the buck
walked cautiously on the other side of the river bank had surely found
its mark. Joseph's heart pumped with the excitement of the hunt and
the thought that his substantial family could finally feast on something
more than their customary fare of potato soup and boiled wheat.

The root cellars of the tiny immigrant hamlet were well provisioned
with garden produce for the long winter, but in the first six weeks of
the new year, no meat had appeared on the Bolander family's table.
Immediately after the volley echoed through the canyon, Joseph caught
a glimpse of the deer darting into a thicket of wild rose brambles and
he sped across the shallow Palouse River to locate the animal.

No sooner had his boots touched the water than Joseph felt his legs
freezing into the ice that suddenly formed around him. He dropped the
rifle and struggled to lift himself beyond the chilling grip as the fluid
outline of an expressionless face formed beneath him and softly called,
"Joseph…, Joseph." The reassuring voice of Peter Bolander abruptly
wakened his oldest son from the reoccurring dream, and the boy smiled

195

with relief at the calm appearance of his father. "Joseph, looks like you just fought the Battle of Borodino and captured every Frenchman within these walls," he reported with the authority of a Cossack soldier. "Now arise and fill the woodbox for your mother with as much enthusiasm."

"You should have tended to that as soon as you returned from school yesterday, Phillip Joseph," called his mother from the adjacent kitchen of the family's three-room house. Catherine Bolander often invoked his given and middle names when expressing regard or displeasure. Her tone definitely indicated the latter.

Peter Bolander turned his head out the door and replied, "Give the lad a few minutes, Mama. Maybe he sailed back across the sea to the Old Country last night."

"No, Papa," Joseph shared, "I got trapped down around the bend of the river chasing that buck again."

"Ah, out hunting again all night," Peter laughed. "Well, time to get going around here instead. Your two youngest brothers have been up for an hour so I'll appoint them your kindling duty this morning. Your mother's right that you've slept in again so we can be grateful that today is Sat-ur-day." Peter pronounced the word deliberately in English as he was among the most conscientious in the Palouse River settlement of Germans from Russia striving to master the new tongue. Most of the dozen others in the area who were Peter's age still conversed in the *schveza* of rural Hesse, a Low German remnant that would hardly be taken for proper speech on the streets of Berlin or even Frankfurt.

The Bolanders' ancestors had emigrated eastward from Hessen over a century earlier at the invitation of Tsarina Catherine the Great in order to colonize Russia's frontier Volga borderlands. After two decades of brutal adjustment to the new conditions in that remote region during the lifetime of Peter's great-grandfather, the colonists had slowly prospered. But they did not mix well with the native Russians, and in the 1870s Tsar Alexander III revoked a series of economic and social privileges so they might better assimilate into the broader Slavic culture that still held them in suspicion as foreigners. Rather than face compulsory schooling in the Russian language and five years of miserable service in the Russian Army, Peter and his two brothers, "Dobb" Conrad and Hannas (Johann), decided to immigrate with their families to America.

Agents representing Midwestern railroads distributed throughout Europe literature about settlement opportunities and the Bolanders were among many who relocated from Eastern Europe to the Midwest in the 1870s. Peter's brother-in-law and his wife, Henry and Paulina Walters, had also joined the vanguard as did Anna's widowed mother whom everyone called Ellevess [the "Old Aunt"]. After enduring six years of drought and cyclones on the Kansas prairies, the Bolanders, Walters, and several other families crossed the plains to Washington Territory in 1881. Here they established a small colony in a protected bend of the Palouse River nestled among the rolling Palouse Hills of southeastern Washington Territory. Now, after a decade in their new home, the immigrants hoped that they, too, would find the security and prosperity earned by their colonist ancestors during Catherine's era. But in February 1892, the prospect was by no means certain.

The evening of his dreamland foray into the icy terror of the river, Joseph's parents gathered with their neighbors after dinner directly across the starlit lane at the home of Dobb Conrad and his wife, Marillis. They did this most every Saturday afternoon during the winter months for weekend fellowship and exchanging news anyone might have received from the Old Country. Just two light snowfalls had blanketed the Palouse Hills that winter. Glistening white crescents appeared on the north sides of the rolling summer fallow and stubble fields seen in every direction from the high basaltic bluffs overlooking the riverside colony.

Dobb Conrad was the eldest of the Bolander men and the only one to have a two-story house. With two upstairs bedrooms and an extra sitting room on the main floor, Dobb Conrad and Marillis's was the customary place for weekend get-togethers. As the men smoked their pipes in the front room and discussed prospects for the fall crop, their wives sat around the table in Marillis's substantial kitchen where the wood stove provided the house's only warmth. Older daughters tended the infants and toddlers upstairs while the other children remained at their own homes under the supervision of siblings like sixteen-year-old Joseph.

"Ya, we left the land of Kaiserina Catherine the Great to come here to the land of President Harrison the Not-So-Great," complained Catherine Bolander. "Did my Peter come here to escape the Russian army so our dear Joseph would go fight in South America?"

"Mama, he's not sending any soldiers to South America," Peter said reassuringly as he looked toward the women while standing in the doorway. "He's keeping the peace and making markets abroad for American produce. That can only help us farmers with the price of wheat."

"And who invited you into the women's council, Herr Bolander?" joked Paulina Walters. "Don't you know after feeding and clothing you men and the children who inhabit your river kingdom of hills and Indians all week long that the women have a right to *prootz* about something?"

"The only weapon our Indian visitors have raised against us is the salmon they trade for Ellevess's apples," Peter laughed. "I just caught a chill and felt all the heat coming from out here."

"*Ah, drham is drham, hinnerem owe is nochmoul drham!* (Ah, home is home, and behind the stove is home even more!)," Ellevess reminded everyone.

"*Jedes heische hot sei weishe* (Every household has its ways), Ellevess," answered Peter; "and we wouldn't even have the woodbox filled at our place if it weren't for Catherine and the children."

"There you are right," observed Ellevess putting down her steaming cup of barley tea. Real tea and coffee were seasonal luxuries, so the women needed to improvise by roasting kernels of grain. "It is a marvel your wives can smile," she continued, "and give your men a warm home and food on your table after so many years of wilderness wanderings."

"And who invited you into the women's council?"

Catherine stirred to say something in defense of her husband, but cleared her throat and rose to fetch more hot water from the ribbed pewter kettle on the stove. As she passed Peter, Catherine raised her eyebrows and looked kindly at him as if to voice her concern about Ellevess's remarks that had turned harmless banter into a reprimand. Peter shook his head ever so slightly. Experience had proven to both the men and womenfolk that it was not wise to second guess words uttered seriously by Ellevess. She was old enough to be the mother of any adult in the group, and no one could question her wisdom or skills as a healer when someone fell ill. But she passed oddly between states of mind—one moment happily singing to herself some ancient Hessen melody passed down the generations, and the next instant interrupting casual merriment by intoning biblical reference.

Catherine had always kept a polite distance from the old woman. She had once ventured to ask her good friend, Anna, about her mother-in-law's strange doings and stories that Ellevess dabbled in spellcasting. "She knows and sees things others do not," Anna had confided with a note of indignation. "Some people are jealous of that and spread rumors, but that's not the way it is with her. You know how she brought the Felker girl back from death's door when were in Kansas, and our men still depend on her for knowing when to plant and such."

Catherine felt badly that her inquiry had offended Anna, but mention of Ellevess's ability to know seeding times contributed to her unease—especially since her husband, Peter, had never mentioned taking such counsel. But Catherine resolved to keep her concerns to herself though she preferred to be with her children anytime they visited the Walters household where Ellevess resided.

Just as Dobb Conrad returned to the subject of the season's favorable rise in grain prices, young Joseph and his sister, Anna, burst through the door into the crowded kitchen. "You'd, you'd better come out here and see what is happening!" the girl exclaimed with a look of alarm.

"What's going on?" demanded Paulina Walters, "Has there been an accident?"

"No," Joseph explained excitedly, "we heard the dogs barking and went out to look around. Anna thought maybe the cougar was back for the sheep so...." Her sister had already disappeared back outside and the men rushed past the boy as the women gathered up their things. "Just look up at the sky," said Anna softly. Ellevess then followed and stood next to the men.

The northern sky was fearfully bright beyond the horizon with fiery curtains of red, yellow, and green that seemed to pulse to some unheard, unearthly music. As one sheet would ripple across and almost

"This is the North Light."

disappear, another would spill forth and take its place. Stars shone brightly above them but all eyes were drawn to the shimmering display in the distance above the scattered-pine shadows of the canyon horizon. The spectators stood momentarily mute until Henry Walters gasped, "Great heavens, is the sky on fire?"

Dobb Conrad wondered aloud, "*Ei du*! What can this be?! Are the skies announcing the coming of our Lord?" Marillis let out a shriek which frightened several of the children who had come outside to cluster around their parents in the frigid February air. Dobb Conrad stepped over to his wife's side and held her tight. "If the Lord has tarried long enough," he said flatly, "then may our households be ready."

Peter Bolander's steady voice then rose above the sobs and whispers. "Tomorrow is the Sabbath," he reminded everyone, "and it is our turn to host Pastor Rehn. We'll gather again at eleven o'clock at your place," he said to Dobb Conrad, "so let's wait and see what Pastor says about all this." For the three years Pastor August Rehn had ministered to his pious flocks in a scattered circuit that also included the rural communities of Endicott, Colfax, and Ritzville. Tomorrow would be his appointed day for the Palouse Colony families near Endicott.

"Father, do we need to feed the animals tonight?" asked Joseph's younger brother, Samuel. "Or can we wait to see what happens in the morning?"

"I'll feed all them tonight, Samuel," Conrad replied. "You go with your parents and the others to your homes now." The confident tone of the children's uncle was reassuring and the families began to disperse.

Soon only Peter and Ellevess remained by the frozen lane pondering the celestial marvel. "What do you think it is?" quietly asked Peter. Ellevess, clad in the brown woolen *halstook* (headscarf) she always wore outside, silently peered above. "Did we come so far these past years," he wondered aloud, "only to now see the end of the world?"

"They are beautiful," Ellevess marveled as if beholding an Old Master's work of art. "Their silence is a wonder," she whispered. Peter felt some relief that the old woman seemed almost calm. She continued, "*Da ist das Nordlicht* (This is the North Light); it comes from power beyond us. The old ones said Aurora's Ghosts travel across *die Regaboga Bryka* (Rainbow Bridge) when its colors blaze in the night sky. They come from the other world to fetch souls." The amber amulet around her neck seemed to pulse beneath the midnight radiance. "When they ride across," Ellevess whispered, "the sky turns to fire."

"I would rather hope they are angels beckoning the Lord's return," Peter offered.

"It is certainly in God's power to bring forth the Second Coming, Peter," said Ellevess. "But remember the Ezekiel's 'fearsome cloud from the north glowing brightly.' The North Light appeared long before even the First Coming. Let us rejoice tomorrow in the promise of His return, but may we also be vigilant for the safety of the innocent in the meantime."

Given the peculiar circumstances of their visit and hint of danger, Peter ventured a personal question he had long pondered but thought too peculiar to previously ask. "Ellevess," he started before seeking a way to politely rephrase his inquiry. "Ellevess, they say you know things because of what happened when you were born." It wasn't so much a question as a statement, and he hoped she would offer some clarification, but Ellevess remained quiet. Peter continued, "I remember Pastor Tellemann telling us back home that reading the stars and such was so much superstition—'*Der Awerglaawe is lauter Duwacksraach*' (Superstition is nothing but tobacco smoke)."

"Ah, yes, Pastor Tellemann," recalled Ellevess; "I sometimes think of him, a kind and wise man. And did he tell you what he would do whenever he had a bad earache?"

"I suppose he went to the doctor," Peter answered.

"No," Ellevess said with a wry smile as she turned to face Peter. "He came to our house so father could blow tobacco smoke into his ear!" Peter laughed nervously and they both gazed again at the fantastic colors that began to fade from view. "Yes, my father was *Braucher*," Ellevess continued, "a healer and knower of the old ways handed down generation by generation from the old days. Some folks spoke against him, but most respected what he knew. Many benefited from his doings which he offered freely to restore life, livestock, crops, whatever. Truth is truth everywhere, Peter, and so it is with *die Brauche*. Papa would tell me, '*Rede wenig, hoere viel*' (Speak little, learn much), and so I tried to do. If some find fault with that, so be it."

Ellevess's voice had turned quieter, and somehow the ground beneath Peter's feet did not feel as cold as it had a few minutes earlier. "I'm probably going numb," he thought and considered walking back across the lane into his house. "No one should be faulted for helping others," Peter offered, "and you've helped us more than most know, Ellevess. Here, let me walk you down to your place."

"Our number is seven," she continued while walking down the lane as if stating the obvious; "and no good can come apart from naming the Father, Son, and Holy Ghost. What is used to bring a remedy varies depending on the need. No two are alike, and I'm not sure many among us who have come to America know of such things. This is the New World, a new day, and a new sky. Most think it is better to bury the old. You have always been kind to me, Peter, but I know others around you—how shall I say," Ellevess smiled, "prefer some distance."

"She's just concerned about the children," Peter said as he looked to the dimly lit windows in his house across the way where he could see Catherine's silhouette through the lace curtains moving about in the kitchen.

"And she is right to do so; you are a lucky man," Ellevess reminded him. "She has you like I had John's father. Our blessings do not depend on where we live. *In Gottes Sagen ist Alles gelegen* (Upon God's grace everything depends). *So is' es* (That's the way it is). And your Phillip Joseph—a bright boy so kind and handsome. He always asks what he can bring me from town."

"If he would but keep the kitchen in kindling," Peter sighed.

"Like most any boy, but his is a special life," Ellevess observed. "May God preserve him and all your household. Perhaps the boy's mind is elsewhere around the family, Peter, but I have seen his work alongside you in the field, and how he cares for the younger ones."

"Yes, if the Lord tarries—and tomorrow may tell, I have thought he might be a pastor, or a teacher to follow Miss Fournier at a school," Peter said.

"Well, whatever our tomorrows," Ellevess answered, "*Wie der Vater, so die Buben; wie der Acker, so die Rueben* (As the father is, so the sons will be; as the field is tilled, so the harvest will be)."

Peter smiled at his people's familiar proverb, but hoped his son's life would be more stable than his had been. Unlike some of the others, he had no regrets over leaving their old homeland for America. But after the evening's peculiar spectacle he was feeling uneasy.

Ellevess interrupted his thinking. "Go see to your anxious ones, Petya," she said. "We've come across the high seas so I can make it past the barn." The two then parted and Peter crunched the few snowy steps to his house. He turned around at the door to see the huddled form of Ellevess, clad in a brown woolen shawl, carefully make her way down the frozen path and disappear into the Walters home.

• • •

A sudden jolt on Joseph's shoulder awakened the boy from deep slumber. He squinted in the bright sunshine beaming through the upstairs bedroom window and heard excitement in his younger brother's voice. "Joseph, Joseph!" Samuel shouted, "We're still here! Mama said we might wake up in heaven this morning, but we're still here."

"Yes, Samuel, I understand," Joseph said wearily while turning his tousled head toward the wall.

"You said to wake you when I got up," Samuel continued, "so you could help Mama and Papa before services."

"Yea," Joseph mumbled; "thanks Samuel, I'll be right down." Joseph had resolved after the previous day's kitchen incident that he would be more mindful of household chores. Catherine Bolander happily greeted her eldest son before he dashed outside to fetch kindling. Joseph then joined his brothers and Anna at the breakfast table. They enjoyed a full breakfast of bacon, milk, and boiled wheat kasha that Catherine made more flavorful for the children by adding a spoonful of honey to each bowl. Eleven-year-old Martin said he had hoped the world would have ended the night to avoid any more of Miss Fourner's arithmetic lessons.

"No jokes about such matters," Catherine scolded.

"I wanted to meet Grandpa and Grandma Bolander," added Anna. Peter's parents had remained in the Old Country, but he had often told of his father's exploits in the tsar's army where Peter Sr. had served in a cavalry unit during the ill-fated Crimean War. Anna repeated her thoughts moments later when his father came in from outside and blew warmth into his red hands.

"So the Lord tarries, *Schodzee* (sweetheart)," Peter explained. "As is written in Scripture, children, 'May we walk in newness of life,' knowing we shall yet gather in the bye and bye with all our loved ones. The colored North Light seldom appears," he added, "so be thankful the spectacle came and passed without any harm to us." Peter considered saying something about the ghosts who crossed Rainbow Bridge but declined making any Sunday reference to Ellevess's musings, especially in Catherine's presence.

A half-hour later the barking of the colony's two mixed-blood shepherds announced Pastor Rehn's mid-morning arrival on horseback shortly before the service typically began. The kindly black-clad minister with close-cropped beard stopped in front of the elder Bolanders' home where Dobb Conrad emerged to greet him and shoo away the yelping dogs that wagged their tails in recognition of the circuit-rider. The two men briefly visited before entering Marillis's spacious kitchen where a slice of warm buttered rye bread and steaming cup of black coffee awaited their special guest. Conversation soon turned to the Northern Lights, and Pastor Rehn reported that he had witnessed the phenomenon with many residents of Plainville where he had spent the night. He then thanked Marillis, arose from the Bolanders' table, and drew a starched white collar from an inside coat pocket to secure around his neck.

Other families from the rural neighborhood arrived a few minutes later and everyone huddled together in the living room. Most crowded close on chairs or stools while Samuel and Martin claimed a small wooden bench brought from the porch. Peter noticed that Henry and Paulina arrived without Ellevess. Paulina mentioned that her mother was unwell after a strangely restless night. Pastor Rehn informally greeted the small assembly and then intoned the sonorous High German of the liturgy so esteemed and familiar to the immigrants. He led them in song and voices of young and old blended in two plaintive tunes from their tattered *Volgagesanbuchen* expressing God's abiding grace.

An Advent sermon followed in which the clergyman reminded his listeners of Mary and Joseph's special care for the baby Jesus in the weeks after his birth. He noted celestial events like Bethlehem's shining star often indicated God's hand in human affairs. Pastor Rehn also mentioned the Old Testament Prophet Ezekiel, and read from chapter one, verse four: "I looked and saw a fearsome cloud from the north glowing brightly all around me with the color of gleaming amber...."

Peter remembered Ellevess's words from the night before and listened intently to the minister's commentary on the forces of good and evil in this present world. He remembered the trials of family separation in the Old Country, how others with whom they set out for America perished at sea, and that Dobb Conrad and Marillis had lost their two children to scarlet fever that first year in the Midwest. Here Peter sat surrounded by all four of his children, and only this week his beloved Katya had told him she was again with child. Why was he so blessed when many others just like him had experienced such loss? How long would his family's good fortune last? He often wondered about such matters on the Sabbath.

When the service ended, Peter and the other adults thanked Pastor Rehn for his message and the men adjourned to the porch to share local news while smoking their pipes. Joseph, Anna, and their younger siblings and cousins enjoyed the sunshine and snow outside while the women readied the customary monthly feast of roast beef with boiled potatoes, carrots, and parsnips in honor of the pastor's presence.

The next morning Samuel again stirred his older brother from sleep. The boys dressed and joined the rest of the family downstairs at breakfast. "Since there's not a cloud on the horizon," Peter Bolander related, "Dobb and I hitched two teams so we can all finish hauling cordwood to the Reinkes and Lairds. We've overdue with some deliveries, but we'll spare the time to take you up the hill if need be."

"That would be far out of your way, Papa," Joseph answered.

"Yes, we'll have a race up the canyon this morning," Anna added. "The fun part will be sliding back down after school." Catherine was still uneasy over the weekend's peculiar events and Pastor Rehn's words. She protested the children's plan and warned of the road's hazardous grade and hairpin curve that descended a thousand feet from the top of the steep bluff of basalt columns interspersed with pine trees and bunchgrass.

"Mother's right," Peter ruled. "Henry or Dobb or me can wait with the team when school is over to bring you all back down." Moments later and all clad in wool coats and black felt boots, the four Bolander children joined the nine-year-old Walters twins—Adam and Sophie—on the trek from their riverside colony to the one-room Allen School. The white clapboard structure had been built the previous year for the two dozen school-age children in the vicinity. The isolated structure and adjacent teacherage stood as a pair of lonely sentinels atop a wind-swept hill one and a half miles south of the colony. Kittie Fourner was in her first year of teaching, but the diminutive schoolteacher had a well-deserved reputation for keeping order and imparting a love of learning to her diverse flock.

Miss Fourner warmly welcomed her pupils who sat attentively at wooden desks framed in black wrought iron which concealed almost everything but the heads of the smaller pupils like the Alice Helm and the twins. The Christmas tree cut by "Shuska" Bafus from a nearby stand of pines still stood in front of the room opposite the teacher's desk. Decorated by the students with white paper snowflakes and strings of red wooden beads, Miss Fourner thought it too lovely to take down before February. After leading the customary formalities of flag salute and opening prayer, she solicited any news from the weekend. Several hands waved to be answered before Sophie shouted out, "We saw the Northern Lights on Saturday night, Miss Fourner. They were beautiful," she giggled, "but I was scared for a while."

"No shame in that, Sophie," Miss Fourner responded. "I spent the weekend in Pullman and we saw them, too. Yes, they were *spectacular.*" As was often the case when encountering a term she thought might be new to the immigrant children, Miss Fourner pronounced it with special emphasis before parsing the meaning. "That word comes from Latin *spectare* which means 'to watch.' So who else 'watched' the *spectacle?*" Everyone's hands again rose with uncharacteristic whispering soon dispelled by Miss Fourner's firm but kind manner. Before she could move on to the day's multiplication lesson, Alice asked if the Northern Lights were really caused by the sun's rays like her uncle had suggested.

"Well, I'm no astronomer, Alice, but I don't think it's exactly the sun's regular rays or else we'd have the *aurora* year-round," Miss Fourner replied with a hint that more word lessons would follow. "A friend of mine at the college in Pullman," she continued, "said this happens when peculiar storms on the sun throw special particles far out in every direction. Some collects at the earth's poles as we *orbit* the sun and these fall down to create such special colors."

"You mean like sunbeam snowflakes?!" exclaimed Martin.

"Well, I suppose it is something like that, Martin," agreed Miss Fourner.

Samuel met that explanation with his mother's skepticism about other science lessons on cause and effect they had studied. "Mama says that just because the tsar sneezes in St. Petersburg," he repeated, "doesn't mean it will rain in Walla Walla."

"Mama is no scientist either," Joseph chided; "but Pastor Rehn says that what we saw can sometimes have other meanings."

"I don't know about that, Joseph, but let me show you all what I mean," offered Miss Fourner. With that she stepped to the middle of the class and knelt down while raising her right hand. "Pretend my raised index finger is the earth, and here comes the sun." With that she raised her left hand and made a fist around which her digital world slowly moved. The primitive orrery aptly demonstrated planetary motion.

"So where's the moon?" wondered Johnny Poffenroth.

"Now you're making it hard on me," laughed Miss Fourner, who then contorted her right little finger and slowly spun it part-way around with her entire arm continuing around the "sun."

Throughout the unexpected lesson, no one had noticed the sky's gradual darkening as the day's brilliant sunshine gave way to ominous clouds swiftly blowing in from the north. A blast of wind shook the building's rafters and Mrs. Fourner glanced outside to see snowflakes blowing sideways. She walked to the door and opened it to a great gust of cold. She immediately closed the door and announced that morning recess would be held inside.

As Miss Fourner watched the boys and girls separate into groups to play games and visit during lunch, she grew apprehensive over the worsening conditions outside and called for Joseph to come to her desk. "Your way back home with Anna and the children is a bit treacherous, Joseph," she said. "Do you think your father will be coming up for you with the weather turning like this?"

"He'd probably want to, Miss Fourner," Joseph replied, "but he and my uncles went upriver this morning to deliver wood. I'm not sure when they might get back."

"Well, my horse won't know the way down if it starts drifting like it soon will if this keeps up," she said apprehensively. "I'll take the others home down the road toward town. You better head out soon with your family and cousins so nobody gets stranded in this."

• • •

Everyone put on their coats, stocking caps, and boots and prepared to return home. The cold afternoon wind bit into their cheeks upon stepping outside, and Miss Fourner saw that almost three inches of fresh snow had already fallen on the handrail in just the past half-hour. Before leaving with the other children, she dashed into the teacherage and emerged moments later with a large ball of cordage. "Joseph, you better take this," she advised. "I've known blizzards where you can't see beyond a few feet so tie yourselves in a row if need be so none of the little ones get lost."

Miss Fourner then gave Anna a hug and nervous smile and returned to gather the other children who lived toward town. Joseph and Anna set out in the other direction with Samuel and Martin, and Sophie and Adam Walters. After a few steps, Anna offered to walk behind the young children and noticed that little Adam was shivering. "Where's your cap?" she asked as they continued in the footsteps of the others.

"It felt so nice this morning I guess I just took off without one," the boy explained.

Joseph overheard them and turned to place his gray woolen cap on the boy's head. "Here, you better take one of my gloves, too," he added.

"Joseph, you'll freeze!" shouted Anna.

"I'll put my collar up and be just fine," he replied. "We need to keep moving."

After ten minutes of trudging down the trail along the steep bluff, Joseph began to lose sight of the surrounding hills. He still felt the flat, frozen road beneath them, but great wisps of fine snow in the eerie silence threatened to disorient his bearings. Joseph paused to pull the cordage from inside his coat, took off his gloves, and tied a series of half-hitches. He then turned to place each child's hand inside the stiffened loops. "Here, Anna," he ordered, "you tie this around yourself and I'll hold on to the other end."

Anna noticed that her older brother's ears were rosy red, and took Sophie's scarf. "For my sake, Joseph, please take this," she implored, and he tied the small garment around his head as best he could. As their march continued, Anna asked if they shouldn't start turning soon.

"Just a few more steps and we'll start heading that way," he replied. "I think I can make out the big pine up ahead. Don't worry; I'm not going to walk us over the cliff." Sure enough, moments later the massive bull pine flanking the road emerged from the swirling whiteness. Here the road turned northeast to descend several hundred yards to the horseshoe curve and final stretch home. "Pa-pa! Pa-pa!" Joseph yelled at the top of his lungs before telling the others to be silent and listen. Nothing was heard but the swish of snow-laden winds. He hollered again but without result. "Most likely they're not back from Reinkes yet," he thought, and plodded farther into the white abyss. Through the lengthening day's diffused light, the sky seemed to merge with the earth. Joseph found it more and more difficult to perceive either distance or direction. He found himself periodically stumbling as he broke trail for the others and at one point Samuel veered to the left and sank to his waist. Were they going up or down? Joseph couldn't really tell.

Down in the colony Catherine Bolander arose again from her cup of tea on the Walters' table and stood near Paulina's polished brass samovar on the oak hutch. She looked out the window and said, "I can't even see our house from here. What if the children are trying to get home in this?"

"No good to fret," Paulina replied. "The men will surely be back anytime now."

Catherine continued gazing silently out the window. "Where *can* the men be?! They've been gone all morning, for heaven's sake," she blurted. "All they have to do is follow the river back down here, but parts of that trail up the hillside aren't much even in good weather. If anything happens to those *Kinder*...."

"Let's hope they'll be staying with Miss Fourner until the storm passes," interrupted Paulina.

"I don't have a good feeling about this," sobbed Catherine. "Do you think we should see Ellevess?"

"I'm not sure what to ask, Catherine," Paulina replied. "She's only come out of her room a couple times since yesterday and still isn't...." But before she could finish, Ellevess's door opened and the old woman walked slowly into the kitchen.

"Ellevess!" Catherine pleaded. "It's the children and a blizzard like back home. They might be caught out in this. You…you know things, Ellevess. What can we do?"

"Mama," Paulina interrupted. "Come and take some tea. You're not well."

"Tea won't make things better," Ellevess said soberly as she sat down at the table. Then she looked beyond both women and issued an order: "Bring me something made of wood belonging to each child." Catherine and Pauline looked blankly at each other only to hear Ellevess repeat the instructions with some urgency. "Something wooden from each child."

Without further consideration, Pauline went into the twins' bedroom while Catherine ran home to fetch objects that belonged to Anna and the boys. In minutes she returned to the table where she and Paulina spread out wooden spoons, toys, and one of Anna's barrettes. Ellevess then stood up, walked to the cupboard, and took out a clean, pressed Pyramid Flour sack. She carefully placed all the objects inside, returned to her room, and put the bag on the bed and knelt down to empty the contents on her heavy brown quilt.

Elevess knelt down by the bed.

Ellevess leaned to open a drawer in the small table near the headboard and took out a crumpled piece of linen. One by one, she thoroughly rubbed each item with the cloth and returned it to the sack. Ellevess then grasped the amber necklace she had been wearing since the weekend and placed the palm of her other hand upon the bag. Catherine and Paulina overheard the old woman's whispered prayer: "*Vater, Sohn, und Heilige Geist; Vater, Sohn, und Heilige Geist* (Father, Son, and Holy Ghost)." She repeated the expression seven times, and then began to hum softly while rocking back and forth.

After trudging through foot-high drifts since turning at the pine tree, Joseph had lost track of time and was startled by Anna's voice. "Joseph, shouldn't we be turning left by now? These drifts are getting too high for Sophie and Adam and we don't dare miss the curve."Joseph didn't reply. His sister added, "Do you want to take my hat for a while?"

Anna sounded as if she were far in the distance, but Joseph understood and turned to assure her they needed to press on a bit farther. The bend in the road had to be just ahead. He explained that turning too early would risk a fatal fall over the bluff. Anna reluctantly complied, and the forlorn band continued to traipse along. Walking in the deeper snow seemed oddly easier now to Joseph, who was proud of this new-found strength though his head tingled with numbness. He felt carried on with scarcely any effort, moving to the tempo of some mournful siren sound beckoning from above with seraphic horns.

"Joseph...Joseph!" The dissonant noise of his sister's yell interrupted his dream, and Joseph struggled to comprehend her words. "Listen to me! It can't be this far," Anna scolded. "If we go beyond the ravine and don't turn down soon nobody is ever going to find us out here! The little ones can't keep this up, Joseph, and neither can I." Anna was now demanding and the children were crying, but Joseph wanted to press on. He turned to drop the rope and free himself from the others, but the line seemed frozen to his hand. He pulled it away with the other and smiled at his sister. "Joseph, what are you doing?" Anna sobbed. "We need you!"

Joseph looked up but began yielding to sleep. Was that Ellevess's voice rousing his muddled thinking? She sang a different song coming from a different direction. He had heard the folk tune many times when Ellevess sometimes rocked him as a child: "*Gott, streck aus dein' milde hand; dass mir kommen an das Land* (God, stretch out Your guiding hand, to lead us safely in this land)."

Joseph sensed a peculiar amber warmth glow within him, and he stared at Anna's trembling arm holding the rope. He then wound it back around his wrist, turned, and followed his sister and the children. Minutes later, they heard the sharp report of a rifle and calls from the men who had gathered at the sharp curve below them to fan out in search of the wanderers. Anna and the children shouted in jubilant recognition and they soon found each other. Within minutes they were returning by wagon down to the colony.

"*Gott Lob and Dank!* (God be praised and thanked!)," exclaimed Catherine as the relieved parents and weary children gathered inside Dobb Conrad and Marillis's warm kerosene-lit kitchen. The men helped Joseph to a chair by the wood stove where he soon recovered to join the others for a satisfying supper. "I was planning to bake tomorrow," Catherine said to Paulina. "Maybe Ellevess would like a loaf of rye bread." Paulina thanked Catherine for the offer and took soup to give her mother. As she stepped outside with the kettle, Paulina noticed the snow had abated. She looked skyward and saw the hazy light of several evening stars.

⌐ Afterword ↝

One of the original Palouse Colony residents, the "Ellevess" of this story, had been born in Russia within months of the famous 1848 meteor shower that was especially bright across the lower Volga. According to some Old World traditions, shooting stars and the aurora borealis were associated with heavenly beings and departed souls who could influence human affairs. Celestial phenomena were thought to foster mystical powers in persons like Ellevess who were born in the year following their appearance. The memorable Northern Lights spectacle mentioned in this story took place on February 12, 1892, and was seen from the Atlantic to Pacific coasts. Period newspaper accounts variously described them as "the most wonderful exposition ever seen on American soil" and the "rumored harbinger of Armageddon."

Dobb and Marillis Conrad's two-story house still stands at the base of the old road to the Palouse Colony between the rural communities of Endicott and St. John, Washington, where heirloom fruit trees and hop vines still thrive. My grandfather's family spent their first weeks in the colony adjusting to the new surroundings due to the generosity of hosts like the Bolanders and Walters—fictitious surnames used here for representative families. Old photographs of some of the women show them wearing amber necklaces, one of the few luxury items brought by Germans from Russia to the United States. In European folklore, amber was the solidified essence of the sun's rays and said to impart special protection to the owner.

Palouse Colony Sunset. *John Clement*

Accounts of the colonists' first sighting of the Northern Lights and the children who survived the blizzard by being roped together were related by Dan Ochs (St. Helena, California, 1974) and Dave Schierman (Walla Walla, Washington, 1972). Their families were among the first Germans to emigrate from Russia to America and the Pacific Northwest, and Dan and Dave recalled their rural Northwest boyhoods in vivid detail. The one-room country school they attended was later converted to a home that still stands in the nearby community of Endicott. Still growing a short distance from its original location overlooking the colony are the progeny of the tree contributed by the Bafus family for the Allen School Christmas. From the stump of the pine that was cut down so long ago, two others grow today in its place.

"I say we just plan on him gettin' a Golden Nichtsie."

The Golden Nichtsie

Even though it was cold outside in the December air, Miss Fournier's fourteen pupils at the two-room Allen School were eager for noon recess. Eleven-year-old Martha Weber and her classmates knew there were only three more days of school before Christmas vacation. They eagerly awaiting recess to make snowmen in the several inches of snow that had fallen overnight. Martha was certain their classroom Christmas tree must be the most beautiful of any around. Country schools dotted the rolling countryside every few miles on roads surrounding tiny Plainville, and local farm families took great pride in these sentinels of learning.

The Webers attended church in town, and Martha looked with excitement to this special week of evening holiday programs both at school and in Plainville. The children had devoted time every afternoon at school for the past week to building holiday dioramas using pine boughs, straw, and balls of colored paper. Beneath an imposing portrait of President Woodrow Wilson on one side of the blackboard stood a wonderfully crafted manger scene. The Holy family and attendant livestock were crafted from folded grain stalks and clothed in brightly colored cloth. On the opposite side of the room near the heavy upright piano stood a magnificent Christmas tree.

The children especially enjoyed the afternoons when they could sing carols and visit the small library adjacent to their room. And today they would draw names for a gift exchange! Miss Fourier usually accompanied her students at the piano but sometimes she let Martha, who had a special gift for music, play other tunes when it was too rainy to play outside at recess. The old instrument had a sharp, tinny sound and two keys didn't work, but Martha enjoyed practicing the hymns she heard at church and happy tunes like those her Uncle Johnny often sang.

"Have you ever seen so many popcorn strings around a tree?" Martha whispered to her sister, Emily, who was two years older and stood nearby at the window to sharpen a pencil.

"Maybe Miss Fournier bought it all up so nobody else has any!" Emily laughed.

The branches of the tall pine were laden with several strings of the creamy white puffs that limply wound round and round from the bottom of the tree to the yellow-painted wooden star on top. Scattered about the branches were some dozen intricate ornaments woven from wheat straw in the shapes of snowflakes, stars, and spiral twirls. Vess Marik, an elderly widow who lived near the school, had recently visited the children to show how to craft the delicate marvels. Small apples of green, red, and yellow hung on the tree by small hooks they had formed from paperclips, and here and there dangled a few precious oranges. Earlier in the month Mrs. Fournier had asked the children to bring a few pieces of fruit from home to decorate for Christmas. Martha and Emily's parents, Adam and Christina Weber, contributed a small box of apples from their orchard which they kept fresh throughout winter in the family's substantial root cellar.

"But I can only spare two oranges," Mrs. Weber told her daughters. "There's one here for each of you. It's a miracle we've been able to get any at the store this time of year."

Neither Miss Fournier, the Weber sisters, nor the rest of the girls approved of the popcorn raids periodically undertaken by some of the boys when Miss Fournier was preoccupied with tending to some student's needs. Twelve-year-old Robert Schlagel seemed to be the ringleader in this mischief. He was the brightest boy around, and popular with everyone. The teacher showed him no special favors but ever encouraged his far-ranging interests. To keep him busy she assigned Robert work on par with the school's oldest students, eighth-graders Margaret Wenzel and Robert's somewhat peculiar cousin, David Schlagel.

The older boy had fuzzy growth around his chin and seemed to prefer being left alone. His parents were among the rural neighborhood's most recent immigrants, and had come from Europe just before the Great War to join Robert's family. Some of the children made fun of David's thick German accent and he clearly struggled to learn English and fit in. Since his parents were late-comers to the area and good farmland was expensive, his father was an itinerant mechanic who struggled to make ends meet for the family. When Robert wasn't around, the other boys sometimes teased David for his clumsiness and stuttering. Martha and the other girls mostly just avoided him.

Everybody seemed to know about Robert's conniving and practical jokes except dear Miss Fourier. He would patiently wait until she stepped across the hall into the small library, or noticed yet again that

David was scribbling aimlessly on his paper or staring out the window. She would amble among the students until reaching David, who regularly shifted his long legs uncomfortably one way and another beneath his wooden desk.

Miss Fournier's quiet comments were familiar to everybody. "Now David," she might say looking down at his paper, "looks like you've made a good start there. Here, let me help you with the next line." Or numbers, or picture, or whatever.

Since Robert sat behind Martha and close to the Christmas tree, she knew what might happen next. Robert would drop his pencil or find some other excuse to move toward to a branch and silently clasp a few of the delicious puffs of popcorn. Martha couldn't help but take notice and furrowed her brow.

She turned around and whispered sternly, "That's stealing pure and simple, Robert!"

"Miss Fournier said it belonged *to all of us*," Robert replied slyly, and with that flipped a piece of popcorn in his fingers right into Martha's face. She winced and turned back around to send her pigtails flying while several of the other children snickered.

"Martha!" Miss Fournier called. "What's the commotion over there?"

"Oh...oh nothing, ma'am," Martha answered curtly, and returned to her work with a shrug.

Martha had to admit that Robert's fun was always good-natured, and she also admired the way he stood up to defend his cousin when others teased him. For some weeks Martha had also harbored a special fondness for Robert. But she seemed to have no vocabulary to express her feelings. The prospect of him ever starting a real conversation seemed out of the question so she need not fear blushing. In all their years growing up together as neighbors, Martha hadn't a single recollection of him being aware of anything more than her name. He seemed to finish regular homework in half the time it took others. So Miss Fourier had challenged Robert the previous year to read the entire "Great Americans" biography series of thick blue hardbound volumes in the bookroom. Just last month their teacher had commended Robert to the entire class for already having read twenty of the set's forty titles.

"Why on earth would he ever hold a conversation with someone like me who still likes picture books?" Martha wondered. Besides that, whenever he did schoolwork with others, Miss Fournier grouped him with the seventh and eighth graders. Martha knew it was wrong to be jealous, but watching her older friends Elizabeth and Margaret so casually visit and laugh with him made her angry.

• • •

Finally the time came after recess snowman building to draw names for the secret friend gift exchange. "I know many of you are related to each other," Miss Fournier explained, "but we're not a very large group and I don't want this to be complicated. So I've put everyone's name on a piece of paper and mixed them up inside the hat," she added. "I'll walk down the rows and have each of you pull one out. And no telling till next Friday at the Christmas program!" She stepped out to the front row and looked down at the youngest member of the class, six-year-old Benjamin Lewis. "Okay, Benny," she said with expectation, "you get to pick first."

Martha shuddered at the exciting prospect of drawing her sister's name. She knew that Emily would be thrilled to receive the pair of white leather ice skates she and Uncle Johnny had found at a thrift shop during the family's annual fall trip to Spokane. They had kept them in a closet at Uncle Johnny's house just down the lane for safe-keeping. The skates were too big for Martha but she and Uncle Johnny thought they would fit Emily just fine. Then Martha was struck by the possibility of drawing Robert's name. She smiled at the prospect of such a moment when he might offer a kind word or two. But then came the dreaded realization that neither she nor her family could afford any gift like she would hope to give—a leather belt with silver buckle, a new book. Yes, that would be the best if....

"Martha Weber!" Miss Fourier cheerfully shouted, "How long do you think I am going to stand here?"

Martha looked up to see her teacher holding the woolen cap, and noticed the bustle of whispers and expressions of surprise across the four other rows beside hers. She reached into the folded fabric and fumbled about to feel the three remaining pieces of torn paper. Martha hesitated a moment and then pulled her hand out with a tight fist around the folded note. Very carefully amidst all the jubilation she slowly opened it to see boldly printed in Miss Fournier's neat handwriting: "DAVID."

Martha's heart sank. Somebody else in the family might as well give the skates to Emily, and there would be no new book to give Robert.

David could hardly read English, and Martha couldn't imagine what on earth she could possibly get that he would like.

Miss Fournier then announced that the class was to begin presenting their Christmas declamations from a list she had shared a month earlier. The first and second graders were to memorize Bible verses about the Holy Child's birth, while the older children were learning holiday poems and brief readings. Martha had selected "The Joy of Giving," a short poem for the season by John Greenleaf Whittier. She had taken her older sister's advice and practiced several times while standing in front of the dresser mirror in their bedroom. But she still fumbled on the last lines and wasn't in any mood now to stand up in front of the entire class.

Little Benny opened the session by stumbling over his lines from "Mary's Song" in the second chapter of Luke ("My soul glorifies the Lord and my spirit rejoices in God my Savior..."). Katie Dolmann followed with a flawless rendering in her cherubic voice of verses from "Zechariah's Song" ("And you, my child, will be called a prophet of the Most High..."). Miss Fourier then called on Margaret to deliver two stanzas from James Russell Lowell's "The First Snowfall." The poem could not have seemed more appropriate given the recent storm that cloaked the hills surrounding the Allen School in white. Only a few south-facing sides exposed chocolate-brown sweeps of bare soil where the piercing wind had carried the snow away. Deep whipped-cream drifts appeared on northern slopes where the children loved to sled during recess.

Miss Fournier herself could quote at length lines from Lowell and other popular New England Schoolhouse poets like Whittier and William Wadsworth Longfellow. When Margaret stood to confess that she had not yet learned her lines, Miss Fournier reminded her firmly that the program was just days away, then seemed to look beyond the children and in hushed tone with fervent gestures spoke words that seemed part of her very being:

The snow had begun in the gloaming,
And busily all the night
Had been heaping field and highway
With a silence deep and white.

Martha closed her eyes and imagined her father and Uncle Johnny hitching two horses to their sleigh for a brisk ride across the hills.

The sound of a whinnying horse tethered outside broke the silent magic of the moment. Their teacher became herself again and Martha was back at school. "Okay, everyone," Miss Fournier said, "time to gather your books and coats and head home. And don't lolligag now that it gets dark so early. And *work on those declamations!*" she shouted as the boys and girls put on their coats, hats, and boots. "Robert, maybe you can tell us tomorrow what the word 'gloaming' means."

"Yes, Miss Fourier," Robert dutifully replied.

"And if you have any popcorn at home maybe you can bring some for what's missing from our Christmas tree," she said matter-of-factly.

"Yea…, yes, ma'am," Robert stammered as he headed out the door.

• • •

Martha fretted all evening long about the gift she needed to get for David Weber. "He's just so strange!" she complained to Emily while washing and drying dishes after supper. "So aren't you going to tell me whose name you drew?" she asked.

"Well nobody's supposed to know until the party," Emily replied. "But of course by tomorrow afternoon Margaret and Elizabeth will have asked around and figured it all out."

"So much for secrets," Martha sighed.

"Well, it turns out that I drew Martha Weber," Emily said flatly.

"How wonderful, Em!" Martha said before pausing. "Of course," she followed, "I don't expect you to get me anything special."

"In that case I'll just take back that diamond brooch," Emily joked.

"Too bad it isn't a belt buckle." Martha said. "Maybe then I'd have something to give."

"What are you two girls fussin' about over there?" interrupted Uncle Johnny from the dinner table, where he and their parents had been quietly visiting. The girls' jovial uncle was their mother's brother and lifelong bachelor who often ate dinner with them.

"Well I'm afraid Martha has got herself in a real fix, Uncle Johnny," Emily explained.

"How so, *Schodzhe?*" he asked. The girls always liked it when their uncle used the elders' colorful Low German *Schveza* (dialect) terms and expressions. *Ich gehe nach die Nushnik* meant, "I'm headed to the out-house," and *die schwartze Feldstievel* were "the black felt boots" that came in handy for outside trips in the winter cold. *Schodzhe* meant "sweetheart."

"Go head, Martha," Emily urged, "tell them."

"Well, first off," Martha began, "I've been having trouble memorizing my lines for the school Christmas program. Even the first graders can say their pieces better than me."

"Now Martha," their mother said reassuringly, "you still have plenty of time to learn your poem. You'll do just fine."

"I know," she agreed, "but I have no idea how to buy a present for our class gift exchange. And of all people I picked David."

"So what's the problem with that?" asked her father.

"I have no idea what he might want and have only saved twenty-eight cents anyway. That's not enough to get anything nice," Martha replied in frustration. "Come Friday night everyone else will have something. He'll be all left out and find out it was supposed to be me."

"So who ever gave you the notion something like that would happen?" asked Uncle Johnny. "Haven't you ever heard about Christmas magic?"

"I'm a little old for that, Uncle," Martha replied with a sniffle.

"Well it's true we don't have a peck of money to buy new things, and time's a little short for you to knit a new pair of socks or mittens. So before you make yourself all sad about it, I say we just plan on him gettin' a Golden Nichtsie."

"A golden what?" wondered Emily aloud.

"A Golden Nichtsie for heaven's sake," Uncle Johnny replied. "Don't folks your age know what a Golden Nichtsie is? What on earth are you going to school for?"

"I guess not to learn that," said Martha as she dried the last plate. "So maybe you'll have to explain it to us."

"Oh, happy to oblige, girls," said Uncle Johnny. "You know the meaning of *nichts*, don't you?"

"Yes," Martha replied slowly, "it means something like 'not,' or 'no.'"

"And 'nothing'!" exclaimed Uncle Johnny with a loud laugh.

"Sooo, we're going to get David a "Golden Nothing'?" asked Martha meekly as she and Emily walked back over to the table.

"Why yes; Golden Nichtsies have saved the day many a time."

"I have no idea what you're talking about, Uncle Johnny," said Martha. "It really doesn't sound like anything that will help me out, and might make matters worse."

"Hey, sweethearts; has your old uncle ever let you down?"

"Of course not," Martha said softly.

"Then there's nothing to be sad about!" Uncle Johnny said loudly. "It's Christmastime so cheer up and show me you believe it."

Martha looked up and managed a slight smile, and both girls walked over to their whiskered uncle and kissed him on his forehead.

"Now that's better," Uncle Johnny said with a grin.

"And it's off to homework and bedtime," instructed their mother.

On their way up the narrow stairway to their bedroom, Martha turned to her older sister and asked quietly, "Do you have any idea what he's talking about?"

"Not at all," replied Emily. "But it is Christmas so who knows what might just happen."

Each morning at school for the rest of the week the children would rush to their festive tree to see what new presents had arrived. By Friday thirteen wrapped gifts of various sizes were spread out beneath the branches. All but one student had a gift. The absence of a package with David's name on it did not seem to especially bother him since David rarely smiled anyway. But Martha thought there was no way to really know what he felt inside. At lunchtime she overheard Robert say how unfair it was that his cousin had been overlooked. "I heard he's getting a Golden Nichtsie," Emily volunteered.

"A golden what?" Robert asked.

"A Golden Nichtsie," Emily repeated as Martha gave her a cross look.

"I've never heard of such a thing," said Benny, who had overheard the conversation.

"Well don't expect to see one either," advised Robert. "I think you're making it all up, Emily Weber."

Martha started to say something just as Mrs. Fournier turned away from putting another log into the stove and called for the students to take their seats.

Martha took her place next to the Christmas tree and opened her reading book. She folded her hands on its open pages and silently said a brief prayer: "Dear Lord, please bless this day and help me to get a present for the program tonight."

The morning's lessons seem to fly by and Miss Fournier allowed a little longer recess time on this last day before Christmas vacation so the children could sled down the steepest slope overlooking the school. The snow was so deep that none of the field stubble was visible and their well-worn track kept most everyone from tipping over. Elizabeth, Margaret, and Emily raced with Robert and the other boys, while Martha joined the other girls building snow forts near the school. She thought

David must be the strongest of the bunch when she saw him trudging back up the hill with Benny on the sled as if he were a horse in harness.

That afternoon the children arranged their classroom for the long-awaited Christmas program. The older boys brought up two dozen wooden folding chairs that had been stored in the basement and arranged them between the students' desks. They also moved two benches along the wall behind the rows of chairs while the girls placed white tablecloths, red candles, and greenery on two small serving tables for punch and cookies. At the end of the day Miss Fournier reminded the children to return that evening by seven o'clock.

As Martha walked by the Christmas tree she glanced down at the presents hoping that by some chance one more present might have appeared there during the day. But nothing seemed to have changed. She bundled up and joined Emily outside for the long walk back home. "Hurry up, you slow-poke," Emily chided her younger sister as she ambled down the stairway.

The Weber family dined early that evening so they could leave in plenty of time for the program. "Eat your fill of soup," Mrs. Weber told the girls, "It's a long cold walk up the canyon."

"You mean we're not taking the sleigh?" Martha asked.

"I'm afraid not," answered Uncle Johnny, who had joined them for the meal. "The road down here has drifted something fierce the last two nights, and we'd be stuck for sure. Why old Sam and Flax might have to wait a month before they can take us for a run out that way."

Uncle Johnny heard Martha's quiet whimper, and turned to hoist her almost to the ceiling. "It's Christmas, my dear!" he shouted. "Why I can just carry you all the way like St. Nick's pack if you get too tired."

Somehow he had found a floppy old red and white Santa hat and placed it on his head. Martha couldn't help but laugh as he swung around to make them both dizzy. In minutes they were out the door with warm clothes and boots with Uncle Johnny humming *Jingle Bells*. They walked along single file for several minutes to reach the narrow swinging bridge that always made the girls a bit nervous when crossing.

"No fears about drowning tonight," Uncle Johnny kidded. "Why that river's frozen so hard we'll probably have ice till August."

Martha carefully grasped the rope lines on both sides of the walkway and carefully stepped along the wooden footboards. She knew better

The stars seemed to sparkle like colored jewels in the frigid air.

than to look down so gazed toward the night sky above the western hills. What a spectacle to behold! The stars seemed to sparkle like colored jewels in the frigid air. Not only were many brightly twinkling like crystals, but others shone red and blue and green. Martha paused for a moment to take in the celestial grandeur and knew she would never forget it.

Shortly afterward they began ascending the canyon trail amdist the sheltering pines toward the school. They stopped for a moment to catch their breath in the stillness. "Maybe it was a night like this when Jesus was born," said Emily. They then heard the voices of their neighbors, the Wenzels. Margaret's parents greeted the Webers and the group trudged on. They soon saw the glowing lights of the Allen School's windows. The children raced to the stairs and entered the beautifully decorated classroom where a crowd of several dozen parents and students had gathered.

Martha welcomed the warmth of the wood stove and joined her classmates for a cup of hot cider and sugar cookies. Her parents visited with friends while Uncle Johnny walked around the room with others to view the students' dioramas and the festive Christmas tree. A few minutes later Miss Fournier announced it was time for the program to begin so everyone took a seat. One by one the students said their pieces starting with the youngest, little Benny and Katie, who did just fine. When Katie finished her verses and the audience applauded, Martha glanced down toward the presents under the tree and noticed something peculiar. A small box wrapped in shiny gold paper rested on top of the one that had Elizabeth's name on it. She could tell something was written on a small piece of paper attached to the box's white ribbon, but she was too far away to read it. But she thought the first letter looked like it might be a "D." Could it be?

After several more recitations it was Martha's time to deliver her poem. She walked to the front of the room and smiled nervously at the crowd. Martha stood up straight, cleared her throat, and began "The Joy of Giving" by John Greenleaf Whittier:

> *Somehow not only for Christmas*
> *But all the long year through,*
> *The joy that you give to others*
> *Is the joy that comes back to you.*
> *And the more you spend in blessing*
> *The poor and lonely and sad,*
> *The more of your heart's possessing*
> *Returns to make you glad.*

Uncle Johnny led everyone in clapping, and Martha returned to her desk delighted that she was finished. For the first time she really thought about the words she had memorized, and how helping others was the most important thing regardless of how popular they might be. A short time later Emily presented her reading and then Mr. Wenzel led the group in singing Christmas carols. Finally only Margaret and David were left. With help from Miss Fournier's prompting, Margaret made it through several stanzas of a holiday poem by Alfred, Lord Tennyson.

After she finished the children were surprised to see David, who had been sitting with his parents on the back bench, walk to the front of the room. Everyone was silent and without introduction the boy began to sing. In a rich tenor of perfect pitch, David sang "Silent Night" in words familiar to all the German immigrant families, followed by the words in English:

> *Stille Nacht, Heil'ge Nacht, Alles schlaeft, einsam wacht,*
> *Nur das heilige Eltern-paar, Das im Stalle zu Bethlehem war,*
> *Bei dem himmlischen Kind, Bei dem himmlischen Kind.*

> *Silent Night, Holy Night, all is calm, all is bright,*
> *Round yon virgin mother and Child, Holy Infant so tender and mild,*
> *Sleep in heavenly peace, Sleep in heavenly peace.*

David began to sing.

David's voice was exquisite, and all the more astounding because he sang calmly and continuously without a single stammer. After a few seconds of stunned silence, everyone rose with Miss Fournier in applause as David returned to his parents and smiled. Miss Fournier then thanked everyone for coming and invited them to enjoy more refreshments while the children could open their presents. The youngsters rushed to the tree where Robert took charge and started reading out names. Martha was one of the first to receive a gift, but she took her time with the wrapping so she could see who received the mystery box. She opened hers enough to see the box was a doll wearing a splendid dress. Just then she heard Robert shout "David!" and hand his cousin a present.

At first David just stared at the golden wrapping as if it were too nice to tear. "Open it up for heaven's sake, David!" yelled Benny who held a new stocking hat. David pulled the paper off and opened the top of a small white box. He gasped and set it down so others could see a gleaming wristwatch that seemed to Martha as if it were made of pure gold.

"*Ein, ein sch...shöne Uhr*," David marveled.

"Yes, it is a beautiful watch," agreed Elizabeth. David handed it to her and motioned for her to pass it around so all could take a look.

Martha returned to her desk to retrieve some papers and felt someone standing behind her. She turned to see Robert standing close by. "That was very nice what somebody did for David," he said with raised eyebrows. "I had never seen a Golden Nichtsie before."

"I guess there's a first time for everything," Martha smiled.

"Hey, maybe you'd like to come to the sledding party we're having at our place tomorrow afternoon," Robert said.

"Well, yes," Martha answered. "That sounds like great fun."

⸎ Afterword ⸎

In the summer of 2015 I attended a relative's wedding in our hometown of Endicott, Washington. Among the many relatives there were two elderly sisters who had been raised at the rural Palouse Colony several miles north of town, but had long since resided out of the area. One of them, Vera Grove Rudd, was a spry ninety-nine years old, and after the ceremony other relatives drove her back in the hills to see their old place. She recalled very specific details about life there many decades ago—the varieties of heirloom apples in the orchard, names of their horses and dogs, and the colors of her mother's favorite irises. Since that time I have made periodic visits to see Vera, who at 101 still has a wonderful sense of humor and vivid recollections that span the past century. In December 2017 I asked her to share a favorite Christmas memory and she said that she very much enjoyed telling her grandchildren and great-grandchildren about the "Golden Nichtsie." I had never heard the expression, so she proceeded to relate this peculiar tale which she had experienced as a girl and I have recast with dialogue and minor details.

APPENDIX I
Emma Schwabenland Haynes Papers, 1927–1982

Manuscripts, Archives, and Special Collections
Washington State University

Emma Schwabenland Haynes (1907–1984) was one of the twentieth century's preeminent historians of the Germans from Russia. She was raised in rural Odessa, Washington, where her Volga-born parents, Rev. J. C. and Mrs. Dorothea (Miller) Schwabenland, ministered for many years at the local German Congregational Church, which was attended by many first-generation immigrants from Russia. Emma was surrounded by the language and cultural traditions of the area's *Russlanddeutschen* and as a young woman used her capacious intellect and engaging personality to research and write her people's history. She received her bachelor's and master's degrees in German and history from the University of Colorado in the 1920s, and completed a thesis titled, "German-Russian on the Volga and in the United States."

Emma undertook graduate studies from 1930 to 1931 at the University of Breslau in Germany, and was among the last Westerners to visit the famine-plagued Volga German villages before Stalin's oppressions closed Russia's borders to foreigners. In the aftermath of World War II, she assisted the Allied prosecution team as translator for high ranking Nazi defendants at the Nuremburg War Crimes Tribunals where she met Thomas Haynes, a Chicago court reporter. The couple married in 1948 and established their home in Germany where they lived for twenty-eight years. During this time Emma traveled throughout Europe searching libraries and archives for original source materials related to her special interests. She became an important American liaison to the *Landsmannshaft der Deutschen aus Russland* (Society of Germans from Russia) and trusted colleague of historian Karl Stumpp and other authorities in the field.

Emma was among a small group of interested American and Canadian citizens including David Miller, Ruth Amen, and Adam Giesinger who organized the American Historical Society of Germans from Russia (AHSGR) in Denver, Colorado, in 1968. She served on AHSGR's founding International Board of Directors and as the organization's representative in Europe until the couple returned to the United States in 1976 to live in

Arlington, Virginia. They relocated to Ventura, California, in 1984. In recognition of her prodigious scholarly contributions, AHSGR named the society's Lincoln, Nebraska, heritage center library in her honor.

I first learned about Emma's remarkable work as a history major at Washington State University when she responded by letter in February 1971 to an inquiry for information I had published in the AHSGR journal. She informed me that a complete list of Yagodnaya Polyana's original settlers had been published in a 1926 issue of the German-Russian historical journal *Heimat im Bild*. Given this information I was able to obtain a copy of the article while Emma began searching the castle archive of the Ysenburg family in Büdingen, Germany, for the original list which had been prepared by the village's schoolteacher, Georg Kromm, in 1912. Emma wrote to me in November 1971 about AHSGR's upcoming international convention in Boulder, Colorado, which I attended the following June. In this way I came to meet Emma and the growing circle of Volga German historians including President David Miller, Gerda Walker, and Arthur Flegel.

When Emma and Tom moved back to the United States in the summer of 1976, my wife Lois and I were living in Tacoma, Washington, where I was completing graduate studies in history at Pacific Lutheran University. Emma alerted us to several rare Russian language works in the Library of Congress by historian Grigorii Pissarevskii about German settlement that were relevant to my research interests, so we traveled to Washington, DC, to investigate and were given a most warm reception by the Hayneses. She further introduced me to core volumes on Volga German history from her personal library including works by Gottlieb Bauer, Gottlieb Beratz, and Gerhard Bonwetsch.

In 1980 Washington State University hosted a regional conference on Northwest Germans from Russia at which Emma delivered the keynote address, and after the gathering we toured several places in the region she had known in her youth. Through subsequent visits and correspondence, she expressed interest in donating volumes from her library not already at the Lincoln AHSGR headquarters to the society's archive, which she did. Emma also expressed hope that an institution in her beloved Pacific Northwest might become home to the substantial balance of her collection. She had already made considerable donations to the Washington, DC, and Lodi, California, AHSGR chapter libraries. Since I had remained in close contact with WSU Manuscripts, Archives, and Special Collections (MASC) staff in Pullman where notable regional studies specialists included Professors David Stratton, Clifford Trafzer, and Donald Messerschmidt, I suggested she consider that institution.

Emma was pleased with the prospect and made arrangements through WSU archivists John Guido and Stephen Balzarini for transfer of materials in 1983 and 1984. Series 1 of her papers consists of research papers and theses, article offprints, and miscellaneous small publications. Series 2 is comprised of correspondence with various authors and researchers in North America, Germany, and Russia. Her papers consist of materials in both English and German, photographs, and other resources for a total of 6.5 linear feet of shelf space in seven containers. The collection is open to the public without restriction. A guide to the collection can be found at wsulibs.wsu.edu/masc/finders/cg573.htm or archiveswest.orbiscascade.org/ark:/80444/xv87212.

In addition to these papers, Emma Haynes donated her library of books, which have been incorporated into the MASC Rare Book Collection at Washington State University.

Richard Scheuerman

APPENDIX II
Glossary of Foreign Terms

The following German and Russian words were commonly used by *usu Leut* and often appear in oral histories and their letters. The very expression by which they were known (*usu Leut*) indicates differences from "High German" (*unsure Leute*) in the medieval "Low German" Hessen dialect they perpetuated well into the twentieth century. For this reason their relict language was studied by several European linguists. Volga Germans also utilized a number of Russia loanwords (*Lehnwörter*) through dealings with their Russian neighbors and changes in education policies beginning in the 1870s requiring boys to study Russian in village schools. Spellings may vary with dialects.

alt (German): old
ambar (Russian): granary
arbuza (R): watermelon
Aussiedler (G): emigrant

babushka (R): grandmother
Belz/Peltz (G): pelt, coat
Belznickle (G): ogre clad in bear coat
bierock/pirog (R): meat-filled dough
bitte (G): please
blina (R): pancakes
badelya (R): bottle
borscht (R): vegetable (beet) soup
Brot (G): bread

chai (R): tea

Deutsch (G): German
Dorf (G): village, town
durak (R): fool, also a card game

Fedda (G): uncle, older man
Feldstievel (G): felt boots
Flaasch (G): meat

Gaul (G): horse
goluptsi (R): stuffed cabbage rolls
Gott (G): God
grossambar (R): communal granary
guberni (R): province

Halstookh (G): headscarf
Heimatland (G): homeland
Heirat/Heirode (G): marriage
herzliche (G): heartfelt, hearty
Hinkel (G): chicken
hinner (G): behind
Hirsche (G): gruel made from grain
Hof (G): yard, home

Kasta (G): large travel trunk
Kerike/Kirche (G): church
khutor (R): farm in the country
Kinder (G): children
Klees (G): dumplings
Koi (G): cow
kolkhoz (R): collective farm
kolonisty (R): colonists
konfekt (G): sweets

kopek/kopeck (R): small Russia coin
Kopf (G): head
kopitze (R): grain shocks
kossár (R): reaper

Leut (G): people
loshka (R): wood spoon

mir (R): village commune
mirskoi skhod (R): village assembly
Mutter (G): mother

neue (G): new
nushnik (R): outhouse

oblast (R): region

pazhalsta (R): please, thank you
pelmeny (R): meat dumplings for
     soup
pituvka (R): pantry table
pood (R): dry unit measure (~36 lbs.)

rout/rud (G): red
ruble (R): monetary unit (100
     kopecks)
Russische (G): Russian

samogón (R): home brew
samovar (R): brass tea vessel
schee/schön (G): beautiful
schlechte (G): bad, hard
Schodzee/Schodzhe/Schodsche (G):
     sweetheart

Schule (G): school
Schulmeister (G): schoolmaster
schwartz (G): black
Schwartzbeeren (G): blackberries
Schweza/Schveza (G): talk, converse
selo (R): village, town
soldat (R): soldier
Sohne (G): son
spasiba (R): thank-you
Suess blina (*Suesspleena*) (G)(R):
     sweet pancakes

Tochter (G): daughter
troika (R): three-horse sleigh, a
     threesome

ukaz (R): official decree
ulitsa (R): street
usu, usa (G): our

Vater/Vader (G): father
varenye (R): stewed fruit stirred into
     tea
verst (R): unit of distance (.66 mile)
Vess (G): aunt, older woman
vorony (R): ravens

Weinachten (G): Christmas
weiss (G): white
Welt (G): world
Wuscht (G): sausage

Yunga (G): young person
zemlyanka (R): earth home

Notes

Introduction

1. Will Durant, *The Reformation: A History of European Civilization from Wyclif to Calvin, 1300–1564* (New York: Simon and Schuster, 1957), 380.
2. Fred Koch, *The Volga Germans: In Russia and the Americas, from 1763 to the Present* (University Park: Pennsylvania State University Press, 1977), 5.
3. It was calculated that Germany's population during the war decreased from 21,000,000 to 13,500,000. Hundreds of villages were left totally unoccupied, thousands of acres in the surrounding fields were left uncultivated, and the peasants were reduced to eating rats and grass, some even resorting to cannibalism.
4. Koch, 5.
5. Hattie Plum Williams, *The Czar's Germans: With Particular Reference to the Volga Germans* (Lincoln, NE: AHSGR, 1975), 6.
6. Nicholas V. Riasonovsky, *A History of Russia* (New York: Oxford University Press, 1969), 275.
7. Wilhelm Würz, "Wie Jagodnaja Poljana gegründet wurde," Heimatbuch der Deutschen aus Russland (1962), 65.
8. "Bericht der Regierung zu Giessen und den Landgrafen" (April 4, 1767), *Acten des Geheimen Staats-Archivs XI*, Abtheilung, Convolut l, in the Hessian State Archives, Darmstadt, West Germany, quoted in Williams, 20.
9. Karl Esselborn, "Die Auswanderung von Hessen nach Russland," *Heimat im Bild* (1926), 84.
10. Emigration from southern Germany at this time was not limited to North America and Russia, rather many also settled in Brazil, Algeria, and elsewhere in Europe. See Ernst Wagner, "Auswanderung aus Hessen," *Ausland-deutschtum und evangelischen Kirche Jahrbuch* (1938).
11. Cited in Grigorii G. Pissarevskii, *Iz istorii inostrannoi kolonizatsii v rossi v XXIII v* (Po neizdannym arkivnym dokumentam), (Moskva: A. I. Snegrirevyi, 1909), 180. *(History of Foreign Colonization in Russia in the Eighteenth Century. Based on Unpublished Archive Documents).*

Chapter 1: The Program of Colonization under Catherine II

1. This program is detailed in Pissarevskii, 38-45.
2. Pissarevskii, 45.
3. A "German suburb" in Moscow developed as early as the sixteenth century following the settlement there of a number of German craftsmen and teachers under the reign of Ivan the Terrible (1533–84). His efforts to modernize the country through such programs were not continued by the early Romanov commercial ties to Western Europe.
4. Karl Stumpp, *The German Russians: Two Centuries of Pioneering* (Bonn, West Germany: Atlantic Forum, 1967), 6.
5. Adam Giesinger, *From Catherine to Khrushchev: The Story of Russia's Germans* (Battleford, Saskatchewan: Marian Press, 1974), 4.
6. Pissarevskii, 48.
7. Gladys Scott Thomson, *Catherine the Great and the Expansion of Russia* (New York: Collier Books, 1965), 119.
8. George J. Eisenach, *Pietism and the Russian Germans in the United States* (Berne, IN: The Berne Publishers, 1948), 17.
9. Pissarevskii, 45.

10. Ibid., 46.
11. Ibid.
12. Ibid.
13. In this manifesto and later legislation directing the immigration program, Jews were forbidden to colonize in the country.
14. Pissarevskii, 48.
15. Ibid.
16. Williams, 38.
17. Pissarevskii, 49.
18. Russia, *Polnoe Sobranie Zakonov Rossiiskoi Imperii* XVI, No. 11,800 (St. Petersburg, 1649-1916). (Collection of Laws of the Russian Empire, in the Hoover Institution Library at Stanford University, Stanford, California).
19. Giesinger, 5.
20. Ibid.
21. Pissarevskii, 52.
22. David G. Rempel, "The Mennonite Commonwealth in Russia: A Sketch of its Founding and Endurance, 1789-1919," *Mennonite Quarterly Review* XLVII (October 1973), 11.
23. Pissarevskii, 51.
24. Giesinger, 9.
25. Williams, 43.
26. Ibid., 45.
27. The perils of this journey are described in Gottlieb Bauer, *Geschichte dor Deutschen in Den Wolgakolonien* (Saratov, 1907), 19; and Gottlieb Beratz, *Die deutschen Kolonien an der Unteren Wolga* (Saratov: H. Schellhorn u. Co., 1915), 41–42.
28. These French recruiters, most of whom proved to be unscrupulous businessmen, included men named Beauregard, DeBoffe, LeRoy, Monjou, Pictet, and Precourt.
29. Koch, 7.
30. While all aspects of Simolin's program were not always above reproach, there developed an intense rivalry between the two recruiting agencies as the Frenchmen were often accused of fraudulent business practices. For a fuller explanation see Pissarevskii, Appendix 17.
31. "Berichte des pruessischen Gesandten in Russland an Koenig Friederich II, 1766," quoted in Williams, 78.
32. "Schreiben der Churfuerstl. Mainzischen Regierung an die Fuerstl. Hessische wegen gemein schaftlicher Massregeln gegen fremde Werber," Mainz, February 7, 1766, found in the Hessen State Archives, Darmstadt, West Germany.
33. Esselborn, 84.
34. Williams, 79–80.
35. Ibid., 84.
36. Pissarevskii, 148.
37. Letter from the government in Giessen to Ludwig VIII, Landgrave of Hessen-Darmstadt, quoted in Esselborn, 88.
38. Ernst Wagner, "Auswanderung aus Hessen," *Auslanddeutschtum und evangelischen Kirche Jahrbuch* (1938), 24–33.
39. Pissarevskii, Appendix 14.
40. Ibid.
41. Pissarevskii, 169.
42. As the equivalent of the foreign minister, the chancellorship was left vacant during most of Catherine's reign as she preferred to assume the responsibility herself, allowing vice-chancellors to execute her wishes although she was influenced to a great degree by various court favorites.
43. Pissarevskii, 168.

44. Ibid., 148.
45. Ibid., 148–49.
46. From *Tagebuch eines Schlitzer Bauern namens Adolf Weissbeck*, in Arthur and Cleora Flegel, "Research in Hesse," AHSGR Work Paper, No. 13 (December 1973), 24–5.
47. Georg Kromm, "Die deutschen Ansiedler an der Wolga," *Schottener Kreisblatt* 15 (February 22, 1920), 1–3.
48. Williams, 81.
49. Ibid.
50. Wagner, 23–33.
51. Würz, 67. Special bonuses were given to families under the liberal terms of settlement.
52. Pissarevskii, 149.
53. Estimates given by Bauer and Beratz. Pissarevskii recorded 22,800 original German colonists to the Volga while Bonwetch suggested a figure of 25,000 was more accurate. Pallas in *Reisen durch verschiedene Provinzen des russichen Reiches in den Jahren 1768-1774* (St. Petersburg, 1771–76) put the number at about 29,000. The first census of the German Volga colonies was taken in 1769 under Count Orlov of the Guardianship Chancery, indicating a population then of 23,109 (10,894 in crown colonies and 12,215 in proprietory with 137 allowed to settle in Saratov).
54. In addition a colony of Moravian Brethren from Herrnhut was established on the Volga at Sarepta, about 200 families founded four colonies in the province of St. Petersburg and 742 Germans from the area of Frankfurt a.M. settled in the Chernigov province.
55. Williams, 99. One of the original 104 colonies was settled by French colonists.
56. Williams, 87.
57. Pissarevskii, 117.
58. Other than colonization in the Josefstal, Fischerdorf, and Jamberg districts near the Dneper River by Germans in 1780 and of Mennonites from Danzig and West Prussia to the Chortitza area from 1789-90, foreign settlement in Russia was suspended until 1804 when renewed efforts begun by Alexander I brought thousands of German settlers to the Black Sea region and later to the Caucasus. Mennonites came to Samara beginning in 1853 when they founded Köppenthal.

Chapter 2: Colonial Development on the Volga

1. Christian G. Züge, *Der russiche Kolonist I* (Zeitz und Naumberg: Wilhelm Webel, 1802), 49.
2. Williams, 107.
3. Beratz, 45.
4. Giesinger, 11.
5. Williams, 109.
6. Beratz, 53.
7. Emma D. Swabenland, "German-Russians on the Volga and in the United States" (unpublished master's thesis, University of Colorado, 1929), 17.
8. Demographic data on these villages is indicated in the following table (from Pissarevskii, 74–83, and Karl Stumpp, *The Emigration from Germany to Rulssia in the Years 1763 to 1862.* Tilbingen [West Germany: by the author], 67–77):

Colony	1769	1772	1912	1926
Balzer	410	479	11,110	11,556
Frank	425	525	11,557	5,191
Hussenbach	438	525	8,080	6,623

Yagodnaya Polyana	312	402	8,845	15,000*
Kolb	107	143	3,800	2,823
Messer	329	397	5,295	3,575
Norka	772	957	14,236	7,210
Walter	382	431	6,660	2,739
Warenburg	524	579	8,312	4,754

*The district population, consisting also of residents in Pobochnaya and Neu-Straub. Stumpp also provides a list of the original immigrants who founded the colonies of Yagodnaya Polyana and Balzer, 77–81.

9. Züge, 14–44.
10. Kratzke was located on the Karamysh. See Williams, 110, for a brief discussion on the disputed location.
11. Kromm also quotes a Saratov document which indicates the colony was founded on September 16, 1767. See George Kromm, *Einwanderliste von Jagodnaja Poljana* (aus Hessen). At the Volgelsberg Museum in Schotten, West Germany, reprinted in Esselborn, 91–92.
12. Würz, 66.
13. Kromm, "Die deutschen Ainsiedler an der Wolga," *Schottener Kreisblatt* (February 22, 1910), 2.
14. Koch, 25, and Mrs. Catherine Luft, oral histories, Sheboygan, WI. June 15–19, 1977.
15. Johannes Schleuning, *Die deutschen Kolonien im Wolgagebiet* (Berlin, 1919), 20.
16. David Schmidt, *Studien Uber die Geschichre der Wolgadeutschen* (Polrowsk, ASSR der Wolgadeutschen: Zentral-Volker-Verlag, 1930), 128–31, 138.
17. Beratz, 178–201.
18. Bauer, 105.
19. Esselborn, 92. Beideck's favorable location near the west bank of the Volga River and its early well supervised founding in 1764 may help explain the optimistic report.
20. Kromm, "Die deutschen Ainsiedler an der Wolga," *Schottener Kreisblatt* (February 25, 1910), 1.
21. Koch, 99.
22. The entire story of Stärkel's experience while captive was recorded by Johannes Stärkel in "Johann Wilhelm Stärkel aus Norka unter der Fahne Pugaschews," Friedensbote (November 1910), 85–88.
23. Bauer, 47.
24. Ibid., 48.
25. Koch, 29.
26. Ibid., 33.
27. Williams, 146.
28. Jacob Volz, *Historical Review of the Balzerer* (York, NE, 1938), 4.
29. Schleuning, 11.
30. Conrad Blumenschein, oral history, St. John, WA, May 6 and 13, 1980.
31. Koch, 55.
32. Blumenschein oral histories.
33. Koch, 183.
34. Ibid., 78, and Henry Litzenberger, oral history, Deer Park, WA, May 4, 1980.
35. Koch, 77.
36. Blumenschein oral histories.
37. Koch, 185–86, and Blumenschein oral histories.
38. Elizabeth Kromm, oral history, Lacrosse, WA, June 10, 1979.

39. Koch, 58.

40. Mrs. C. P. Morasch, oral history, Endicott, WA, April 23, 1971, and Susan M. Yungman, *Faith of Our Fathers* (by the author, 1972), 9.

41. Mr. and Mrs. John Schierman, oral history, Vulcan, Alberta, July 2, 1977.

42. Elizabeth Kromm, oral history, LaCrosse, WA, June 10, 1979.

43. August Markel, oral history, Endicott, WA, June 19, 1970, and Blumenschein oral histories.

44. Luft oral histories.

45. Mrs. A. P. Morasch, oral history, Endicott, WA, March 4, 1980.

46. Alec Reich, oral history, Endicott, WA, April 2, 1969.

47. Blumenschein oral histories.

48. Henry Litzenberger, oral history, Deer Park, WA, May 4, 1980.

49. Koch, 190.

50. Koch, 68–69, quoting statistics given by Bonwetsch, Pallas, and Beratz.

51. Aleksandr Avgustovich Klaus, *Nashii Kolonii: Opyty materialy po isotorii i statistike inostfannoi kolonizatsii v rossi* (St. Petersburg: Tipografiia V. V. Nusval't, 1869), 190–95. (*Our Colonies: The Lessons of Materials Based on the History and Statistics of Foreign Colonization in Russia*).

52. Giesinger, 54.

53. Klaus, 189–95.

54. Blumenschein oral histories.

55. George J. Eisenach, *Das religiöse Leben unter den Russland deutschen in Russland und America* (Marburg an der Lahn, West Germany: Buchdruckerei Hermann Rathmann, 1950), Appendix I, 214–16.

56. Betty Scott, unpublished papers, Mission, KS.

57. Henry Litzenberger, oral history, Deer Park, WA, May 4, 1980.

58. Grigorii G. Pissarevskii, *Vnutrennoi rasporiadok v koloniiakh povolzh'ia pri Ekaterine II* (Varshava: Tipografiia varshavskago uchebnogo okruga, 1914), 10. (*Internal Order in the Volga Colonies during the Reign of Catherine II.*)

59. Bauer, 64. These debts had been incurred largely through loans for home construction and operating expenses at the time of settlement. The slow recovery from the early period of drought and corruption in the collection of crown taxes delayed final liquidation of the debt until the 1840s, after a special investigation had been made into the matter.

60. Rempel, 58.

61. Beratz, 104.

62. Rempel, 58.

63. Ibid.

64. Ibid., 63.

65. Koch, 93.

66. Giesinger, p155–56. For an extensive treatment of the history of Lutheranism throughout the Russian and Soviet periods, see Edgar C. Duin, *Lutheranism under the Tsars and Soviets*, 2 vols. (Ann Arbor, Michigan: University Microfilms, 1975).

67. Ibid., 157.

68. Ibid., 405. For a complete listing of the pastorates for each Volga German colony see Karl Stumpp, "Verzeichnis der ev. Pastoren in den deutschen und gemischten—vor allem in Städten—Kirchenspielen in Russland bzw. der Sowejetunion, ohne Baltikum und Polen," *Heimatbuch der Deutschen aus Russland* (1969/72), 276–389.

69. Eisenach, *Pietism and the Russian Germans*, 40. For a full discussion of the activities of some of these missionaries in the Volga colonies, see Eisenach, chapter 3.

70. Ibid., 39.

71. Ibid., 40.

72. Giesinger, 161.

73. Eisenach, *Pietism and the Russian Germans*, 41.

74. This popular collection of 823 hymns is still in use in Lutheran congregations in the Soviet Union.
75. Koch, 147.
76. For catechetical instruction the Lutheran Consistory allowed Reformed colony schools use of Rogue's Catechism, see *Schul- und Küster Schülmeister Instruction in der evangelischen Kolonien des Saratovschen und Samaraschen Gouvernments* (Moskva: Moskovischen Evangelischen Lutherischen Consistorio), undated.
77. Koch, 123.
78. Timothy Kloberdanz, "Funerary Beliefs and Customs of the Germans from Russia," *AHSGR Work Paper, No. 20* (Spring 1976), 65.
79. Koch, 154–55.
80. Giesinger, 173.
81. Eisenach, *Pietism and the Russian Germans*, 66. This book gives a complete study on the origins and development of the German Russian pietistic movement.
82. Ibid., 65, and Catherine Luft, oral history, Sheboygan, Wisconsin, June 19, 1977.
83. Ibid., 67–68.
84. Ibid., 69–70.
85. Koch, 205; Center for Volga German Studies, cvgs.cu-portland.edu/history/biographies/s/staerkel_wilhelm.cfm
86. Eisenach, *Pietism and the Russian Germans*, 71.
87. Emma S. Haynes, "Researching in the National Archives," *AHSGR Journal II*, no. 1 (Spring 1979), 4.
88. George Burgdorff, *Erlebnisse als Missionar oder Reiseprediger in Russland* (Hillsboro, KS: M. B. Publishing House, 1924), 93, 151.

Chapter 3: Immigration to the United States

1. Bauer, 163.
2. Harm Schlomer, "Inland Empire Russia Germans," *The Pacific Northwesterner* VIII (Fall, 1964), 60.
3. It was argued by some government authorities that the terms "century" and "forever" were synonymous in vernacular use during the time of Catherine II's reign. See Koch, 199.
4. Harry G. Scholz, "The German Colonists of Russia: The Repeal of Russia's Law of the Colonists in 1871 and its effect on the German Colonist Population," (unpublished master's thesis, Chapman College, Orange, CA, 1969), 29. Several Mennonite delegations journeyed to St. Petersburg from 1871 to 1874 requesting continued exemption on religious grounds but met with little success until 1875 when conditional exemptions were allowed. See Rempel, 80. The complete text of the 1871 Ukase is found in: *Russia, Polnae Sobranie Zakonov Rossiiskoi Imperii* XLVI, no. 49, 705. (St. Petersburg, 1649–1916).
5. Rempel, 78–79.
6. Giesinger, 227.
7. Scholz, 37–38.
8. For a discussion of this earlier migration see Williams, 180–181.
9. Williams, 189.
10. Koch, 205.
11. Emma S. Haynes, "Germans from Russia in American History and Literature," *AHSGR Work Paper* 15 (September 1974), 11–13.
12. Koch, 206–207.
13. Bonwetsch, 114.
14. Scholz, 40.
15. Bonwetsch, 109.

16. Norman E. Saul, "The Arrival of the Germans from Russia: A Centennial Perspective," *AHSGR Work Paper*, No. 21 (Fall 1976), 4–5.
17. Marcus Lee Hansen, *The Immigrant in American History* (Cambridge: Harvard University Press, 1940), 72. Timber cultures provided a quarter-section grant to any settler who planted 40 acres of trees although this was reduced to 10 acres in 1878. One could obtain title to 640 acres at $1.25 per acre under the terms of the Desert Land Act if it was placed under irrigation within three years of the filing date.
18. Norman Saul, "The Migration of Russian-Germans to Kansas," *Kansas Historical Quarterly* XL, No. 1 (Spring 1974), pp. 50-53.
19. *Hays City Sentinel*, August 16, 1876.
20. *Topeka Daily Blade*, December 13, 1875.
21. SS *Ohio* Manifest (to Baltimore, November 23, 1875).
22. SS *City of Montréal* Manifest (to New York, January 6, 1876). This group of nearly 200 Volga Germans was under the leadership of Peter Ekkert, a Mennonite missionary.
23. Saul, "The Arrival of the Germans from Russia," 7.
24. The terms "Kansas colony" and "Nebraska colony" are to be interpreted in the broader sense of the terms as it was from the general areas of Rush and Barton County, Kansas, and Hitchcock County, Nebraska, that Volga German immigration to the Pacific Northwest began.
25. SS *Mosel* Passenger List (to New York, October 24, 1876). The spelling of many Volga German names was altered after their arrival; Scheuermann to Schierman, Brach to Brack, Pfaffenroth to Poffenroth, etc.
26. From Peter Brack's autobiography, typescript copy, sent to Richard Scheuerman with letter from Laurin Wilhelm, Lawrence, KS, April 27, 1974.
27. Leta Ochs, scrapbook clippings, Endicott, WA.
28. Grace Lillian Ochs, *Up From the Volga: The Story of the Ochs Family* (Nashville: Southern Publishing Company, 1969), 29.
29. Mrs. Elizabeth Repp, oral history, Endicott, WA, April 1, 1971.
30. *Russell Record*, December 7, 1876.
31. Richard Sallet, *German-Russian Settlements in the United States* (Fargo: North Dakota Institute for Regional Studies, 1974), translated by LaVern J. Rippley and Armand Bauer, 23–24.
32. Johann Hoezler, "The Earliest Volga Germans in Sutton, Nebraska and a Portion of their History," *AHSGR Work Paper* 16 (December 1974), translated by Arthur Flegel, 16.
33. Williams, 177.
34. Saul, "The Arrival of the Germans from Russia: A Centennial Perspective," 5.
35. *The London Times*, February 1, 1876.
36. The names of these Volga German settlers appear in Hoezler, 16–17.
37. SS *Donau* Manifest (to New York, August 5, 1876), and Roy Oestrich, unpublished papers, Ritzville, WA. Scheibel was originally from the village of Messer.
38. Pauline B. Dudek, "Further Notes on the Wagon Train from Nebraska to Washington," *AHSGR Journal* 11, no. 3 (Winter 1979), 44.
39. SS *Wieland* Passenger List (to New York, June 5, 1878). Historian Harland Eastwood has contributed significantly to the Nebraska colony story both in the Midwest and Washington State in works like *Herr Kanzler's Kinder* (2006).
40. For settlement conditions in this area, see Frederick C. Luebke, *Immigrants and Politics: The Germans of Nebraska, 1880-1900* (Lincoln: University of Nebraska Press, 1969).
41. Roy Oestrich, unpublished papers, Dudek, 45.
42. *Endicott Index*, November 29, 1935.
43. Dave Schierman, oral history, Walla Walla, WA, July 9, 1972.
44. Enoch A. Bryan, *Orient Meets Occident: The Advent of the Railways to the Pacific Northwest* (Pullman, WA: The Student Book Corporation, 1936), 141–42.

Chapter 4: Arrival in the Pacific Northwest

1. Henry Villard, *The Early History of Transportation in Oregon* (Eugene: University of Oregon Press, 1944), 7–38.
2. Ibid., 40.
3. Ibid., 43.
4. Ibid., 50.
5. Ibid., 65.
6. Ibid.
7. Bryan, 141.
8. Ibid., 109.
9. The Northern Pacific constructed a short track between Ainsworth and Wallula in order to reach the coast on the Oregon Railway and Navigation Company line.
10. Bryan, 144.
11. Villard, 89.
12. David Lavender, *Land of Giants: The Drive to the Pacific Northwest, 1740–1940* (Garden City, NY: Doubleday and Company, 1958), 380.
13. Bryan, 148.
14. *Forty-fifth Annual Reunion of the Association of the Graduates of .the United States Military Academy at New York, June 12th, 1914* (Saginaw, MI: Seeman and Peters, Inc., 1914), 105–110 and Mrs. Hazel (Tannatt) Engelland, oral history, Lacey, WA, April 20, 1978.
15. Villard, 85.
16. James B. Hedges, *Henry Villard and the Railways of the Northwest* (New Haven: Yale University Press, 1930), 127.
17. Bryan, 149–51.
18. Villard, 97.
19. Ochs, 26, Mrs. Karl L. Scheuerman, oral history, Endicott, WA, June 8, 1975; Mrs. Leta Ochs, oral history, Endicott, WA, April 23, 1971; 1883. Territorial Census Records, Whitman County, W.T.; and Anna Weitz file.
20. Ochs, 36–38.
21. Letter, R.W. Mitchell, Colfax, W.T. to Tannatt, Portland, OR, May 10, 1881.
22. Letter, Tannatt, Dayton, W.T. to Villard, May 10, 1881.
23. Notation by Tannatt on Mitchell letter, forwarded to Villard, May 11, 1881.
24. Letter, Carl Brobst, interpreter at Culbertson, Hitchcock County, Nebraska to J. E. Shepherd, Oregon Railway and Navigation Company, San Francisco, California, May 10, 1880; quoted in Hedges, 124.
25. Roy Oestreich file.
26. *Ritzville Journal·Times*, "Adams County Pioneer Edition," September 15, 1949; Ruth J. Thiel, "Memories of my Father," unpublished typescript and Roy Oestreich file.
27. *Ritzville Journal·Times*, "Adams County Pioneer Edition," September 15, 1949, 1–3. Evidence suggests that John H. Koch and Henry H. Rehn were among the group that went to Portland. See Dudek, 45.
28. Roy Oestreich file. Ritz was originally from Pennsylvania, born in Lancaster County in 1827. He came west during the California gold rush but in 1850 moved to Winchester Bay, Oregon after reading about strikes along the Umpqua River. Instead, all he found were Indians and dense forests so he turned to trapping. He went north to Canada's Fraser River gold district in 1858. Four years later he opened a tree nursery in Walla Walla which developed into a profitable enterprise and later acquired extensive land holdings. He died in 1889.

Chapter 5: Regional Settlement and Expansion

1. Richard D. Scheuerman, "Patterns of Settlement in the Palouse Country, 1860–1915" (Unpublished Manuscript, 1980), 8.
2. Donald W. Meinig, *The Great Columbia Plain: A Historical Geography, 1805–1910* (Seattle: University of WA Press, 1968), 245.
3. Ibid., 238, 245.
4. Bryan, 161.
5. *Walla Walla Statesman*, October 4, 1882, 1.
6. *Walla Walla Statesman*, September 30, 1882, 3.
7. *Endicott Index*, August 16, 1935, and Henry Litzenberger oral history, J. O. Oliphant file. The Henry Dayton Smiths were the first permanent settlers in the Endicott area. Smith filed a homestead and timber claim in 1878 on land just west of the future townsite and moved there from Walla Walla in the fall of 1879. Smith's wife, Jenny, was the daughter of Major and Mrs. R. H. Wimpy, who had come west in a wagon train after the Civil War. The Smith home near Endicott became known as the Halfway House due to its location between Walla Walla and Spokane and they provided lodging and meals for freighters and other travelers. When the Oregon Improvement Company began surveying operations along Rebel Flat in July, 1880, the local agent, John Courtright, arranged for employee accommodations at the Halfway House. Jefferson T. Person also arrived in the summer of 1880 and later in the year opened the first store in the community.
8. *Endicott Index*, November 29, 1935, 1.
9. T. R. Tannatt, scrapbook clippings, 1878–83.
10. *Walla Walla Statesman*, October 21, 1882, 3.
11. Anna Weitz file.
12. Possibly by members of the Palouse bands who once owned huge herds along the lower Snake River but were defeated by Colonel George Wright in the Interior Indian Wars of 1855–58. In the 1880s they consisted of a few hundred individuals who remained in their homeland.
13. *Endicott Index*, December 6, 1935, 1.
14. Bryan, 163.
15. Letter, Tannatt to C. H. Prescott, Portland, OR, April 27, 1882.
16. *Endicott Index*, December 6, 1935, 1, and Anna Weitz file.
17. Henry J. Winser, *Guide to the Northern Pacific Railroad and its Allied Lines* (New York: G. Putnam's Sons, 1883), 219–20.
18. Jacob Adler, oral history, Tekoa, WA, January 2, 1973.
19. Meinig, 272.
20. Dave Schierman, oral history, Walla Walla, WA, July 9, 1972.
21. This being the northwest corner of Section 9, Township 17 N., Range 41 E.W.M., see *Whitman County Auditor Reports*, 1885–1890.
22. Anna Weitz file.
23. Dave Schierman oral history.
24. C. G. Schmick, oral history, Colfax, WA, April 14, 1969, and as related in Schlommer, 61–62.
25. *Palouse Gazette*, April 24, 1885, 3.
26. Dave Schierman oral history.
27. Gordon L. Lindeen, "Settlement and Development of Endicott, WA to 1930" (Unpublished Master's Thesis, State College of WA, 1960), 80.
28. Dave Schierman oral history.
29. Meinig, 406–07. The raising of Turkey Red, a hard red wheat, was introduced in America by Mennonites who emigrated from Russia to Kansas in the 1870s. It later revolutionized the Midwest grain industry.

30. Carrie Adell Strahorn, *Fifteen Thousand Miles by Stage* (New York, 1911), 304–305.
31. *Ritzville Journal-Times*, "Adams County Pioneer Edition," September 15, 1949.
32. Roy Oestrich file, newspaper clipping quoting *The West Shore*, April 1883.
33. Meinig, 339. For an extensive sociological study on the German Russians in the Ritzville area, see Elmer Miller, "The European Background and Assimilation of a Russian-German Group" (Unpublished Master's Thesis, State College of WA, 1929).
34. Roy Oestreich file.
35. Winser, 219.
36. Jean Roth, "Walla Walla, WA," *Unsere Leute Von Walter* I (June 1978), 15; and Mr. and Mrs. George Gradwohl Jr., oral history, Walla Walla, WA, March 18, 1978.
37. Sallet, 48.
38. Wanda Jane Schwabauer, "The Portland Community of Germans from Russia," unpublished typescript, May 1974, 18, 25, 33.
39. Sallet, 48, 61.
40. Meinig, 277.
41. Ibid., 372.
42. Ibid. For a detailed study of settlement in the Odessa area, see Oscar M. Undeberg, "Odessa, WA: A History of its Settlement and Development to 1920" (Unpublished Master's Thesis, WA State University, 1970).
43. Jacob Weber, oral history, Quincy, WA, April 17, 1980.
44. Faye Morris, *They Claimed a Desert* (Fairfield, WA: Ye Galleon Press, 1976), 46.
45. Sallet, 123.
46. Mr. and Mrs. Leo Lautenschlager, oral history, Brewster, WA, April 17, 1980.
47. SS *Hungaria* Passenger List (to New York, May 15, 1888).
48. Mrs. Elizabeth Repp, oral history, Endicott, WA, April 1, 1977.
49. Mr. and Mrs. Alfred Poffenroth, oral history, Calgary, Alberta, July 5, 1977.
50. *Mecca Glen Memories* (Ponoka, Alberta: Mecca Glen Centennial Committee, 1968), 223–25, quoting Henry Scheuerman oral history.
51. Mr. and Mrs. Walter Scheuerman, oral history, Bashaw, Alberta, July 1, 1977.
52. *Mecca Glen Memories*, 222, 225.
53. *The Calgary Herald*, May 25, 1957, 7.
54. Jacob Meininger, Jacob Miller, and Jacob Rehn, private oral histories, Tacoma, WA, April 4, 1978.
55. Dale Wirsing, *Builders, Brewers and Burghers: Germans of WA State* (Washington State American Bicentennial Commission, 1977), 40.
56. Sallet, 31.
57. Among Volga German families in the Big Bend country, one finds the names Adler, Amen, Bauer, Bastrom, Becker, Benzel, Bitterman, Boos, Braun, Dewald, Eckhardt (Ekhart), Fink, Gettman, Gradwohl, Greenwalt, Hardt, Heimbigner, Hilzer, Hoffman, Hornberg, Hopp, Horst, Ils, Kanzler, Kembel, Kiez, Kinzel, Kissler, Koch, Kramer, Krehn, Lesle, Lenhart, Maier, Melcher, Miller, Oestreich, Pfeiffer, Rehn, Rogel, Rosenoff, Rudy, Schauerman, Schoessler (Schessler), Schmidt, Starkel, Steinmetz, Stumpf, Thaut, Thiel, Wacker, Wagner, Walter, Weber, Wertemberger, Werzel, Wilhelm, Wolsborn, Zeller, and Zier.
58. Volga German family names in the Palouse country include Adler, Appel, Aschenbrenner, Bafus, Benner, Beutel, Blumenschein, Daubert, Dippel, Fisher, Geier, Gerlitz, Getz, Green, Helm, Hergert, Holstein, Kaiser, Kleweno (Klaveno), Koch (Cook), Konschu, Kromm, Langlitz, Lautenschlager (Lauten), Leinweber, Litzenberger, Luft, Lust, Machleit, Merkel, Moore, Morasch, Miller, Ochs, Poffenroth (Pfaff), Rausch, Reich, Repp, Ruhl, Schaeffer, Scheuerman (Schierman), Schukart, Stang, Wagner, Weitz, and Youngman.

59. Sallet, 123. German families from the Volga who settled in the Walla Walla area included those named Amen, Buterus, Daerr (Daire), Dietz, Fox, Frank, Fries, Gies, Gottwig, G radwohl, Hamburg, Hill, Ills (Els), Mueller (Miller), Oswald, Reiter, Roth, Schmidt, Schneidmiller, Schoessler (Schlesser), Schreiner, Streck, Volz, Walter, and Zier.

60. Elaine Davidson, "Autobiography of Wilhelm (William) Frank," *Unsere Leute Von Kautz* 1 (May 1979), 17–21 and Mr. and Mrs. William Schneidmiller, oral history, Walla Walla, WA, April 13, 1980.

61. Art Eichler, oral history, Yakima, WA, June 31, 1979.

62. Sallet, 112.

63. Ibid., 123.

Chapter 6: Pioneering Mission Work

1. Sallet, 112.

2. According to estimates for 1930, Evangelical Volga German membership nationally was as follows: Lutheran, 45 percent; Congregational, 30 percent; other Protestant denominations, 25 percent. See Koch, 120.

3. Eisenach, *A History of the German Congregational Churches*, 131.

4. Ibid., 46, quoting *The Home Missionary*, December 1881, 229.

5. Ibid., 46–48.

6. Ibid., 56. Two other German Congregational Churches were organized at Ritzville: Zion (1888) and Philadelphia (1912).

7. Ibid. The Walla Walla Congregation disbanded in 1884 but was reorganized in 1896.

8. Congregational work in Colfax was begun by the pioneer missionary of the Home Missionary Society, Rev. Cushing Eels, in the summer of 1874. The Plymouth congregation was organized there by him in July 1877 following his move from Puget Sound where he had been active in Indian mission work. The Congregational Association of WA Territory was formed in 1879 and a meeting on September 5 of that year in Colfax established a regional district which became known as the Upper Columbia Conference. Active in Congregational mission work in the area during the 1880s were Rev. George H. Atkinson, who had entered service in the Oregon Country in 1848, Rev. Thomas W. Walters who continued Eel's work in Colfax in 1882, and Rev. Jonathan Edwards who in 1886 had accepted a call to the Spokane Falls congregation.

9. *Minutes of the Congregational Association of Oregon and Washington 1887*, Portland, 1887, 51.

10. Eisenach, *A History of the German Congregational Churches*, 57. Rev. Gottfried Graedel, longtime WA German Congregational Conference missionary, wrote that the Endicott council was led by Rev. Atkinson, Walters, and Edwards.

11. Ibid., 290.

12. Ibid., 136.

13. Ibid., pp. 99–103. The following ministers and delegates represented the seven churches at the Portland Conference: 1) Portland Ebenezer: P. Yost, C. Yost, Mr. Krueger, and Rev. J. Koch; 2) Beaverton Bethany: Mr. Graf, Mr. Siegenthaler, and Rev. John Graef; 3) Endicott Evangelical Congregational: Rev. J. Hergert; 4) Seattle First German: Rev. J. Biegert; 5) Beaver Creek (Oregon) St. Peters: Mr. Grossmueller, Rev. R. Staub; 6) Ballard (Washington) German Congregational: Rev. G. Graedel; and, 7) Stafford (Oregon) German Congregational: Mr. Wolf and Mr. Schatz. Also present were Superintendent Eversz, who was elected moderator, Rev. G.F. Graedel, elected scribe, and Rev. C.F. Class. The large number of churches in the Odessa area was due to both widespread rural settlement of Russians German and the fact that the churches were often organized according to regional origin in Russia as the Volga and Black Sea Germans established separate congregations in the town and surrounding countryside.

14. Ibid., 161.
15. U. Clifford Nelson, *Lutheranism in North America, 1914–1970* (Minneapolis: Augsburg Publishing House, 1972), 3.
16. For a detailed history of the Joint Synod, see C. V. Sheatsley, *History of the Evangelical Lutheran Joint Synod of Ohio and Other States* (Columbus, OH: Lutheran Book Concern, 1919).
17. Theodore C. Moeller, "The Development of Lutheranism in the Pacific Northwest with Specific Reference to the Northwest District, The Lutheran Church—Missouri Synod, Part I," *Concordia Historical Institute Quarterly* XXVIII (Summer 1955), 58–62.
18. Ibid., 65.
19. Ibid., 63.
20. Walter H. Hellman, ed., *The Story of the Northwestern District of the American Lutheran Church* (Dubuque, IA: Wartburg Press, 1941), 10.
21. *The Lutheran Standard*, May 28, 1887, 176. Hereafter cited as *LS*.
22. Hellman, 10.
23. Ibid.
24. Revs. A. Krause, H. Rieke, G. F. Pauschert and Groschupf, *Denkschnft zum Silber-Jubiläum des WA Distrikts der Ev. Luth. Ohio Synode, 1891–1916* (Columbus, OH: Lutheran Book Concern, 1916), 74. Hereafter cited as *DWD*.
25. *LS*, February 28, 1891, 75.
26. *LS*, May 28, 1887, 176.
27. Rev. John Groschupf et al., *A Brief History of the Emmanuel Lutheran Church*, Spokane, WA, 1939, 5.
28. Verhandlungen des WA Distrikts (Columbus, OH: Lutheran Book Concern, 1914), 72. At the Archives of the American Lutheran Church, Dubuque, Iowa.
29. Ibid., undated, 33.
30. *LS*, May 21, 1892, 21. This summary is in reference to the work of Pastors Mollenauer and Schneider in the Big Bend area.
31. Hellman, 10.
32. Moeller, 66.
33. Rev. H.J. Gieseke et al., *A Brief History of Zion Lutheran Church (Missouri Synod) at Endicott, Washington*, 1941, 3.
34. Moeller, 66.
35. Rev. R. H. Eckhoff et al., *Seventy-five Blessed Years, 1890–1965* (Zion Lutheran Church Anniversary Booklet), Tacoma, WA, 1965, 3.
36. *LS*, August 5, 1 893, 243.
37. *LS*, June 14, 1890, 1708.
38. *DWD*, 66–70.
39. Ibid.
40. *LS*, June 7, 1890, 178. The school mentioned is probably a reference to the parochial school opened by Rev. Wolf at Trinity Lutheran Church in Tacoma during the summer of 1889. Professor Henry L. Wittrock, who had emigrated from Germany to Detroit, Michigan, accepted a call to become the first teacher at the Tacoma school and built it into a highly respected academy. See Hellman, 30, for a discussion of Wittrock's work and the history of the institution.
41. *LS*, June 14, 1890, 1708.
42. Schuh's vehement response to this can be seen in his report published in the *Lutheran Standard*, December 12, 1891, 395. Earlier that year he had written, "Here is an opportunity to cast bread upon the waters and after many days it shall return. There is so much to do that it is fairly confusing. The only discouraging feature in this work is the great cry of the people for pastors and our in ability to serve them. May the Lord of the harvest send us help out of Zion!" *LS*, February 28, 1891, 75.

43. *LS*, June 14, 1891, 1708.
44. *DWD*, 82.
45. Letter, Rieke to Groschupf, May 5, 1890.
46. Ibid.
47. Hellman, 10–11.
48. Ibid., 9.
49. *DWD*, 3–4. The pioneers present who effectuated the organization of the district at the Tacoma conclave, in the order in which they entered service in the Far West, were: Pastors F.N. Wolf, Tacoma; A.H. Horn, The Dalles; H.H. Rieke, Genesee; P.F. Hein, Spokane; C. Lembke, Lake Bay; A. Krause, Tacoma; L. H. Schuh, Tacoma; Groschupf, Genesee; C.F. Vollmer, Walla Walla; E. Hasse, Leber; J. Willers, Tacoma; and Teacher H.L. Wittrock, Tacoma. Pastor C. Pitzler from Fairfield was formally excused due to his inability to attend. District officers elected for the first synodical year were: Pastors L.H. Schuh, president; P.F. Hein, vice-president; A. Krause, secretary; C.F. Vollmer, treasurer; and Groschupf, chaplain.
50. *Verhandlungen der ersten Versammlung des WA—Distrikts der Allgem. Ev. Luth. Synode van Ohio u. a. St.* (Columbus, OH, 1891), 8–10.
51. *LS*, December 9, 1891, 402.
52. *LS*, November 19, 1892, 373 and *LS*, April 16, 1892, 131. At this time, when immigration to eastern Washington was rapidly peopling the land, the mission fields labored in by many of these Lutheran pastors were still great. The following listing demonstrates the extent of their work in 1892 (dates indicate the years the churches were constituted):
    Rev. P. H. Hein: Spokane (Emmanuel, 1889).
    Rev. H. Rieke: Fairfield (Zion, 1890), Farmington (Christ Lutheran, 1896) and Spangle.
    Rev. Groschupf: Cameron (Emmanuel, 1888), Genesee (St. John's, 1888), Uniontown, Palouse and Moscow (Emmanuel, 1902). Together with Rev. Rieke: Endicott (Trinity, 1890) and Colfax (Peace, 1902).
    Rev. W.H. Kropp: Sprague (St. John's, 1891), Lind (Good Hope, 1903) and Ritzville (Emmanuel, 1891).
    Rev. L. H. Mollenauer: Reardan (Emmanuel, 1891), Davenport (Zion, 1891), Egypt (Christ Church, 1891), Almira and Wilbur (St. Paul's 1900).
    Rev. A.F. Gillman: Walla Walla (Emmanuel, reorganized 1890). Sixteen families withdrew from Walla Walla's Emmanuel Lutheran Church in 1896 to establish a more centrally located congregation which became Christ Lutheran Church. One pastor served both congregations until the growth of the Christ Lutheran, largely due to the influx of Volga Germans, enabled them to call Rev. C. Wellsandt as their first permanent pastor in 1912. See Rev. Foege and others, Emmanuel Lutheran Church 15th Anniversary, Walla Walla, 1963 and *DWD*, 82–84.
53. Moeller, 67. Rev. Theiss had also organized St. Paul's Lutheran Church in Portland in 1889 but a debate arose over the possible relocation of the church and the synod into the Ohio Synod, calling Rev. C.F.W. Allwardt as their new pastor. See *DWD*, 54.
54. Ibid., 58.
55. Gieseke et al., 3.
56. *Oregon-WA Distrikt, Synodal-Bericht*, 1901. (Translated by K. Lorenz, St. Louis: Concordia Publishing House, 1901, 5).
57. Moeller, 76.
58. Ibid., 77.
59. Gieseke and others, 3.
60. Doering journal entries forwarded with letter to Mission Board, 1902, as quoted in Moeller, 74–75.
61. Ibid.
62. *DWD*, 22.

63. Ibid., 26.
64. U.S. Bureau of Census, *Religious Bodies, 1916*, Part I, *Abstract*, 1919, 324.
65. Ibid., 323.
66. Hellman, 23.
67. Riasanovsky, 540-41.
68. Emma D. Schwabenland, *A History of the Volga Relief Society* (Portland, OR: A.E. Kern & Co., 1941), 127, hereafter cited as *VRS*. Hoover's American Relief Administration distributed $61,500,000 worth of food, clothing, and medicine in Russia in response to the Soviet's appeal for aid during the famine. The Volga Relief Society was one of many groups that raised funds for the starving populace in Russia at this time as Quaker, Catholic, and Mennonite organizations also joined the effort.
69. Bonwetsch, 122 and *VRS*, 30.
70. Letter in the possession of the author, translated by Karl Scheuerman.
71. Mr. and Mrs. George Repp file, quoted in *VRS*, 33.
72. *VRS*, 34. Officers elected at the Portland meeting included John W. Miller, president; David Hilderman, vice-president; George Repp, secretary, and John H. Krieger, treasurer (replaced by Gottfried Geist a week later).
73. Ibid., 34–35.
74. Ibid., 36–39. The following excerpt is from the Volga Relief Society's financial statement of contributions as of December 1922 (see *VRS*, 82):

Oregon

Portland	$29,576.86
Salem	15.00
Ruckles	15.00

Washington

Odessa	$4,184.83	Warden	$206.75
Walla Walla	2,456.95	Ralston	154.50
Ritzville	2,384.00	Seattle	120.55
Endicott	1,415.50	Wapato	50.00
Dryden	1,203.51	Snoqualmie	50.00
Waterville	930.00	Sunnyside	20.00
Tacoma	597.50	Blaine	15.00
Quincy	418.60	Wilkinson	12.50
Alkali Flats	315.00		

75. *VRS*, 69.
76. Mr. and Mrs. George Repp file, quoted in *VRS*, 93.
77. Ibid., 91–92.
78. Ibid., 87–88.
79. Sallet, 105.
80. Mr. and Mrs. George Repp file, quoted in *VRS*, 122.

Bibliography

Books and Pamphlets

Bauer, Gottlieb. *Geschichte der Deutschen in den Wolgakolonien*. Saratov, 1907.

Beratz, Gottlieb. *Die deutschen Kolonien an der Unteren Wolga*. Saratov: H. Schellhorn u. Co., 1915; 2nd ed., Berline: Verband der wolgadeutschen Bauern, G.m.b.H., 1923.

Bonwetsch, Gerhard. *Geschichte der deutschen Kolonien an der Wolga*. Stuttgart: Verlag van J. Englehorns Nachf, 1919.

Bryan, Enoch A. *Orient Meets Occident: The Advent of the Railways to the Pacific Northwest*. Pullman, WA: The Students Book Corporation, 1936.

Burgdorff, H. George. *Erlebnisse als Missionar oder Reiseprediger in Russland*. Hillsboro, KS: M. B. Publishing House, 1924.

Collard, Rev. Ernest et al. *Peace Lutheran Church Fiftieth Anniversary, 1909–1959*. Tacoma, WA, 1959.

Duin, Edgar C. *Lutheranism under the Tsars and Soviets*. 2 vols. Ann Arbor, MI: University Microfilms, 1975.

Durant, Will. *The Reformation: A History of European Civilization from Wyclif to Calvin, 1300–1564*. New York: Simon and Schuster, 1957.

Eastwood, Harland. *Herr Kanzler's Kinder*. Ritzville, WA: By the Author, 2006.

Eckhoff, Rev. R. H. et al. *Seventy-five Blessed Years, 1890–1965*. Zion Lutheran Church Anniversary Booklet. Tacoma, WA, 1965.

Eisenach, George J. *A History of the German Congregational Churches in the United States*. Yankton, SD: The Pioneer Press, 1938.

———. *Pietism and the Russian Germans*. Berne, IN: The Berne Publishers, 1949.

———. *Das religiöse Leben unter den Russlanddeutschen in Russland und Amerika*. Marburg an der Lahn, W. Ger.: Buchdruckerei Hermann Rathmann, 1950.

E(rbes), J. and P. S(inner). *Volkslieder und Kinderreime aus den Wolgakolonien*. Saratov: Buchdruckerei Energie, 1914.

Fairchild, Henry Pratt. *Immigration*. New York: John Wiley and Sons, Inc., 1925.

Foege, Rev. W. et al. *Emmanuel Lutheran Church 75th Anniversary*, Walla Walla, 1963.

Forty-fifth Annual Reunion of the Association of the Graduates of the United States Military Academy. Saginaw, MI: Seemans and Peters, Inc., 1914.

Gieseke, Rev. H. J. and others. *A Brief History of Zion Lutheran Church (Missouri Synod) at Endicott, Washington*. N.p.: 1941.

Giesenger, Adam. *From Catherine to Krushchev*. Battleford, Saskatchewan: Marian Press, 1974.

Groschupf, Rev. John et al. *The Story of Fifty Years: A Brief History of the Emmanuel Lutheran Church, 1889–1939*. Spokane, WA, 1939.

Hansen, Marcus Lee. *The Immigrant in American History*. Cambridge, MA: Harvard University Press, 1940.

Haxthausen, August von. *Studien über die inneren Zustaende des Volkslebens und insebsondere der laendlichen Einrichtungen Russlands*. Hanover, 1847–1852. Translated by Eleanore L. M. Schmidt in *Studies on the Interior of Russia*. Chicago: University of Chicago Press, 1972.

Hedges, James Blain. *Henry Villard and the Railways of the Northwest*. New Haven, CT: Yale University Press, 1930.

Height, Joseph S. *Paradise on the Steppe*. Bismark, ND: North Dakota Historical Society of Germans from Russia, 1972.

Hellman, Walter H., ed. *Fifty Golden Years: The Story of the Northwest District of the American Lutheran Church, 1891–1941.* Dubuque, IA: Wartburg Press, 1941.

Klaus Aleksandr Avgustovich. *Nashii kolonii: Opyty materialy po istorii i statistike inostrannoi kolonizatsii v rossi.* St. Petersburg: Tipografiia V.V., Nusval't, 1869.

Koch, Fred C. *The Volga Germans: In Russia and the Americas, From 1763 to the Present.* University Park: Pennsylvania State University Press, 1977.

Krause, Revs. A., H. Rieke, G. F. Pauschert, and P. Groschupf. *Denkschrift zum Silber-Jubiläum des Washington Distrikts der Ev. Luth. Ohio Synode, 1891–1916.* Columbus, OH: Lutheran Book Concern, 1916.

Lavender, David. *Land of Giants: The Drive to the Pacific Northwest, 1750–1950.* Garden City, NY: Doubleday and Co., 1958.

Luebke, Frederick C. *Immigrants and Politics: The Germans of Nebraska, 1880–1900.* Lincoln: University of Nebraska Press, 1969.

Mecca Glen Memories. Ponoka, AB: Mecca Glen Centennial Committee, 1968.

Meinig, Donald W. *The Great Columbia Plain: A Historical Geography, 1805–1910.* Seattle: University of Washington Press, 1968.

Morris, Faye. *They Claimed A Desert.* Fairfield, WA: Ye Galleon Press, 1976.

Nelson, E. Clifford. *Lutheranism in North America, 1914–1970.* Minneapolis: Augsburg Publishing House, 1972.

Ochs, Grace Lillian. *Up From the Volga: The Story of the Ochs Family.* Nashville: Southern Publishing Association, 1969.

Pallas, Peter Simon. *Reisen durch verschiedene Provinzen des russischen Reiches in den Jahren 1768–1774.* St. Petersburg, 1771–1776.

Pissarevskii, Grigorii G. *Iz istorii inostrannoi k olonizatsii v rossii v X VIII v. (Poneizdannym arkhivnym dokumentam.)* Moskva: A. I. Snegirevyi, 1909.

———. *Vnutrennii rasporiadok v koloniiakh povolzh' ia pri Ekaterine II.* Varshava: Tipografiliia varshavskago uchebnago okruga, 1914.

Protokoll der im Jahr 1889 zu Saratov abgehaltenen 16-ten combinirten Synode der bei den Wolga-Präposituren. Saratov: Prapositur der Wolga, 1889.

Raugust, W.C., R. Hoefel, Rev. A. Rehn, and Rev. A. Hausauer. *History of the Pacific Conference of Congregational Churches of Washington, Oregon and Idaho, 1897–1964,* 1964.

Riasanovsky, Nicholas V. *A History of Russia, 2nd ed.* New York: Oxford University Press, 1969.

Sallet, Richard. *Russian-German Settlements in the United States.* Fargo: North Dakota Institute for Regional Studies, 1974. Translated by LaVern J. Rippley and Armand Bauer.

Schleuning, Johannes. *Die deutschen Kolonien im Wolgagebiet.* Berlin, 1919. Reprint, Portland, OR: A.E. Kern & Co., 1922.

Schmidt, David. *Studien uber die Geschichte der Wolgadeutschen.* Pokrowsk, ASSR der Wolgadeutschen: Zentral-Völker-Verlag, 1930.

Schnaible, Rev. Fred, et al. *A History of Trinity Lutheran Church, 1887–1975.* Dedication Anniversary Booklet. Endicott, WA, 1975.

Schul- und Küster-Schülmeister Instruction in den evangelischen Kolonien des Saratovschen und Samaraschen Gouvernments. Moscow: Evangelisch-Lutherischen Consistorio, n.d.

Schwabenland, Emma D. *A History of the Volga Relief Society.* Portland, OR: A.B. Kern & Co, 1941.

Sheatsley, C.V. *History of the Evangelical Lutheran Joint Synod of Ohio and Other States.* Columbus, OH: Lutheran Book Concern, 1919.

Snowden, Clinton. *A History of Washington: The Rise and Progress of an American State.* 6 vols. New York: The Century History Company, 1909

Strahorn, Carrie A. *Fifteen Thousand Miles by Stage.* New York, 1911.

Stumpp, Karl. *The Emigration from Germany to Russia in the Years 1763 to 1862.* Tübingen, Germany: by the author, 1973.

————. *The German-Russians: Two Centuries of Pioneering.* Trostberg, Ger.: A. Erdl, 1967. Translated by Dr. Joseph Height.

Thomson, Gladys Scott. *Catherine the Great and the Expansion of Russia.* New York: Collier Books, 1965.

Villard, Henry. *The Early History of Transportation in Oregon.* Eugene: University of Oregon Press, 1944.

Volz, Jacob. *Historical Review of the Balzerer.* York, NE, 1938.

Wagner, Rev. Albert F. et al. *Emmanuel Lutheran Church Diamond Anniversary.* Ritzville, WA, 1965.

Weitz, Anna. *History of the Evangelical Congregational Church, 1883-1963.* Endicott, WA, 1963.

Williams, Hattie Plum. *The Czar's Germans: With Particular Reference to the Volga Germans.* Lincoln, NE: The American Historical Society of Germans from Russia, 1975.

Winsor, Henry J. *The Great Northwest: A Guidebook and Itinerary for the Use of Tourists and Travellers Over the Lines of the Northern Pacific Railroad.* New York: G. P. Putnam's Sons, 1883.

Wirsing, Dale R. *Builders, Brewers and Burghers: Germans of Washington State.* The Washington State American Revolution Bicentennial Commission, 1977.

Yungman, Susan M. *Faith of Our Fathers.* By the author, 1972.

Zorrow, William F. *Kansas: A History of the Jayhawk State.* Norman: University of Oklahoma Press, 1957.

Züge, Christian Gottlob. *Der russiche Kolonist.* I. Zeitz und Naumberg: Wilhelm Webel, 1802.

Periodicals and Official Minutes

Davidson, Elaine, ed. "Autobiography of Wilhelm (William) Frank," *Unsere Leute Von Kautz* I (May 1979), 17–21.

Dudek, Pauline B. "Further Notes on the Wagon Train from Nebraska to Washington," *AHSGR Journal* II, no. 3 (Winter 1979), 44–46.

Esselborn, Karl. "Die Auswanderung von Hessen nach Russland," *Heimat im Bild,* 1926, 83–104.

Flegel, Art and Cleora. "Research in Hesse," *AHSGR Work Paper* No. 13 (December 1973), 21–27.

Haynes, Emma S. "Germans from Russia in American History and Literature," *AHSGR Work Paper* No. 15 (September 1974), 4–20.

————. "Researching in the National Archives," *AHSGR Journal* II, no. I (Spring 1979), 4–7.

Hoezler, Johann. "The Earliest Volga Germans in Sutton, Nebraska and a Portion of their History," *AHSGR Work Paper* No. 16 (December 1974), 16–18. Translated by Art Flegel.

Kloberdanz, Timothy. "Funerary Beliefs and Customs of the Germans from Russia," *AHSGR Work Paper* No. 20 (Spring 1976), 15–20.

Kromm, Georg. "Die deutschen Ansiedler an der Wolga," *Schottener Kreisblatt,* Redaktion, Druck und Verlag von Wilhelm Engel, Schotten, Ger., Nos. 15–17, 21 (February, March 1910).

Moeller, Theodore C. Jr. "The Development of Lutheranism in the Pacific Northwest with Specific Reference to the Northwest District, the Lutheran Church-Missouri Synod, Part I," *Concordia Historical Institute Quarterly* XXVIII (Summer 1955), 49–86.

Oregon-Washington Distrikt, Synode-Bericht, 1901 (Missouri Synod). Translated by K. Lorenz, 1901. District Archives, Portland, OR.

Rempel, David G. "The Mennonite Commonwealth in Russia: A Sketch of its Founding and Endurance, 1789–1919," *Mennonite Quarterly Review* XLVII (October 1973) and XLVIII (January 1974)

Roth, Jean. "Walla Walla, Washington," *Unsere leute Von Walter* I (June 1978), 15.

Saul, Norman E. "The Arrival of the Germans from Russia: A Centennial Perspective," *AHSGR Work Paper* No. 21 (Fall 1976), 4–11.

———. "The Migration of Russian-Germans to Kansas," *Kansas Historical Quarterly* XL, no. 1 (Spring 1974), 38–62.

Schlomer, Harm. "Inland Empire Russia Germans," *The Pacific Northwesterner* VIII (Fall 1964), 57–64.

Stärkel, Johannes. "Johann Wilhelm Stärkel aus Norka unter der Fahne Pugachews," *Friedensbote* (November 1901), 685–688.

Stumpp, Karl. "Verzeichnis der ev. Pastoren in den deutschen und gemischtenvor allem in Städten-Kirchenspielen in Russland bzw. der Sowjetunion, ohne Baltikum und Polen," *Heimatbuch der Deutschen aus Russland,* 1972, 276–389.

Verhandlungen des Washington Distrikts (Ohio Synod), 1891–24, Columbus, Ohio. Archives of the American Lutheran Church, Dubuque, Iowa.

Wagner, Ernst. "Auswanderung aus Hessen," *Auslanddeutschtum und evangelischen Kirche Jahrbuch,* 1938, 24–33.

Würz, Wilhelm "Wie Jagodnaja Poljana gegrundet wurde," *Heimatbuch der Deutschen aus Russland,* 1962, 65–66.

Manuscript Materials

Frank, John W. "A Brief History of the Russian-Germans in the Evangelical and Reformed Church." Bachelor of Divinity thesis, Eden Theological Seminary, Webster Grove, Missouri, 1945.

Lindeen, Gordon L. "Settlement and Development of Endicott, Washington to 1930." Master's thesis, Washington State University, 1960.

Miller, Elmer. "The European Background and Assimilation of a Russian-German Group." Master's thesis, State College of Washington, 1929.

Scholz, Harry G. "The German Colonists of Russia: The Repeal of Russia's Law of the Colonists in 1871 and its effect on the German Colonist Population." Master's thesis, Chapman College, Orange, CA, 1929.

Schwabauer, Wanda J. "The Portland Community of Germans from Russia." Typescript photocopy, 1974.

Schwabenland, Emma D. "German-Russians on the Volga and in the United States." Master's thesis, University of Colorado, Boulder, 1929.

Scheuerman, Richard D. "Patterns of Settlement in the Palouse Country, 1860–1915." Unpublished manuscript, 1980.

Swanson, Robert W. "A History of Logging and Lumbering on the Palouse River, 1870–1905." Master's thesis, State College of Washington, 1958.

Thiel, Ruth. "Memories of My Father." Mimeographed typescript, undated.

Undeberg, Oscar M. "Odessa, Washington: A History of its Settlement and Development to 1920." Master's thesis, Washington State University, 1970

Vogt, Don. "Whitman County, Washington Germans from Russia." Unpublished manuscript, 1980.

News Articles

Calgary Herald. Calgary, Alberta. May 25, 1957.

Endicott Index. Endicott, WA. 1919, 1928, 1935–36.

Hays City Sentinel. Hays City, KS. August 16, 1876.

London Times. London, England. February 1, 1876.

Lutheran Standard. Columbus, OH. 1887–95.

Palouse Gazette. Colfax, WA. 1882–85.
Ritzville Journal-Times. "Adams County Pioneer Edition," September 15, 1949.
Russell Record. Russell, KS. December 7, 1876.
Topeka Daily Blade. Topeka, KS. December 13, 1875.
Walla Walla Weekly Statesman. Walla Walla, WA, 1882.

Public Documents and Papers

Church Anniversary Bulletins of the American Lutheran Church. North Pacific District Archives, Seattle, WA.
Hesse, *Acten des Geheimen Staats-Archives, XI*, Abhteilung, Convolut I. Hessen State Archives, Darmstadt, West Germany.
Kromm, Georg, Ed. *Einwanderliste van Jagodnaja Poljana (aus Hessen)*. Vogelsberg Museum, Schotten, West Germany.
Russia, *Polnoe Sobranie Zakonov Rossiisk oi Imperii. Sankt Peterburg, 1649-1916*. Hoover Library and Institute, Stanford University, Stanford, CA.
Oliphant, J. Orin. Unpublished papers. Manuscripts, Archives, and Special Collections, Washington State University Libraries, Pullman.
Oregon Improvement Company. *Annual Business Reports, 1881-1890*. Library, Special Collections, University of Washington, Seattle.
Oregon Improvement Company Letter File. Manuscripts, Archives, and Special Collections, Washington State University Libraries, Pullman.
Tannatt, Thomas R. Private letter file and scrapbook clippings, 1878-1883. Manuscripts, Archives, and Special Collections, Washington State University Libraries, Pullman.
U.S. Bureau of the Census. *Thirteenth Census of the United States: 1910. Abstract*, 1912.
U.S. Bureau of the Census. *Religious Bodies: 1916*, Part 1. *Abstract*, 1919.
U.S. National Archives. *Manifests of Vessels arriving at New York, 1820–1897*. SS *Ohio* (to Baltimore) (November 23, 1875), S.S. *City of Chester* (July 10, 1876), SS *Donau* (August 5, 1876), SS *Mosel* (October 24, 1876), SS *Frisia* (December 8, 1876), SS *Hungaria* (May 15, 1888), SS *Wieland* (June 5, 1878), SS *City of Montreal* (January 6, 1876).
Washington Territorial Census. *Whitman County, 1883* (Microfilm copy). Manuscripts, Archives, and Special Collections, Washington State University Libraries, Pullman.
Weitz, Anna B. Unpublished papers. Manuscripts, Archives, and Special Collections, Washington State University Libraries, Pullman.
Whitman County *Auditor Reports, 1885-1892*. Whitman County Courthouse, Colfax, WA.

Oral Histories

Adler, Jacob. Tekoa, WA, January 2, 1973.
Bafus, Mrs. John. Endicott, WA, April 29, 1980.
Balderee, Eva Litzenberger. Spokane, WA, June 10, 1993.
Bergman, Jack. College Place, WA, August 2, 2015.
Blumenschein, Mr. Conrad. St. John, WA, May 6 and 13, 1980.
Engelland, Hazel (Tannatt). Lacey, WA, April 20, 1978.
Eichler, Art. Yakima, WA, June 31, 1979.
Gradwohl, Mr. and Mrs. George, Jr. Walla Walla, WA, March 18, 1978.
Greenwalt, Mr. and Mrs. John. Quincy, WA, April 2, 1976.
Koch, Peter. Portland, Oregon, June 15, 1977.
Kromm, Elizabeth. Lacrosse, WA, June 10, 1979.
Lautenschlager, Mr. and Mrs. Leo Brewster, WA, April 17, 1980.
Litzenberger, Henry. Deer Park, WA, May 4, 1980.

Luft, Catherine. Sheboygan, WI, June 15-19, 1977.
Lust, Martin. Colfax, WA, April 7, 1975.
Markel, August. Endicott, WA, June 19, 1970.
Meininger, Jacob. Tacoma, WA, April 4, 1978.
Miller, Jacob. Tacoma, WA, April 4, 1978.
Morasch, Mrs. A. P. Endicott, WA, March 4, 1980.
Morasch, Mrs. C. P. Endicott, WA, April 23, 1971.
Ochs, Ed. Cashmere, WA, March 17, 1977.
Ochs, Mr. and Mrs. Dan. St. Helena, CA, February 16, 1974.
Ochs, Leta. Endicott, WA, April 23, 1971.
Oestreich, Mr. and Mrs. Roy. Ritzville, WA, April 1, 1978.
Poffenroth, Mr. and Mrs. Alfred. Calgary, AB, July 5, 1977.
Rehn, Jacob, Tacoma, WA, April 4, 1978.
Reich, Alec. Endicott, WA, April 2, 1969.
Repp, Elizabeth. Endicott, WA, April 1, 1971.
Repp, Jim. Colfax, WA, June 20, 2016.
Rieke, Mr. and Mrs. H.H. Cashmere, WA, October 10, 1975.
Rudd, Vera Grove. College Place, WA, September 15, 2017.
Scheuerman, Karl. Endicott, WA, December 10, 1969.
Scheuerman, Una Mae. Endicott, WA, June 8, 1975.
Scheuerman, Mr. and Mrs. Walter. Bashaw, AB, July 1, 1977.
Schierman, Dave. Walla Walla, WA, July 9, 1972.
Schierman, Mr. and Mrs. John. Vulcan, AB, July 2, 1977.
Schmick, Conrad G. Colfax, WA, April 14, 1969.
Schneidmiller, Mr. and Mrs. William. Walla Walla, WA, April 13, 1980.
Weber, Jacob. Quincy, WA, April 17, 1980.

Private Files and Correspondence

Dudek, Pauline. Letter to the author. Bladen, Nebraska, March 1, 1978.
Hausauer, Rev. Albert. Unpublished papers. Odessa, WA.
Haynes, Emma S. Letter to the author. Arlington, VA, November 19, 1977.
Horst, Alec. Unpublished papers. Tacoma, WA.
Miller, Earl. Unpublished papers. Endicott, WA.
Ochs, Leta. Scrapbook clippings. Endicott, WA.
Oestreich, Roy. Unpublished papers. Ritzville, WA.
Reich, Evelyn. Unpublished papers. Colfax, WA.
Roth, Jean. Unpublished papers. Seattle, WA.
Scheirman, William. Letter to the author. Overland Park, KS, February 10, 1977.
Scheuerman, Richard D. Unpublished letters from Russia, 1920–1940. Richland, WA.
Scott, Betty. Unpublished papers. Mission, KS.
Wilhelm, Laurin P. Letter to the author. Lawrence, KS, April 27, 1974.

Index

Includes Part I only. Notes in italics indicate illustrations.

About the Authors

Richard D. Scheuerman is director of the Franklin County Museum in Pasco and president and co-founder of Palouse Heritage, which in 2015 reestablished Palouse Colony Farm on land settled by his Volga German ancestors in eastern Washington. A career historian and professional educator, he has published numerous books and articles, most on the history and agriculture of the Inland Pacific Northwest. He is co-author with Michael O. Finley of *Finding Chief Kamiakin: The Life and Legacy of a Northwest Patriot* (WSU Press, 2011).

Clifford E. Trafzer is Distinguished Professor of History and the Rupert Costo Chair in American Indian Affairs at the University of California, Riverside. Trafzer has been an archivist and museum curator, and he is the author or co-author of many books, including *A Chemehuevi Song: Resiliency of a Southern Paiute Tribe*. In spring 2019, the University of Oklahoma Press will publish his book, *Fighting Invisible Enemies: Health and Medical Transitions among Southern California Indians*.

Together, Scheuerman and Trafzer are authors of the WSU Press books *Renegade Tribe: The Invasion of the Inland Pacific Northwest* (1986), which was revised, updated, and re-released in 2016 as *The Snake River Palouse and the Invasion of the Inland Northwest* and *River Song: Naxiyamtama (Snake River–Palouse) Oral Traditions from Mary Jim, Andrew George, Gordon Fisher, and Emily Peone*.